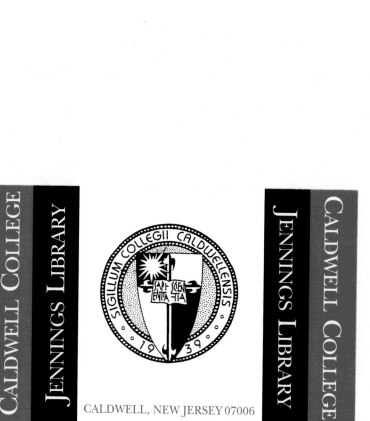

THE FOREST
IN FOLKLORE
AND MYTHOLOGY

THE FOREST
IN FOLKLORE
AND MYTHOLOGY

ALEXANDER PORTEOUS

DOVER PUBLICATIONS, INC.
Mineola, New York

Bibliographical Note

This Dover edition, first published in 2002, is an unabridged republication of the work originally published by The Macmillan Company, New York, in 1928.

Library of Congress Cataloging-in-Publication Data

Porteous, Alexander.
   [Forest folklore, mythology, and romance]
   The forest in folklore and mythology / Alexander Porteous.
      p. cm.
   Originally published: Forest folklore, mythology, and romance. New York : Macmillan, 1928.
   Includes index.
   ISBN 0-486-42010-8 (pbk.)
    1. Trees—Folklore. 2. Trees—Mythology. 3. Forests and forestry—Folklore. I. Title.

GR785 .P67 2002
398'.368216—dc21

                                 2001028839

Manufactured in the United States by Courier Corporation
42010805
www.doverpublications.com

CONTENTS

CHAPTER I

FORESTS OF ELD

Archæan Forests ; Primeval and Tropical Forests ; Cosmogonic and
Traditional Forests.

THE earliest vegetation of our globe must have been of the
simplest possible type, as during the Archæan Age the earth
still retained much of its original internal heat, and the
resulting close, warm and damp climate, with the super-
abundant quantity of carbonic acid gas in the atmosphere,
would be favourable to the growth and development of Fungi,
Moulds, Algæ, Mosses and similar plants. Judging from the
analogy of after ages, when gigantic plants appeared during
the Carboniferous Era, and enormous reptiles had their being
throughout Jurassic times, probably these now lowly plant
forms attained dimensions far exceeding those of our loftiest
forest trees of the present day. If one can imagine the forests
of that period, there would probably have been seen enormous
toadstools with their domed summits extending over many
yards ; patches of gigantic mosses pushing up their vast spore
urns into the murky sky ; or mighty masses of cellular moulds
ramifying in every direction and producing thickets of globular
spore cases borne on long cellular stalks. Absolute silence
would reign in the cimmerian gloom ; no song of bird would
be heard, no chirp of insect, nor rustle of leaf, for none of
these yet had being. Even during the tempests which must
often have raged through these forests, no crash of falling

trees would resound; the soft cellular tissue would sink noiselessly to earth. In the waters which in all likelihood at that time constituted the greater part of the surface of the globe, strange and gigantic forms of algæ would rear themselves above the surface, and all the various forms of vegetation would be of one uniform sombre hue. During unnumbered æons, from these simple cellular plants were gradually evolved the mighty piniferous (if they may be so called) forests of the Carbonaceous Age, and, later, the highly organised trees of the forest which are now familiar to us.

Each succeeding geological period had its own peculiar type of vegetation which had all been leading up to that immense development of plant life known as the Carboniferous period, the remains of which form our coal seams. Never before or since had there been such an exuberance of plant life. So luxuriant was the plant growth over the whole globe that to the inhabitants of other planets this world would probably be known as the green star. A strange picture indeed, these forests, with their towering reeds and their gigantic club-mosses, must have presented had there been human eye to see. In addition to the damp steamy atmosphere, an ever-clouded sky hung over these forests, reaching from pole to pole. During the daytime a pallid light would shed a lurid glimmer through the shadowy recesses, bringing into relief here and there the naked trunks of *Sigillarias*, while, above, the hirsute arms of the *Lepidodendrons* would wave ghostlike in the gentle breeze, or toss wildly when a hurricane swept through the forest carrying destruction in its path.

As the milleniums passed, other epochs of time held their sway, until at the close of the glacial periods forests as we now know them covered the land, and, apart from their utilitarian purposes, a very wealth of romance lies hidden within their bosky depths. There, the voice of Nature speaks to the weary wayfarer; the rustling and whispering of the leaves; the sad, yet sweet, cooing of pigeons; the melody of song-birds, or the distant cawing of rooks; the hum of innumerable insects : all impart a feeling of rest, and the strife and jealousies of the world seem far removed. Here in the sunny glades of the forest the ground is carpeted with mosses and flowers, while all around the view is bounded by gigantic trunks of trees each clad with many-coloured lichens, and the whole canopied with leafy boughs whence the feathered orchestra of the woods pour forth their divine melody. It is recorded that the monk of Hildesheim, doubting how with God a thousand years could be as yesterday, listened to the melody of a bird in the green wood during three minutes, and found that in these three minutes three hundred years had flown.

To a wanderer in forest solitudes a sense of mystery is often perceived which lures him on and on into the verdant depths of the woodland world. On a brilliant summer day the tremulous throbbing of the air, seemingly full of whisperings and sighings from an unseen host, appears like the pulsation from the mighty heart of the forest, while, all around, sunlight and shadow form a tangled web of enchantment, which is deepened by soft elusive perfumes floating on the damp zephyrs. In fancy he may feel drawn back to the early primitive ages, when the forest deities would have had a very real existence to him, and he would understand the inner meaning of those oracles which were often spoken in the glades of the primeval woods.

Every season of the year imparts its own peculiar beauty to the forests. In early spring a shimmer of tenderest green spreads over them, especially when a forest of Beeches is breaking into leaf, as if the wand of an enchanter had been waved over it. These tints gradually deepen with the advent of summer, when in the hot noontide hours the tired wanderer may repose in the cool shade, lulled to rest by the hum of insects and the music of rustling leaves. When autumn comes, what an inimitable palette of gorgeous colour is spread out before the eye, albeit but the symptom of decay ; and when winter holds the land in its icy grasp, even then the forest has a grandeur and a grace all its own, especially when the branches and twigs glitter in the sunshine with hoarfrost, or gracefully bend under a dazzling weight of snow. It has been said that the forest knows all and is able to teach all, and there is a French proverb to the effect that the forest, which always listens, has the secret of every mystery, while a Latin proverb of the Middle Ages says : *Aures sunt nemoris, oculi campestribus oris*, and similarly the German : *Das Feld hat Augen, der Wald hat Ohren*.

In Asia vast forests yet exist in many unexplored quarters in much the same condition as they did in primeval ages, and in their depths myth and superstition still hold full sway. According to Pliny (*Nat. Hist.*, Bk. vi. c. 34) there were forests beyond the shores of the Red Sea in which the city of Ptolemais was situated near Lake Monoleus, which city had been built by Philadelphus for the pursuit of the elephant, and that in consequence it had been called Epitheras. When Timour the Tartar subdued the Kingdom of Kashgar, he marched to a distance of about 1,440 miles towards the north-east of Samarcand, crossing the River Irtish, into the depths of these forests, and in them his emirs erected a rude memorial to commemorate their exploits.

Palestine is one of those ancient seats of civilisation which in former times contained numerous forests, but which now, owing to the ravages of war and the improvidence of the people except in a few districts, is a comparatively bare and treeless land. The Old Testament has many references to forests, the best known of which were those of Mount Lebanon, and the venerable Cedars growing thereon are perhaps the most solemnly impressive trees in the world. A full century before the days of King Solomon one Zekar-baal reigned as king in the city of Byblus on the Syrian coast, which city was said to have been founded by the great god El, and to have been the oldest in Phœnicia. An Egyptian merchant named Wen-Ammon traded with the king, and kept a record of his transactions written on papyrus. He records that he stayed for some time with the king at Byblus, and on his leaving they exchanged presents, he receiving a supply of timber which had been felled in the forests of Lebanon. There was also a sacred Cedar Forest at Elam. (See Art. " Paradise," *Jewish Ency*.)

There are numerous references to forests in the sacred writings of India. Thus we are told, that among the Brahmins, students of the Vedas had to study each Veda for twelve years, although he might study one only. When his course was complete he had to choose which of the four orders of Brahmins he would enter. If he chose that of the hermit he had to live in the forest, practise austerities, live on roots and fruits, never enter a village or pass over ploughed ground, and dress himself in skins, or coverings made of bark. This hermit life was considered to be the culmination of their existence. The ascetic life was also highly recommended, as a great portion of it was passed in the forests. If, however, the forest dweller did not find the desired liberation in the forests, then he became a mendicant, indifferent to everything, and concentrating his whole mind on Brahma. One of the precepts given to attain this high life is : " Let him not desire to live, let him not desire to die ; let him wait for his appointed time as a servant waits for the payment of his wages." [1]

Buddha was one of the god Vishnu's incarnations, and it is told that in his youth he was never so happy as when sitting alone in the depths of the forests lost in meditation ; and it was in the midst of a beautiful forest that he was shown the four great truths.

Various forests of India have become celebrated through the legend of Buddha, among others that of the Mṛigadava, concerning which the following is related : The King of Benares was passionately fond of the chase, and killed so many animals that the king of the animals remonstrated with him and offered to provide one animal for him every day if he would give up the hunt. The king accepted that condition, and they commenced to consult Fate as to the animals destined

[1] G. T. Bettany, *The Great Indian Religions*, 1892, p. 49.

for the table of the king.   One day Fate designated a fat roe.
The roe objected, and pointed out that if they killed her they
would take two lives at once.   The king of the animals, who
was the Bodhisattva himself, the future Çakky-amuni, on
hearing this, was eager to offer himself as a sacrifice to the king
in place of the roe.   The king, touched by his generosity
renounced his pretensions, and gave the order that nothing
was to be claimed or hunted in the Mṛigadava.[1]

A form of the legend of Buddha, telling how his high destiny
had been foretold and mentioning the objects that led him
to adopt the ascetic life, these being a dead man, a decrepit
old man, and a religious recluse, relates how he left his palace
at night after a last look at his sleeping wife Yasodhara, and
the son just born to him, and wended his way to the forests
of Magadha.   In these forests he passed seven years in extreme
asceticism, after which he became the Buddha.[2]

There is a tract of forest country called Nṛisinhavana,
situated to the north-west of Madhyadeça, composed of
Palaça trees, of which the derivation of the name is uncertain.
On one hand it was considered that the forest was sacred to
Vishnu under his name of Nṛisinha, which means half-man
and half-lion, as he had that form in his fourth incarnation ;
while the other view is that the forest was inhabited by a
savage people called Nṛisinha, who were fabulous men-lions.[3]

The whole of the interior of Ceylon is one huge tropical
forest where trees peculiar to the Tropics are found growing
side by side with those of the Temperate Zone.   The Cotton
plant or shrub attains almost to the dimensions of a tree,
which justifies the statement of Herodotus (Book III, 106),
when speaking of India, that " certain wild trees there bear
wool instead of fruit, that in beauty and quality excels that
of the sheep ; and the Indians make their clothing from
these trees."   A remnant of the aborigines of Ceylon still
inhabit the forests.   These are the Veddas or " hunters."

[1] De Gubernatis, *Mythologie des Plantes*, vol. i. p. 78.
[2] *Marco Polo's Travels*, Yule, vol. ii. p. 263.
[3] Weber, *Indische Studien*, ix. 62.

They live in caves or in huts made from bark, and formerly their clothing consisted of bark. Ages ago they seem to have inhabited hollow trees, as in Singhalese the word for a hollow tree is *rukula*, and the same word now means a house.

Many of the tropical forests give a faint conception of what vegetation was like in the days of the world's youth. " Neither the season, nor the flight of time, leaves a mark upon the forest ; virgin in the days of which we cannot guess the morn, virgin in our days, virgin it will remain in the days of generations yet unborn." [1] Mr. Maxwell, speaking of the eerie feeling that comes over the wanderer in these shades, says : " So little do you see that the feeling comes over you that you are alone in the midst of mysterious hidden things. The feeling that immediately follows this is that these mysterious things are not merely hidden, but are specially hidden from you. The circle that moves with you is the veil built up against you. You could imagine that you were a trespasser, or at all events are regarded as such. Then you have the horrible feeling that from behind the tree-trunks watching eyes are looking upon you. It is bad enough at any time if you are alone and all is quiet ; it is worse as the sun sinks and light fades ; it is worst if by any ill chance you happen to know that you have lost not only your way, but your sense of direction. At all times you may see things happen of which the reason is hard to divine."

Java lays claim to be the finest and most interesting tropical island in the world, and with reason, for, apart from the luxuriant forests which clothe the mountains to their summits, in these forests are found, buried in the jungle, the remains of ancient cities, with vestiges of the temples and statues which once adorned them. They all point to a high degree of civilisation, and it is known that for untold centuries Brahmanism was the religion of the land, until it was superseded by Mahommedanism in or about the year 1478.

Mr. H. M. Stanley, in his journey for the relief of Emin

[1] George Maxwell, *In Malay Forests*, 1911.

Pasha in 1887, when crossing Africa through the primeval forest, expressed the eerie feelings that beset one when alone in these gloomy depths, similar to those mentioned by Mr. Maxwell when writing of the Malay forests. Stanley wrote that " an awe of the forest rushed upon the soul and filled the mind. The voice sounded with rolling echoes as in a cathedral. One became conscious of its eerie strangeness, the absence of sunshine, its subdued light, and marvelled at the queer feeling of loneliness, while inquiringly looking around to be assured that this loneliness was no delusion. It was as if one stood amid the inhabitants of another world." [1]

Hermann von Wissmann also speaks of the apprehensions besetting one in these wilds. He says : " Be it imagination, be it excitement of the nerves, the slightest sound which at night interrupts the deep quiet seems to startle you. The piercing shrieks of the nocturnal monkey, the splashing of a fish pursued by a crocodile, or the deep thundering of the hippopotamus, causes the auricular nerves to be continually on the alert." [2]

It is to Dr. Alfred R. Wallace that we are most indebted for his glowing descriptions of the Brazilian forests, particularly those of the River Amazon and the Rio Negro, through which he travelled in 1848. In his accounts of the forests of the Amazons he says : " Perhaps no country in the world contains such an amount of vegetable matter on its surface as the valley of the Amazon. Its entire extent, with the exception of some very small portions, is covered with one dense and lofty primeval forest, the most extensive and unbroken which exists upon the earth. . . .

" The forests of no other part of the world are so extensive and unbroken as this. Those of Central Europe are trifling in comparison ; nor in India are they very continuous or extensive ; while the rest of Asia seems to be a country of thinly wooded plains, and steppes, and deserts. Africa con-

[1] *In Darkest Africa*, vol. ii.
[2] *Through Equatorial Africa*, p. 33.

tains some large forests, situated on the east and west coasts, and in the interior south of the Equator ; but the whole of them would bear but a small proportion to that of the Amazon. In North America alone, is there anything approaching to it, where the whole country east of the Mississippi and about the great lakes is, or has been, an almost uninterrupted extent of woodland.

" In a general survey of the earth, we may therefore look upon the New World as pre-eminently the land of forests, contrasting strongly with the Old, where steppes and deserts are the most characteristic features." [1]

The Australian " Bush " gives an impression of mystery and awe in its very name. The " Great Hush and Mystery," as it has been called, has been the scene of many tragedies. Hunger and thirst, and often death, have been the lot of many who, in the past, had endeavoured to penetrate its secrets. It is the uncleared country, the parts covered with trees or brushwood, and the name is derived from the Dutch word *booch*, meaning a wood or forest. The common use of the word, however, is to indicate the open country as distinguished from towns and their environments. In the more sterile regions amid the rocky mountain tracts, or in the sandy plains of the interior, the forests degenerate to what is called the " scrub," where the country is covered with miserable stunted trees and scanty brushwood of unpromising and forbidding aspect.

Many forests of fabulous fame have been mentioned in classical writings and by the authors of old romances. Hindu mythology tells of a great cosmogonic forest, the principal tree in which is the mighty Jambu, which bears an immortal fruit as large as an elephant, resembling gold, and of which the seeds produce pure gold. In this celestial forest, in the field of flowers of light, the plant of immortality grew, and from this plant Dhanvantari, the physician of the gods, extracted the divine ambrosia.

---

[1] *Travels on the Amazon and Rio Negro*, p. 303.

One of the most ancient traditional forests of which we have any knowledge was the Forest, sometimes called the Grove, of Eridhu. It is frequently mentioned in the Assyrian tablets, and as Babylonian tradition placed the site of the Garden of Eden in its vicinity, it was believed that the Tree of Life grew therein. In a hymn to Hea one line reads : "In the mighty thickets we have smelled his good wind." There was also a city of Eridhu which about the year 4000 B.C. was one of the chief cities of Babylonia. In those days this city was situated at the mouth of the Euphrates, but during the centuries which have elapsed the river has gradually formed an alluvial delta, and now the site of the city is considerably far inland, and the only signs of its former existence are the mounds of Abu Shahrein, situated on the eastern bank of the river.

The great Epic of Ancient Chaldea is known as the Izdubar Legends, dating fully 2000 B.C., and many of the scenes and adventures related in it are represented as taking place in the forests. The tablets recording the Epic were discovered by the late Mr. George Smith in 1872, and he was of opinion that Izdubar, who was a mighty hunter, was the Nimrod of the Bible. It has long been recognised that the adventures of Herakles (Herculus) in Greek mythology are simply a copy of those of Izdubar which was brought from Babylonia to Greece by the Phœnicians.

The chief incident in the Epic relates to the overthrow of the tyrant Khumbaba, the King of the Elamites, who had conquered the land. The Epic records that Izdubar, when at Erech, the capital of Shumur, or Southern Chaldea, and the Shinar of the Bible, had a curious dream which was interpreted to him by a peculiar being called Hea-bani. This Hea-bani seems to have been a kind of satyr who lived in the forests and was on intimate terms with the wild beasts. These two then arranged to overcome Khumbaba, and set out on their journey to find him. His dwelling was far away in a forest of Pines and Cedars. In this forest, also, the gods and the spirits had their abode. After various adventures they arrived at the confines of the forest which surrounded the palace of Khumbaba, and the Epic relates : " He stood and surveyed the forest of Pine trees, he perceived its height, of the forest he perceived its approach, in the place where Khumbaba went his step was placed on a straight road and a good path. He saw the land of the Pine trees, the seat of the gods, the sanctuary of the angels. In front of the seed the Pine tree carried its fruit, good was its shadow, full of pleasure, an excellent tree, the choice of the forest," and so on. This particular Pine appears to have been that known as the Black Pine of Eridhu, the Tree of Life, and will be noticed further on. The travellers then entered and passed through the forest. They evidently encountered Khumbaba and slew him, but the tablets recording this are so mutilated that it is impossible to reconstruct the narrative. Further on, however, it is stated : " We conquered also Khumbaba, who in the forest of Pine trees dwelt."

Towards the end of the Epic, Hea-bani is again mentioned, as addressing certain trees which, Professor Sayce says in his edition of Mr. Smith's volume on *The Chaldean Account of Genesis*, p. 257, " are supposed to have the power of hearing and answering him. Hea-bani praises one tree and sneers at another, but from the mutilation of the text it does not appear why he acts so. We may conjecture he was seeking a charm to open a door he mentions, and that according to the story this charm was known to the trees."

After his victory over Khumbaba, Izdubar was proclaimed king in Erech. The goddess Istar fell in love with him, but he rejected her advances, whereupon she caused grievous trials to fall upon him, and, in addition, slew Hea-bani. Izdubar then resolved to consult his ancestor Hâsisadra, who lived far away in the land of the immortals. He accordingly travelled through strange lands, encountering on the way certain super-natural beings known as Scorpion-men. These, understanding that he was under the protection of the gods, allowed him to continue his journey. He came at last to a wonderful forest situated on the shores of the ocean—the waters of death. The trees of this forest bore as fruit emeralds and other precious stones, but they were guarded by two maidens named Siduri and Sabitu. These mistrusted Izdubar and refused him access to their dwelling. The ocean on the shores of which he found himself separated the land of the living from the land of the dead, but Urubêl, the ferryman, pitying him, took him across and landed him on the immortal shore. Here he met his ancestor, who gave him full instructions how to act, by following which he gained all his desires, and returned safely to Erech.

Alexander the Great, during his wanderings, is said to have encountered a forest of Maidens or Flower-Women.[1]

Dante describes the Cimmerian Forest, that infernal forest where the knotted, dark-leaved trees spoke to the wanderer when he endeavoured to pluck a twig.

When Orpheus was lamenting the loss of Eurydice and fingering his lyre in the abandonment of his grief, ancient tradition relates how, as soon as the first melancholy strains were heard, a forest of Elm trees sprang up, under one of which he reposed after his expedition to Hades had failed.

---

[1] Lewis Spence, *Dictionary of Mediæval Romance*, p. 319.

CHAPTER II

FABULOUS FORESTS

Forests of Romance and Myth.

THE Romances of the Middle Ages contain many allusions to forests famous in myth, and enchanted forests full of magic. Several of them are connected with the quest for the Holy Grail, and relate the adventures of the gallant knights who figure in Arthurian Romance as having undertaken that quest. The enchanted Forest of Broceliande in Brittany may be considered as a type of all that is best in romance, and the legends connected with it teem with the chivalry of bygone ages. It is for ever associated with the name of Merlin, being reputed to contain his tomb, or rather the place of his enchantment, as legend tells that he was enchanted by Vivien, the Lady of the Lake, and entombed under a great stone. Merlin, wandering through the forest, came to a beautiful fountain and sat down on its brink to rest. To him came Vivien, whose mother, wife of the lord of Broceliande and also a fay, had prophesied that the wisest man in the world should love her. He would grant all her desires but could never compel her to consent to his. Merlin told her many of his magic secrets, and promised to meet her in a year's time. He did so, and this time his love overpowered all his wisdom. She desired yet more wisdom, which he imparted. Finally she desired to know an enchantment which would eternally bind him to her. He taught her, and so it came about that he was for ever lost and withdrawn from the world of men.[1]

A ruined dolmen, called the *Perron de Belenton*, is supposed to represent the tomb of Merlin, and close beside it is the

[1] Lewis Spence, *Legends and Romances of Brittany*, pp. 64–70.

fountain of Belenton or Baranton, where Merlin was said to have met the fay. Beside the fountain was a marvellous step or slab of stone, and an Oak tree, from which hung a golden basin, overshadowed it. A mediæval writer said of this spot : " Oh, amazing wonder of the Fountain of Brecelien ! If a drop be taken and poured on a certain rock beside the spring, immediately the water changes into vapour, forms itself into great clouds filled with hail ; the air becomes thick with shadows, and resonant with the muttering of thunder. Those who have come through curiosity to behold the prodigy wish that they had never done so, so filled are their hearts with terror, and so does fear paralyse their limbs. Incredible as the marvel may seem, yet the proofs of its reality are too abundant to be doubted." Huon de Méry claimed to have beheld all the marvels by taking water from the fountain and sprinkling the step. Robert de Wace, however, hearing of the wonders of this forest, went expectant into it, but did not appear to have seen or heard anything out of the ordinary. He wrote :

> " Thither I went in search of wonders,
> The forest I saw, the earth I saw,
> I sought wonders but found none,
> Foolishly I returned, foolishly
> I went back. Foolishly I went,
> Foolishly I returned thence,
> I sought foolishness. A fool
> I held myself."

The Welsh Romance of the Lady of the Fountain, found in the *Mabinogion*, evidently treats of the same theme. One of King Arthur's knights called Kymon set out one day in quest of adventures. He came to a great tree, under which sprang a fountain by the side of which was a marble slab. On the slab lay a silver bowl. He had been instructed to empty this bowl, full of water from the fountain, on the slab. No sooner had he done so than a terrific storm of hail followed, which nearly made an end of him, and stripped the tree bare of leaves. As soon as the hail ceased, numerous birds resting on the leafless tree poured forth a ravishing melody, and a black knight made his appearance who worsted him in combat, after which he returned home. This has been compared to the rain-making ceremonies found in the folklore of many races. Another enchanted fountain was situated in the Forest of Arden, and was said to have been created by Merlin in order that Sir Tristram might be cured of his passion for Isolta. That knight, however, never drank of it, yet its virtue remained.

The scene of the French romance of Lancelot du Lac, or Lancelot of the Lake, is also placed in the Forest of Broceliande. It relates how the queen of King Ban left her new-born son, Lancelot, on the banks of a lake while she tended her husband on his deathbed. When she returned she found the child in the arms of a lovely lady who, heedless of her entreaties to return him, plunged with him into the lake and disappeared. This lake was an illusion, and the art of creating it had been taught by the devil to Merlin, who, as already narrated, had passed on his knowledge to the fay Vivien, also known as Dame du Lac. The lake concealed a forest in which the lady had many fair palaces, and in one of these Sir Lancelot was educated in all knightly matters, and in due time became one of the famous knights of King Arthur's Court.

It is related that Alexander the Great and Floridas went to reside with Dame du Lac in her enchanted castle in the forest in order to be cured of their wounds, and that the fortnight they spent with her seemed to be but one night.

Another of King Arthur's knights was Sir Launfal who, it is said, was displeased with the king when he married the lovely but frail Gwennere. She ignored him when she was distributing gifts, whereupon Sir Launfal left the Court, and after a time happened to ride into a " fair forest." Here, being overcome by the heat, he lay down under the shade of a tree and fell into a reverie, from which he was aroused by the approach of two charming maidens sumptuously attired. They invited him to meet their mistress, the beautiful Dame

Tryamour. He did so, and the lady, falling in love with him, gave him many valuable gifts of magical powers. Afterwards he returned to the Court of King Arthur, but again had the misfortune to offend the queen. He was timely rescued from her vengeance by Dame Tryamour with whom he departed, and the romance concludes :

> " Thus Launfal, withouten fable,
> That noble knight of the rounde table,
> Was taken into the faërie ;
> Since saw him in this land no man,
> Ne no more of him tell I ne can,
> For soothè without lie."

This enchanted Forest of Broceliande is the haunt of one of the most malignant of the beings with which popular fancy has peopled the woods. This is the Korrigan who, under the guise of a fair and lovely maiden, may often be encountered beside the sylvan streams and fountains, but only at night as she shuns the day. By her fatal wiles she has the power to enthral the hearts of the noblest of men, who are doomed to perish for the love of her. Her powers of enchantment were unparalleled. By aid of her wand the forest recesses in which she dwelt became changed into a sumptuous palace containing all that could delight and charm the ear and eye. Here throughout the night her hapless victim was royally entertained, but the first rays of dawn dissolved the charm. The woods resumed their wonted aspect, while the fair maiden was transformed into a hideous hag. The Breton romance of Sir Roland relates how that knight rode unattended through the forest in haste, a league ahead of his troop, lest he be late for the crusade. He had taken a vow never to touch a lady's hand except with his mailed glove, nor ever to press a maiden's lips. Darkness overtook him on the way, and seeing a brilliantly illuminated castle, he entered it. A lady of dazzling beauty accosted him and entertained him sumptuously during the livelong night. He had almost succumbed to her wiles, but while in the act of bending to salute her lips she shrank from him. She had seen the earliest flush of dawn appearing in the east, and with that the whole scene became transformed. The castle walls melted into tree trunks, the couches became grassy banks, and the rugs and carpets were revealed as mossy forest paths. Looking down on the lady a fearful countenance of baffled hate and rage met Roland's gaze, and with a hideous shriek the Korrigan fled into the forest depths. Roland fell on his knees and, clasping his rosary, returned thanks for his great deliverance. Thus was he found when his troop rode merrily into the glade.

Another enchanted forest is mentioned in one of the Folk-tales of Brittany called " The Castle of the Sun." There was once a peasant who had a family of six sons and one daughter. The youngest son Yvon, and the daughter Yvonne, being delicate and gentle, were treated as drudges. One day, when Yvonne was taking the cattle to pasture, she met a handsome stranger who married her and took her away. After a year the brothers desired to see their sister and set off in search of her, leaving Yvon behind. Riding on, they came to a wide-spreading forest, in which they lost themselves. They found an old woman tending a large fire, who said that her son, a giant, could direct them to their sister. The giant led them to a great plain, where he deserted them. They were bewildered there, but, after many wanderings and adventures, they at last succeeded in returning home. Yvon then set out to find his sister. He had similar experiences, but, being bold and resolute, he at last came to a palace of crystal in the forest where his sister lived. She told him she was happy, except that her husband was absent every day going she knew not whither. When the latter returned that evening he and Yvon became very friendly, and Yvon asked if he might accompany him on his journey next day. He agreed, but on the condition that " if you touch or address anyone save me you must return home." They then set off, and Yvon saw many strange sights, " but that which seemed strangest of all to him was the sight of two trees lashing each other angrily with their branches, as though each would beat the other to the ground. Laying his hands on them, he forbade them to fight, and lo ! in a moment they became two human beings, a man and wife, who thanked Yvon for releasing them from an enchantment under which they had been laid as a punishment for their perpetual bickering." Yvon, by thus disenchanting the trees, had failed to observe the one condition, and had to return to his sister's palace. Then he was sent home, and on reaching his native village found his dwelling gone. On asking for his father, an old man replied : " I have heard of him. He lived in the days when my grand-father's grandfather was but a boy, and now he sleeps in the churchyard yonder." Yvon then realised that his visit to his sister had been one of generations.[1]

The Arthurian romances mention another mythical forest called Inglewood.

Mr. Thomas Keightley gives the following tradition of Périgord : " Embosomed in the forest of the Canton of La Double near the road leading from Périgueux to Ribérac is a monument named Roque Brun. It consists of four enormous rocks placed two and two, so as to form an alley ten feet long and six wide. A fifth rock, higher and thicker than the others, closes this space on the west. The whole is covered by a huge mass of rock, at least twelve feet by seven, and from three to four feet thick. There can be no doubt of its being the work of man, and it is remarkable that the stone composing it is different from that of the soil on which it stands. The tradition of the canton, however, is that many thousand years ago there was a Fée who was the sovereign of the whole country, and having lost her husband in this very place, she resolved to bury him on the spot. She therefore called six of her pages and ordered them to fetch each one of these stones, and to place them in the order which they still maintain. They instantly obeyed, and they carried and arranged the huge masses as easily as if they had been only rose-leaves. When

[1] Lewis Spence, *Legends and Romances of Brittany*, pp. 131–37.

the tomb was completed, the Fairy ascended it, and turning to the east, she thrice cursed, in a voice of thunder, whoever should henceforth dare even to touch this monument of her royal spouse. Many an instance is still recorded by the peasantry of those who dared and were punished." [1]

The Forest of Colombiers in Poitou is associated with the myth of Melusina. Mr. Keightley, in narrating the legend,[2] tells how Melusina was the daughter of Elinas, King of Albania, and the beautiful Fay Pressina. Melusina, having offended her mother, was condemned by her to become a serpent from the waist downwards on every Saturday until she met a man who should love her so much that he would consent to marry her under the promise of never seeing her on a Saturday. She then wandered through the world in search of this man until she came to the Forest of Colombiers. Here all the Fays of the district met her and told her they had been waiting for her to reign over them. Count Raymond, while wandering in the forest, met her in the moonlight and, attracted by her beauty, married her, having first taken the requisite oath never to endeavour to see her on a Saturday. Unfortunately he violated his oath, whereupon Melusina told him that, obedient to the decree of destiny, she would have to leave him and flit about the earth as a spectre in pain and suffering until the day of doom. She would only become visible when one of his race was about to die at Lusignan, her parting words being : " But one thing will I say to thee before I part, that thou, and those who for more than a hundred years shall succeed thee, shall know that whenever I am seen to hover over the fair castle of Lusignan, then will it be certain that in that very year the castle will get a new lord ; and though people may not perceive me in the air, yet they will see me by the Fountain of Thirst ; and this shall be so long as the castle stands in honour and flourishing— especially on the Friday before the lord of the castle shall die." Having thus spoken she vanished with loud wailing

[1] *Fairy Mythology* (1884), p. 472.　　　[2] *Ibid.*, 480.

and lamentation, and ever since she has only been seen as a spectre of the night. Many tales are told of the various appearances she has made, frequently in the form of a serpent with markings of blue and white.

In the Forest of Longboel in Normandy, when the wind blows melodiously through the trees, the peasants imagine they hear the voices of the ancient verderers, the guardians of the forest, the spirits of whom return to their old familiar haunts ; and in the Forest of Fontainebleau *le grand veneur* is still supposed to hunt, and may be heard on stormy nights (*v. Wild Huntsman*).

A very charming French romance is that of Huon de Bordeaux. Huon, during his travels, met one Gerasmes in Syria and inquired of him the way to Babylon. He was told that there were two roads—one long and safe, the other, which led through a forest, short, but dangerous, as it was so full of Fairie mysteries that few people could traverse it. Oberon, King of the Fairies, dwelt in it. He was three feet in height, with an angelic face, and was wont to meet any wayfarer through the forest and endeavour to persuade him to speak to him. If he succeeded in getting one to speak to him, that hapless wight was lost for evermore. Should, how-ever, the traveller's resolve of silence hold good, Oberon, in the words of the romance, " will be passing wroth with you. For before you have left the wood he will cause it so to rain, to blow, to hail and to make such right marvellous storms, thunder and lightning, that you will think the world is going to end. Then you will think that you see a great flowing river before you, wondrously black and deep ; but know, sire, that right easily will you be able to go through it without wetting the feet of your horse, for it is nothing but a phantom and enchantments that the dwarf will make for you, because he wishes to have you with him, and if so be that you keep firm to your resolve not to speak to him, you will be surely able to escape." Huon followed for some time the advice given him, but after experiencing the storms, he resolved to wait for and speak to Oberon. Shortly afterwards he met the dwarf, who informed him that he was the son of Julius Cæsar, and that at his birth all the fairies had been invited save one. This one, in revenge for the slight, decreed that he would not grow after his third year, but afterwards repenting, and to make what amends she could, she bestowed upon him the most comely countenance. The romance concludes by Oberon going to Bordeaux, and helping to reconcile Huon to King Charlemagne.

The *Orlando Furioso* of Ariosto tells how Count Orlando on seeing the fair Angelica immediately fell in love with her, although he was already married. Angelica, meantime, had lost her heart to the young Medoro, and while strolling with him in the forest he carved their names upon a tree growing beside a fountain. Orlando, hearing how Angelica despised his love, betook himself with his grief into the depths of the forest, where he gave vent to his anguish in shrieks and groans :

> " All night about the forest roved the count,
>   And at the break of daily light was brought
> By his unhappy fortune to the fount
>   Where his inscription young Medoro wrought.
> To see his wrongs inscribed upon that mount,
>   Inflamed his fury so, in him was nought
> But turned to hatred, frenzy, rage, and spite."
> Canto xxiii. St. cxxix. 1–7.

Drawing his sword, he destroyed the carving, and

> " So fierce his rage, so fierce his fury grew,"

that, discarding his weapon, he tore down with his hands many of the forest giants—Pines, Oaks, and others. In his frenzy he became a terror in the forests and ravaged them throughout the land of France.

The romance of the twin brothers Valentine and Orson tells how they were born in a wood near Orleans, and that Orson was carried off by a bear, which suckled him. Owing to this upbringing he became the terror of France when he grew to manhood, and was called the Wild Man of the Forest.

Tasso, in his great poem " Jerusalem Delivered," relates (Book XIII) how the forest was enchanted by Ismeno the sorcerer. He peopled it with demons, who had instructions to guard the trees from the Christians. Godfrey, the leader of the Christian host, desirous of obtaining timber for use in his siege, at first sent workmen to fell the trees, and on their failing to do so, sent his soldiers, but all returned in a state of terror. Alcastus then, in a boastful spirit, set out for the enchanted forest, vowing that no terrors could daunt him. His boast was premature, and, being utterly overcome by the strange weird sights he beheld, he was fain to return humiliated and abject in spirit. Some others then attempted the task, but in vain. Tancred almost succeeded, but even he failed in the end. At last, as told in Book XVIII, Rinaldo proceeded alone to the enchanted forest, resisted the temptations, and thus broke the spell. The Christians were then enabled to hew the trees, and form their siege weapons.

The Forest of Compeigne will ever be memorable as the scene of the signing of the armistice between Germany and France and her allies on November 11, 1918, which marked the close of the Great War. In the midst of the forest a clearing has been made, one stone slab placed showing where Marshal Foch's train drew up, and another showing where that of the German delegates came to a standstill. Between them, and in the centre of the clearing, is another larger slab bearing an inscription indicating that on this spot an end was made of German ambition to bring the free peoples of Europe under German subjection.

Gervase of Tilbury, writing in the thirteenth century, as quoted by Mr. Keightley,[1] mentions a forest which had some supernatural attributes. He says : " There is " (" Otia Imperialia apud *Leibnitz* Scriptores rerum Brunsvicarum," vol. i, p. 982)

[1] *Fairy Mythology* (1884), pp. 284–85.

" in the county of Gloucester a forest abounding in boars, stags, and every species of game that England produces. In a grovy lawn of this forest there is a little mount, rising in a point to the height of a man, on which knights and other hunters are used to ascend when fatigued with heat and thirst, to seek some relief for their wants. The nature of the place and of the business is, however, such, that whoever ascends the mount, must leave his companions, and go quite alone.

" When alone, he was to say, as if speaking to some other person, ' I thirst,' and immediately there would appear a cupbearer in an elegant dress, with a cheerful countenance, bearing in his stretched-out hand a large horn, adorned with gold and gems, as was the custom among the most ancient English. In the cup, nectar of an unknown but most delicious flavour was presented, and when it was drunk, all heat and weariness fled from the glowing body, so that one would be thought ready to undertake toil instead of having toiled. Moreover, when the nectar was taken, the servant presented a towel to the drinker, to wipe his mouth with, and then, having performed his office, he waited neither for a recompense for his services, nor for questions and inquiry.

" This frequent and daily action had for a very long period of old times taken place among the ancient people, till one day a knight of that city, when out hunting, went thither, and having called for a drink, and gotten the horn, did not, as was the custom, and as in good manners he should have done, return it to the cupbearer, but kept it for his own use. But the illustrious Earl of Gloucester, when he learned the truth of the matter, condemned the robber to death, and presented the horn to the most excellent King Henry the Elder, lest he should be thought to have approved of such wickedness, if he had added the rapine of another to the store of his private property."

This tale clearly appears to be a version of the Grail Legend.

Sherwood Forest in Nottinghamshire, will ever be famous as the scene of the exploits of bold Robin Hood and his Merry

Men, and the little tinkling wild-blown bell which guided the Black Knight to the cell of the clerk of Copmanhurst.

The Forest of Ben Bulben was famous in Irish romance as the arena wherein a boar perpetrated many atrocities. This boar happened to be the transformed stepbrother of Dermot, and the legend relates how it roamed the forest until one day, chancing to meet Dermot, it slew him.[1]

There is a tradition that when Napoleon, during his Russian campaign, had, after leading his army three times running against the Monastery of the Holy Trinity, near Moscow, arrived at the gates of Tröitsa, a thick forest suddenly sprang up before him. He vainly endeavoured to penetrate the forest, was constantly misled, and after having been practically lost in it for three days, succeeded, after great difficulty, in regaining the road back to Moscow.

Similar narratives are found in the fairy tales of other countries. Thus, there is a popular English tale which runs : " At break of day, when the giant's daughter was fleeing with the prince, the giant in pursuit, she exclaimed that she felt her father's breath on her back, he being so close at hand. She said to the prince, ' Put your hand quickly into the ear of the grey filly and throw behind you what you will find there.' It is the point of a thorn,' he said. ' Throw it behind you,' she reiterated. He did so, and a forest of blackthorns twenty miles long immediately sprang up. So dense was it that a weasel could scarcely slip through. When the giant came to it he lacerated his head and neck so severely that he had to give up the pursuit."

Again, we are told how the wandering princess, aided by a magic wand, opened a path through an impenetrable hedge, and continued her journey. The evil being following her thought to pass through in his turn, but the hedge closed in on him and lacerated him.

In Perrault's tale of " The Sleeping Beauty in the Wood," it is narrated that " scarcely had the Prince advanced towards

[1] Lewis Spence, *Dictionary of Mediæval Romance*, p. 30.

the wood when all the great trees, the briars and the thorns, moved aside of themselves to let him pass. He went on towards the Castle at the end of a grand avenue into which he had entered, and what greatly surprised him was that no one could follow him, because the trees had closed in again as soon as he had passed."

CHAPTER III

FORESTRY

Ban Forests or Royal Forests ; Early Forestry ; The Moon's Influence ; Ancient Foresters ; Forest Customs.

ALTHOUGH the words " forest " and " forestry " are now generally understood to be connected with trees, yet the former does not necessarily mean wooded ground or natural woodland, but has been considered to have been derived from the Latin *foris*, meaning " out-of-doors," and thus the unenclosed open land. Dr. Wedgwood, however, considered it to be a modified form of the Welsh *gores*, *gorest*, waste or waste ground, whence the English word *gorse*, i.e. " whin " or " furze," was derived, as being the product of waste land. In the early Norman, Plantagenet, and Tudor days the word had a much wider and more significant meaning, and as many of these wastes were clothed with trees and undergrowth, the word " forest " was in course of time applied to a great wood. Marrwood, in his *Lawes of the Forest* (1598), described a forest as " a certen territorie of wooddy grounds and fruitfull pastures, priviledged for wild beasts and foules of forrest, chase, and warren, to rest and abide in, in the safe protection of the king, for his princely delight and pleasure." Another definition speaks of a forest as extensive waste lands which include a certain amount of woodland and pasture within which the right of hunting was exclusively reserved for the king, and which was subject to a special code of laws.[1] The ancients, on the other hand, called a large tract of country covered with trees a *sylva*, from whence is derived the word " sylviculture."

In the Middle Ages the Emperors of Germany and other royal personages were the first to enclose large tracts of land, in which they preserved deer and other game for the purpose

[1] J. Charles Cox, *The Royal Forests of England*, 1905.

of hunting. They made many forest laws concerning boundaries, pasturage, right to feeding swine on mast, damage done to trees, etc. These tracts were known as Ban Forests. King James I. of England was the first who enclosed a part of Windsor Forest, and he incurred much obloquy thereby.

These Ban Forests, or Royal Forests, of the Middle Ages seem to have been originally heathen groves over which the king eventually asserted a right, and withdrew the holy wood from use by the people. Gibbon says : " The royal forests were reserved for the more important purposes of the chase ; and the trees, says Nicetas, were guarded by the eunuchs, like the groves of religious worship." [1]

In Alsace, a royal ban forest existed at Dreieich (from the heathen worship of three Oaks) for a very long period, and its charter was one of the most primitive.

Prescott, speaking of the Forests of Mexico, mentions a tale of one of the ancient kings of Tezcuco, Nezahualcoyotl by name, who reigned in the fifteenth century. He says : " It was common for him to ramble among [his subjects] in disguise, like the celebrated caliph in the ' Arabian Nights,' mingling freely in conversation, and ascertaining their actual condition with his own eyes.

" On one such occasion, when attended only by a single lord, he met with a boy who was gathering sticks in a field for fuel. He enquired of him ' why he did not go into the neighbouring forest, where he would find a plenty of them.' To which the lad answered, ' It was the king's wood, and he would punish him with death if he trespassed there.' The royal forests were very extensive in Tezcuco, and were guarded by laws full as severe as those of the Norman tyrants in England. ' What kind of man is your king ? ' asked the monarch, willing to learn the effect of these prohibitions on his own popularity. ' A very hard man,' answered the boy, ' who denies his people what God has given them.' Nezahualcoyotl urged him not to mind such arbitrary

[1] *History of the Decline and Fall of the Roman Empire* (1847), vol. iv. p.192.

laws, but to glean his sticks in the forest, as there was no one present who would betray him ; but the boy sturdily refused, bluntly accusing the disguised king at the same time of being a traitor, and wishing to bring him into trouble." The end was that the king sent for the boy and his parents, commended the former for his respect for the laws, and praised the parents for their praiseworthy upbringing of their son. He also " mitigated the severity of the forest laws, so as to allow persons to gather any wood they might find on the ground, if they did not meddle with the standing timber." [1]

The forests of the primeval world consisted of many varieties of trees and shrubs, and when the older plants reached their limit of life they disappeared, others taking their place. This natural regeneration of the forests went on uninterruptedly for untold ages, until at length mankind appeared, and by his interference the areas under trees became considerably reduced with accompanying alterations in the climate of the various countries and in the productiveness of their soil. Humboldt said that by felling the forests on the sides of mountains, men in every climate prepared two calamities for future generations, these being want of fuel and scarcity of water. Trees, he says, by the radiation from their leaves in a cloudless sky, surround themselves with a cold and misty atmosphere. As they shelter the soil from the direct action of the sun, evaporation is checked and the water collects to form copious springs. On the other hand, when forests are destroyed, the undergrowths of grass and moss vanish also, with the result that the water produced by heavy rains has an unimpeded course down the hill-sides, and torrents and inundations are the natural sequence.

The earliest recorded instance of Forestry operations, in which trees were transplanted to a foreign land, is found in the records of an Egyptian expedition to the Land of Punt, now known as Somaliland, during the reign of Queen Hatasu, of the Eighteenth Dynasty. The object of this expedition

---

[1] *The Conquest of Mexico*, ed. 1844, vol. i. p. 9.

seems to have been to explore the lands from which incense was brought, and the history of the expedition was depicted on the walls of the Temple of Hathor at Deir-el-Bahari. It reads : " Laden was the cargo to the uttermost with all the wonderful products of the Land of Punt, and with the different nut-woods of the divine land, and with heaps of the resin of incense, with fresh incense trees, with ebony," and so on. It is said that thirty-one of these incense trees, well packed in tubs, were drawn on board the vessels, and that it took six men to drag one of the tubs. An inscription of a later date, 1200 B.C., records how Rameses III., of the Twentieth Dynasty, says : " I have planted trees and shrubs to the end that the people should sit under their shade."

In ancient days the state of the moon, whether it was waxing or waning, was considered to be of great importance in connection with the felling of timber. Pliny, borrowing from Theophrastus, says that the very best time to cut down trees is when the moon is in conjunction with the sun, that day being called the *interlinium*, or sometimes the " moon's silence." He says that Tiberius Cæsar took advantage of that belief to fell the Larches in Rhætia which he required to rebuild the bridge of the Naumachia, which had been destroyed by fire. Cutting the trees at the time of the rising of the Dog Star was also said to be favourable, and the timber used for building the Forum of Augustus was cut at that time. Cato (*De Re Rustica*, chaps. xvii, xxxi, xxxvii) gives instructions regarding timber as follows : " When you root up the Elm, the Pine, the Nut-tree, or indeed any other kind of tree, mind and do so when the moon is on the wane, after midday, and when there is no south wind blowing. The proper time for cutting a tree is when the seed is ripe, but be careful not to draw it away or plane it when the dew is falling." He then proceeds to say : " Never touch the timber except when the moon is on the change, or else at the end of the second quarter : at these periods you may either root up the tree, or fell it as it stands. The next seven days after the full moon are the best

of all for grubbing up a tree. Be particularly careful not to
rough-hew timber, or indeed, to cut or touch it, unless it is
perfectly dry ; and by no means while it is covered with frost
or dew." [1]

Even in comparatively recent times the wane of the moon,
or when it is *wadel*, was considered to be the best time for
tree-felling. The underlying idea seemed to be that as the
moon grew less in the sky so the amount of sap in the wood
decreased or flowed downwards, leaving the wood dryer, much
in the same manner as the waters of the ocean are affected
as seen in the tides. Jacob Grim mentions that in a calendar
printed by Hupfuff (Strasbourg, 1511) appears the following :
" With the moon's wedel 'tis good to begin the hewing of
wood," and he adds that the same precept is still given in
many modern forest-books, and full-moon is therefore called
holz-wadel : " In the bad wädel (crescent moon) fell no
timber." [2] Thus, in early times, carpenters rejected wood
which had been cut when the moon was waxing, alleging that
at that time it was full of moisture. The Forest Laws of
France had formerly a regulation that trees must only be felled
when the moon was on the wane, and even yet in some parts
the opinion is held that wood cut soon after new moon will
not dry. In some parts of the world, however, the opposite
is said to be the case. Thus, some tribes in East Africa use
posts for their hut-building which had been cut while the
moon was waxing, as they considered them very durable, and
some German foresters hold the same opinion.

It is said that in Demarara there is a tree resembling
mahogany called Walala, which is much influenced by the
phases of the moon. If the tree be cut down at new moon,
the wood is tough and very difficult to split, but if the moon
is full at the time, the wood is soft and splits very easily.[3]

The first forester of whom there is any authentic notice was
one Ûni or Una, an Egyptian, whose name appears in the

[1] Pliny, *Nat. Hist.*, bk. xvi. c. 75.
[2] Grim, *Teut. Myth.*, ed. Stallybrass, 1882–88, vol. ii. p. 714.
[3] *Ibid.*

inscription on his tomb. This is one of the most ancient historical texts known, and was discovered by Mariette in the necropolis of Abydos. It takes us back to about the year 3500 B.C., and Ûni was Forester or Inspector of the Woods of the Royal Domain to King Pepi or the Pharaoh Teta. The woods of which he had charge were " probably lands with plantations of palms or acacias, the thinly wooded forests of Egypt, and also of the vines which belonged to the personal domain of the Pharaoh.[1]

Much later, and in another country, another Forester, named Asaph, is mentioned. Nehemiah, when about to rebuild the wall of Jerusalem, obtained letters from Artaxerxes the king, " and a letter unto Asaph, the keeper of the king's forest, that he may give me timber to make beams for the gates of the palace which appertained to the house, and for the wall of the city, and for the house that I shall enter into. And the king granted me, according to the good hand of my God upon me." [2]

In the Ancient Assyrian inscriptions is found the text of the legend of the infancy of Sargina the First, King of Agani, who reigned about the fifteenth or sixteenth century B.C. The king tells how he was born in a secret place, and his mother placed him in an ark of bulrushes well sealed with bitumen, and then threw him into the River Euphrates. The river bore him along on its stream to the dwelling of Akki, the water-carrier, who rescued him and brought him up as his own son. Afterwards he placed him among a tribe of Foresters or Woodmen, and the goddess Ishtar made him the chief or king over them.[3] The record, being partly obliterated, does not specify how many years he reigned over this tribe. This tale bears a close resemblance to that of Moses being found among the bulrushes, and probably both had the same origin, the latter being likely a later adaptation.

Death has been symbolically regarded as a forester, and has

---

[1] Professor Maspero, *The Dawn of Civilisation*, p. 417.
[2] Nehemiah ii. 8.   [3] *Records of the Past*, 1874, vol. v.

been called *holz-meier*, or wood-mower, by Kaiserberg. In a folio written in 1521, called *De arbore humana*, he says : " Wherein easily, and to the glory of God, ye may learn to await blithely the wood-cutter Death." And again : " So is Death called a village-mower or wood-mower, and justly hath he the name, for he hath in him the properties of a wood-cutter, as, please God, ye shall hear. The first property of the village-mower is communitas, he being possessed in common by all such as be in the village, and being to serve them all alike. So is the wood-cutter common to all the trees, he overlooketh no tree, but heweth them all down."

As may be expected many various customs peculiar to different forests, yet sometimes similar, prevail among forest-dwellers throughout the world, but only a few can be referred to here.

In the Neilgherry Mountains, M. Elie Reclus tells us,[1] when a Toda woman has been pregnant for seven months she and her husband retire into the recesses of the forest where they select a certain tree. Beneath this tree they light a lamp, and the wife then kneels and receives a tiny bow and arrows, which she places at the foot of the tree. After partaking of the evening meal the two spend the night in the forest as if to place the child under the protection of the forest deities. As soon as the child is born, the father takes three leaves from the tree, twists them to form cups and pours a little water into one. With this he moistens his lips, and pours the rest equally into the other two leaves. The mother drinks from one, and the infant is made to drink from the other. " Thus," says M. Reclus, " father, mother, and child, earliest of Trinities, celebrate their first communion, and drink the living water, more sacred than wine, from the leaves of the Tree of Life." Next morning the mother and child take up their abode in a hut in the forest, where they remain until it is new moon, and this may be for· a day or a month. The mother then goes home, and the father in turn repairs to the forest, where he remains during the duration of a moon.

[1] *Primitive Folk.*

A Malayan tribe, called the Arucans, do not bury their dead in the earth, but carry the body into the forest, where they place it on the top of four wooden pillars, and a tree is planted near it. This tree is usually the *Pavetta Indica*, and they have the curious custom of allowing none but naked females to be present at the planting of the tree.

In one part of the island of Papua, when youths of marriageable age are engaged in making their drums, they are compelled to live alone in the forest and to observe certain rules. It was believed that if the youth " ate a red banana it would choke him, and the drum would give a dull stifled note ; if he tasted grated coco-nut, the white ants, like the white particles of the nut, would gnaw the body of the drum." [1] Other rules, also, required to be observed, as, if not, the drum would be a failure.

In one of the ancient kingdoms of Ethiopia lying south from Egypt, called Gingiro, there was usually great reluctance to assume the sovereignty over the tribe, and Dr. J. G. Frazer [2] quotes from *The Travels of the Jesuits in Ethiopia*, collected and historically digested by F. Balthazar Tellez (London, 1710), pp. 197 *et seq.*, the following : " They wrap up the dead king's body in costly garments, and killing a cow put it into the hide ; then all who hope to succeed him, being his sons, or others of the royal blood, flying from the honour they covet, abscond and hide themselves in the woods. This done, the electors, who are all great sorcerers, agree among themselves who shall be king, and go out to seek him. When entering the woods, by means of their enchantments, they say a large bird called *liber*, as big as an eagle, comes down with mighty cries over the place where he is hid, and they find him encompass'd by lyons, tygers, snakes, and other creatures, gather'd about him by witchcraft. The elect, as fierce as those beasts, rushes out upon those who seek him, wounding and sometimes killing some of them, to prevent

[1] Dr. J. G. Frazer, *The Golden Bough*, " The Magic Art and the Evolution of Kings," Part I, vol. i. pp. 134–35.
[2] *Ibid.*, Part II, " Taboo and the Perils of the Soul," pp. 18–19.

being seiz'd. They take all in good part, defending themselves the best they can, till they have seiz'd him. Thus they
carry him away by force, he still struggling and seeming to
refuse taking upon him the burthen of government, all of
which is mere cheat and hypocrisy."

There is a custom among the natives of the Forest of
Uregga, traversed by Stanley during his second expedition
into Africa,[1] that when a man's wife dies he puts a thick
daub of charcoal paste over his face, which must be kept on
for two years and a half. A woman who loses her husband
does the same, and, in addition, wears bands of withered banana
leaves round the forehead.

On some parts of the West African coast the king of the
tribe is regarded as the divinity. He controls the weather
and raises storms or allays them. He must live alone in the
forest, and must never lie down to sleep, because, if he left
his seat, the wind would not blow, and consequently navi-
gation would cease.

When the king of the Ho tribe, in Togoland, dies, it is
considered necessary to bury him with the utmost secrecy so
as to prevent his enemies from violating his grave and cutting
off his head. To achieve the end in view a false burial takes
place with much ceremony in or near the king's house, while
the real burial is performed by stealth in some secret spot
in the forest, only one of the king's daughters and a few
trustworthy friends knowing where that spot is. Some other
African tribes have the same practice.

The island of Fernando Po in the Bight of Biafra is very
densely wooded, and in some parts the natives have the curious
custom of burying their dead in the forests with the heads
just sticking up out of the ground.

Many of the Indian tribes of North America believed that
their Medicine Men were endowed with supernatural attributes, as it was not possible for all and sundry to obtain such
a distinction. Far from it. Anyone desirous of attaining that

[1] *Through the Dark Continent.*

dignity had to receive tuition from the older adepts in the art, and also to undergo the most severe trials. These took place in the depths of the forest. The novice had to fast until he almost succumbed from starvation, and had to wound and otherwise torture himself in various ways. The effect of all this was to induce dreams in which spirits figured, and to cause him to believe that they gave him various messages. After passing all the tests successfully he was initiated into the mysteries of the profession, and thus became a full-fledged Medicine Man.[1]

Some of the North American forests were often the scene of a race for a bride. The bride would ride into the forest pursued by her suitors, and the one who could capture her was the lucky one. Needless to say, she usually allowed herself to be caught by the favoured one.[2]

Among certain of the Brazilian tribes the belief is prevalent that moonlight is injurious to babies, consequently immediately after a baby is born the mother retires with it into the thickest part of the forest where the light of the moon cannot penetrate.[3]

[1] James C. Strong, *Wah-Kee-Nah and her People*, 1893, pp. 72–73.
[2] *Ibid.*

[3] Coroados, J. B. von Spix and C. F. Ph. von Martius, *Reise in Brazilien*, vol. i. p. 381.

CHAPTER IV

GROVES

Earliest Temples ; Druids ; Classic Groves.

WHEN the earliest progenitors of the human race had at length evolved from a purely savage state they would no doubt begin to consider the why and wherefore of their existence, and would have vague glimmerings of some power higher than themselves whom it was necessary to propitiate and to worship. They saw the sun in the heavens travelling daily, as they thought, from east to west, pouring out its fervent heat upon them, enabling them to see their surroundings, and causing all vegetation to grow and flourish in its beams. Need one wonder that the sun was considered to be a most powerful deity, and that adoration was especially due to him. They considered it unlawful to build temples wherein to worship the sun because no temple could be spacious enough for him, and one of their sayings ran, *Mundus universus est templum solis*—the whole world is a temple of the sun. As the various forces of Nature impressed their power on the mind of primitive man, other gods or goddesses presiding over each of these forces were gradually evolved, and all of them were at first worshipped in the open air.

The popular conception of the character of a grove is an assemblage of beautiful trees which together impart a peculiar beauty to the scene ; and the external forms of these trees possess so much beauty, and their overhanging boughs afford so welcome a shelter, that we need not wonder if in early ages groves were considered as fittest temples for the gods, and it was believed by the ancients that ghosts and spirits took a delight in making their appearance there. The poet Waller wrote :

" In such green palaces the first kings reign'd ;
Slept in their shades and angels entertain'd.
With such old counsellors they did advise,
And by frequenting sacred groves grew wise ;
Free from th' impediments of light and noise,
Man thus retir'd, his noblest thoughts employs."

Professor Hehn believes that Europe owes much to Asia in
the matters of its forest flora, and particularly that the evergreen trees of Greece and Italy were not indigenous to these
countries, but were due to the sacred groves surrounding the
temples of the Oriental gods and goddesses, and that thus the
Laurel had followed in the wake of the worship of Apollo,
the Cypress and the Myrtle in that of Aphrodite or Astoreth
of the Zidonians, and the Olive in that of Athena.[1] Later
on we shall see how these trees came to be associated with the
worship of those divinities, though it is probable that in the
case of the Olive its value to mankind had a great part in the
superstitions and beliefs which surrounded it at a very early
period.

Originally, hills and mountains were considered the most
befitting spots for worship, as being nearer to the heaven
where the divinities resided, and, in course of time, to beautify
these holy hills, trees were planted upon them, and from this
arose the consecration of these groves ; but the worship of,
and in, groves seems to have at first arisen from the veneration
paid to natural groves. These holy hills were the " high
places " mentioned in the Bible as being forbidden, and the
prohibition, in Deuteronomy xvi. 21, as to planting groves
near the altar, arose from the perversion of these groves to
the purposes of idolatry. The patriarchs of the Bible probably
retired to groves in which to worship God, and, in the Oak
grove at Mamre, we are told (Genesis xviii.) that Abraham
entertained God Himself. We are also told that Abraham
raised an altar to Jehovah near a grove of Terebinths in the
Valley of Hebron. In many instances an idol was placed on
the holy hill and was surrounded by the trees. We read

[1] Hehn and Stallybrass, *Wanderings of Plants and Animals.*

(2 Kings xviii. 4), " He removed the high places and brake the images, and cut down the groves." It would appear that the idol itself was sometimes called a grove, as—" Ahab made a grove " (1 Kings xvi. 33) ; also—" And they set them up images and groves in every high hill and under every green tree " (2 Kings xvii. 10) ; and again—" And they left all the commandments of the Lord their God, and made them molten images, even two calves, and made a grove, and wor- shipped all the host of heaven, and served Baal " (2 Kings xvii. 16). We read, further, that Manasseh " built up again the high places which Hezekiah his father had destroyed ; and he reared up altars for Baal, and made a grove, as did Ahab king of Israel. . . . And he set a graven image of the grove that he had made in the house " (2 Kings xxi. 3, 7). Later on it is recorded that Josiah " brought out the grove from the house of the Lord, without Jerusalem, unto the brook Kidron, and burned it at the brook Kidron, and stamped it small to powder, and cast the powder thereof upon the graves of the children of the people.

" And he brake down the houses of the sodomites, that were by the house of the Lord, where the women wove hangings for the grove " (2 Kings xxiii. 6, 7). The priests who officiated at the idolatrous ceremonies carried on in these groves were called prophets of the grove.

Tacitus remarks that the Israelites, having been driven forth from Egypt by the oracle of Jupiter Ammon, found themselves abandoned in a wild and barren desert. There they were much distressed from want of water until Moses noticed a herd of wild asses going up to a rock shaded with a grove. He followed them, and, noticing the state of the herbage, succeeded in opening up copious springs of water. Probably these were the twelve wells of Elim.

One of the Grail Legends, that of Guyot, tells that a temple dedicated to the Grail was erected on a high hill in the centre of a thick wood or grove, as symbolic of the holiness of that place which no one could enter except by Divine favour.

Evelyn [1] says that Paradise itself was but a kind of nemorous temple or sacred grove planted by God Himself and given to man. It was a place consecrated for sober discipline, wherein to contemplate those mysterious and sacramental trees which they were not to touch with their hands; and in memory of them holy men might plant and cultivate groves where they could invoke the deity. In Ireland, in the shadow of groves of Oak trees, St. Columba planted the Monasteries of Derry and Durrow, these names being derived from the Oak. Mr. S. Baring-Gould [2] quotes the following from a manuscript in the British Museum: " Paradise is neither in heaven nor on earth. The book says that Noah's flood was forty fathoms high, over the highest hills that are on earth; and Paradise is forty fathoms higher than Noah's flood was, and it hangeth between heaven and earth wonderfully as the ruler of all things made it. And it is perfectly level both in length and breadth. There is neither hollow nor hill; nor is there frost nor snow, hail nor rain; but there is *fons vitæ*, that is, the well of life. When the calends of January commence, then floweth the well so beautifully and so gently, and no deeper than man may wet his finger on the front, over all that land. And so likewise each month, once when the month comes in the well begins to flow. And there is the copse of wood, which is called Radion Saltus, where each tree is as straight as an arrow, and so high, that no earthly man ever saw so high, or can say of what kind they are. And there never falleth leaf off, for they are evergreen, beautiful, and pleasant, full of happiness. Paradise is upright on the eastern part of this world. There is neither heat nor hunger, nor is there ever night, but always day. The sun there shineth seven times brighter than on this earth. Therein dwell innumerable angels of God with the holy souls till doomsday. Therein dwelleth a beautiful bird called *Phœnix*; he is large and grand, as the Mighty One formed him; he is the bird over all birds."

[1] *Sylva*, p. 214.
[2] *Curious Myths of the Middle Ages*, 1875, pp. 255–6.

It is worthy of note that the word " Paradise " is the Sanskrit
para desa, and means " high land."

The solemn seclusion of a forest grove seemed to primitive
man to be a place of worship set apart by Nature, and these
groves appear to have been the only and the earliest temples.
In fact, it has been remarked that the architect, when he
designed his vistas of slender columns spreading out into and
supporting roofs of tracery, might well be supposed to have had
in his mind's eye some beautiful recollection of the arcades
of Nature's palaces in the sombre forests, where the twisted
trunks of the trees, the fretwork of their branches and the
leafy covering formed by their leaves supply all the requisites
of a grand and lofty temple, fit for the worship of that great
First Cause who formed them.[1]   A poet says :

> " Groves were planted to console at noon
> The pensive wanderer in their shades. At eve
> The moonbeams, sliding softly in between
> The sleeping leaves, is all the light he wants
> For meditation,"

and thus all who sought a refuge

> " From the world retired,
> Conversed with angels and immortal forms."

In Central and Northern Europe dark groves composed of
ancient trees, and situated in the midst of gloomy forests,
were, as said previously, the only temples, but these had been
rendered holy by the awe and reverence with which they had
inspired each succeeding generation. An invisible deity dwelt
in them who made his power felt in the storms which swept
over them, or in the sunshine which flooded the woodland
glades.

In our own country, and throughout a great part of Northern
Europe, the worship of the Druids was carried on for many
centuries. It was an article in their creed that it was unlawful
to build temples to the gods, or to worship them within walls

---

[1] Elisha Noyce, *Outlines of Creation*, 1858, p. 214.

and under roofs. Consequently all their places of worship were in the open air, and were generally on high ground from whence they could view the heavenly bodies to which much of their adoration was directed. But lest they be incommoded by the winds and rains, distracted by the view of external objects, or disturbed by the intrusion of unhallowed feet when they were instructing their disciples, or performing their religious rites, they made choice of the deepest recesses of groves and woods for their most sacred places, and groves were often planted for that purpose with those trees in which they most delighted. The chief of these was a strong and spreading Oak, for which tree the Druids had a very high and superstitious veneration. These sacred groves were watered by some consecrated fountain or river, and were surrounded by a ditch or mound to prevent the intrusion of strangers. No one was permitted to enter these consecrated groves except through the passages left open for the purpose. These passages were guarded by Druids of an inferior standing to prevent intrusion into the sacred mysteries. Some of the groves were circular, others were oblong, and they were large or small, according to the number of worshippers in the district. In the centre of the grove was a circular area enclosed with one or two rows of large stones set perpendicularly in the earth, which constituted the temple, within which the altar stood on which the sacrifices were offered.

An Oak coppice or grove near Loch Siant, in the island of Skye, was at one time held so sacred that no person would venture to cut even the smallest twig from it.

Sacred groves of Hazel trees formerly existed in the vicinity of Edinburgh and Glasgow, the memory of which is still perpetuated in the name Calton, from the Gaelic *calltunn*, " hazel."

When temples of stone were first begun to be erected an opening was left at the summit of the roof as reminiscent of the holy grove open to the sky, and, evidently with the same idea, Strabo mentions that the Celts unroofed their temples once a year. Many of the ancient churches are said to have owed their origin to miraculous lights having been seen in a grove or wood during the night, these lights being so arranged as to show the ground plan of the future building.[1] It will thus be recognised that the *templum nemorale*—the grove used as a temple—was the only temple primitive man knew, and

> " In the resounding wood
> All vocal beings hymned their equal god."

Many of the smaller forests or woods of Germany are considered to have been holy groves where in ancient times sacrifices were made under certain trees, and in which the bards were inspired to prophesy. Thus we find the Odenwald or Odinswald, the grove sacred to Odin.

In a sacred grove on the mountains it was alleged that witches used to assemble on a certain day to attend to the boiling of salt, as at one time this process was under the care of special priestesses. It afterwards became associated with witchcraft, because witches were believed to hold their assemblies beside salt springs.

Among the Semnones, who lived on the banks of the River Oder and were the principal tribe of the Suevi, a particular reverence was paid to a peculiarly sacred grove situated in Saxony. Tacitus [2] tells us that no person entered this grove without being bound with a chain, as an acknowledgment of his inferior nature and the power of the deity residing there. If he accidentally fell, it was not lawful for him to be lifted or to rise up. He had to roll himself out of the grove along the ground. It was believed that from that spot the nation had its origin—that there was the residence of the Deity, the Governor of all. This grove became known as the Sonnenwald or wood of the Semnones, and at certain periods many of the tribes who were of Suevic blood sent representatives thither, and in the recesses of the grove the memory of

[1] Grim, *Teut. Myth.*, ed. Stallybrass, vol. iv. p. 1313.
[2] *The History*, etc., Oxford trans., p. 331.

the common origin of all was celebrated by human sacrifices
and other savage observances.

Throughout the whole of ancient Germany the groves
dedicated to certain deities were forbidden to be entered by
anyone except the officiating priests or soothsayers,[1] and the
gods were believed to sit enthroned on the trees of these sacred
groves.[2]

Owing to worship having been conducted in groves the gods
were in many cases supposed to be attended by wild animals.
Thus Wotan was attended by a wolf and also by a raven, while
the attendant of Froho was a boar.[3]

Within the sacred groves of Germany the natives kept their
battle standards, which appear to have been images of the
heads of wild animals, or, perhaps, of the whole animal, and
it is considered that they were representative of their deity,
as it was held to be degrading to the latter to represent him
in human form, or to confine him within walls. When a war
was about to be waged these images were brought forth from
the grove and carried before the army.

Ancient writers speak of groves as being tenanted by supernatural beings, and that wayfarers, when passing through their
sombre and gloomy shades, hear the voices of these beings
as the breeze rustles the heavy foliage, or the wind causes the
branches to sway and creak. As time wore on each separate
tree was believed to be the residence of some individual sylvan
deity. The ancients were wont to bury their dead in the
shade of the sacred grove. Certain groves of the Samagitians
were held to be so sacred that, if any of the trees were injured
or the birds and animals disturbed by anyone, it was believed
that the spirits of the grove would cause that person's hands
and feet to become deformed.

Jacob Grim mentions a charm used by herdsmen taken from
a manuscript of the fifteenth century. It runs thus : " To day
my herd I drove Into Our Lady's grove, Into Abraham's

[1] Grim, *Teut. Myth.*, ed. Stallybrass, vol. ii. p. 648.
[2] *Ibid.*, vol. i. p. 430.   [3] *Ibid.*, vol iv. p. 1309.

garden ; be good St. Martin This day my cattle's Warden, May good St. Wolfgang, good St. Peter (whose key can heav'n unlock), Throat of wolf and vixen block, Blood from shedding, bone from crunching ! Help me, the holy one, Who ill hath never done, and his V holy wounds Keep my herd from all wood-hounds ! " [1]

In Scandinavia the god Baldur the Beautiful was worshipped in a sacred grove near the Sogne Fiord. The profanation of this grove by Frithjof is mentioned in the Frithjof Saga.

There was a grove, Hoddmimir's Grove, in the dreary realms of Hel, where certain sinless beings were held ready to repeople the world after the last dread catastrophe, the twilight of the gods.

In the Scandinavian countries groves and trees were appointed as the residence of the Elves after they had been worsted in a conflict with superior beings. In other countries groves were much frequented by fairies and other beings of popular superstition.

Seneca wrote : " If you come upon a grove of old trees that have shot up above the common height, and shut out the sight of the sky by the gloom of their matted boughs, you feel there is a spirit in the place, so lofty is the wood, so lone the spot, so wondrous the thick unbroken shade " (*Epist.* iv. 12, 3). It was in this spirit that Greece and Italy became, above all other countries, the lands of sacred groves with all their poetical associations, and the veneration in which they were held is shown by the fact that Xerxes, when passing through Achaia, forbade his army to do any act of devastation in a grove dedicated to Jupiter which they passed.

Roman shepherds, when they celebrated the festival of the Parilia for ensuring the welfare of their flocks and herds, prayed that they might be forgiven if they had entered a sacred grove or fed their sheep on the leaves of a holy tree.

The myth of Cupid and Psyché relates that Venus, being jealous of the beauty of Psyché, caused her to be exposed on

[1] *Teut. Myth.*, ed. Stallybrass, vol. iii. p. 1241.

a high rock from whence she would be carried away by a monster, but one of the Zephyrs rescued her, and wafted her gently away to a charming valley. Here she fell asleep, and on awaking beheld a grove containing a fountain, and a stately palace close at hand. A voice told her it was hers, and she entered it and retired to rest. Shortly after, an unseen youth tenderly addressed her, and she became his wife. Her jealous sisters persuaded her that her lord was a serpent, and she proceeded to endeavour to destroy him. When he was asleep she approached his couch and was amazed to see Love (Eros or Cupid) himself. A drop of oil from her lamp awakened him, and he flew away. Psyché, however, caught him by the leg as he ascended, but could not retain her hold, and as she lay on the ground Cupid, from the top of a Cypress tree, reproached her for her curiosity. They were eventually reconciled, and became the parents of Pleasure.

It was in a grove that Endymion was espied by the goddess Silene, or the Moon, who then and there fell in love with him, as the poet Fletcher says :

> " How the pale Phœbe, hunting in a grove,
> First saw the boy Endymion, from whose eyes
> She took eternal fire that never dies."

Poggius, an Italian, who wrote in the fifteenth century, says that originally the Tarpeian Rock was in the centre of a savage and solitary thicket or grove ; that in the time of Virgil it was crowned with the golden roofs of a temple ; and that in the writer's time it had reverted to its original wild state of thorns and brambles.

The ancient Athenians held consultations regarding matters of the gravest importance within the shadow of groves, and Philo mentions a certain religious sect, the θεωρητικοί, who were given to contemplation, and who were wont to retire into the solitudes of woods and groves.

In the Slavonic groves a perpetual fire was kept burning in honour of the god Piorun.

Mr. Edward B. Tylor remarks that full well the Turanian tribes of Siberia know the gods of the forest. " The Yakuts hang on any remarkably fine tree iron, brass, and other trinkets ; they choose a green spot shaded by a tree for their spring sacrifice of horses and oxen, whose heads are set up in the boughs ; they chant their extemporised songs to the Spirit of the Forest, and hang for him on the branches of the trees along the roadside offerings of horsehair, emblems of their most valued possession. A clump of larches on a Siberian steppe, a grove in the recesses of a forest, is the sanctuary of a Turanian tribe. Gaily-decked idols in their warm fur-coats, each set up beneath its great tree swathed with cloth or tinplate, endless reindeer hides and peltry hanging to the trees around, kettles and spoons and snuff-horns and household valuables strewn as offerings before the gods—such is the description of a Siberian holy grove at the stage when the contract of foreign civilisation had begun by ornamenting the rude old ceremonial it must end by abolishing." [1]

In the sacred groves of the Ostiacks of Siberia everything seems to have been forbidden ; one could not hunt or fish, or even take a drink of water. Among them seven Larch trees constituted a sacred grove. Everyone who passed by had to leave an arrow in the grove, or suspend furs from the trees. A Russian who once cut down a tree in one is said to have died the day after his sacrilege.

There is a rivulet known as the Holy Wöhhanda which has its source in a sacred grove near Ilmegerve, a village of Esthonia. No one dares to cut down a tree, or even to break a twig in this holy place. Should one do so he is sure to die within the year. Both the rivulet and the spring from which it flows are carefully cleaned once a year, and it is said that if anything is thrown into the spring the weather at once becomes stormy. [2]

[1] *Primitive Culture*, 1871, vol. ii.
[2] Grim, *Teut. Myth.*, ed. Stallybrass, vol. ii. p. 598.

In Poland a sacred grove was called *rok* and *uroczysko*, and when invasion threatened, rods cut from the grove were sent around to summon the neighbours, much after the same fashion as the fiery cross was wont to be sent round in Scotland.[1]

The City of Vienna arose round a sacred grove, the last remaining tree of which, a venerable Oak, the *Stock am Eisen*, stands in the centre of the city.

In Lithuania holy groves were often maintained near the villages, and it was considered a deadly sin to break off a branch therein, and that he who did so would either die suddenly or be crippled for life. In the year 1386, Yagello, Grand Duke of Lithuania, adopted Christianity as the religion of his country, and felled the sacred groves. But for many centuries afterwards the heathen rites and festivals continued to be carried on in secret in the gloomy depths of the Lithuanian forests.

W. Mannhardt speaks of an old sacred grove consisting of Fir trees, near Dorpat in Russia, where, when rain was wanted, three men used to climb up the tree. One hammered on a kettle to imitate thunder, another struck two burning sticks together, making sparks fly, so as to resemble lightning, and the third sprinkled water from a vessel with a bunch of twigs, to imitate rain. This latter was called the rain-maker.[2]

The Moslem heaven, among other delights, comprised numerous groves, and the tale is told of an Arabian youth who, embracing his relatives on leaving for the field of battle, exclaimed : " Farewell, we shall meet again among the groves and fountains which God has provided for His elect." [3]

In India, and particularly in Bengal when the primitive forest was felled, care was always taken to leave several majestic trees standing, forming sacred groves, wherein the various woodland spirits might find refuge. Almost every village in India has a grove near it in which is situated a temple dedicated to one or other of the many Hindu divinities.

[1] Grim. *Teut. Myth.*, ed. Stallybrass, vol. i. p. 77.
[2] *Antike Wald-, und Feldkulte*, p. 342, note.
[3] Gibbon, *Decline and Fall of the Roman Empire*, ed. 1847, vol. iii. p. 471.

As these temples are inhabited by the officiating priests fruit trees form a considerable proportion of the constituents of the groves. The Khonds of Bengal cannot understand building a house for the deity, and consequently groves are used for that purpose, and kept sacred from the axe. These sacred groves in or near every village are generally composed of Sâl trees (*Shorea robusta*). Each village dedicates its grove to the forest god.

M. Gerson da Cunha, in his *Life and System of Gautama Buddha* (London, 1875), writes regarding the death of Buddha thus : " He then retired to Kuçinagara, and entered a grove of Sâl-Trees ; there, during the night he received a gift of food from an artisan named Chanda, and was seized with illness. At early dawn next day, as he turned on to his right side with his head to the north, the Sâl-Trees bending down to form a canopy over his body, he ceased to breathe."

In Assam each Mundari village has its sacred grove, and the gods of the grove " are held responsible for the crops, and are especially honoured at all the great agricultural festivals." It is believed that if a tree of the grove is cut down, the gods in their anger will withhold rain.[1]

Mr. W. W. Skeat mentions a grove of Durian trees near Jugra in Selangor in the Malay Peninsular, in which the villagers assemble on a certain day. One of the local wizards strikes the most fruitless tree, and says : " Will you now bear fruit or not ? If you do not, I shall fell you." Another man who has climbed a Mangosteen tree, replies for the Durian, saying : " Yes, I will now bear fruit. I beg you not to fell me."[2]

Confucius completed his commentaries on the ancient books of China in the solitude of a grove of Apricot trees. After having done so, he erected an altar there, and thanked Heaven for having allowed him to bring his cherished scheme to a happy issue.

[1] Villault, *Relation des costes appellés Guinée* (Paris, 1699), pp. 266 *et seq.*
[2] *Malay Magic*, pp. 198 *et seq.*

In Africa, as in other countries, almost every village has its sacred grove which the priests alone might enter. Barth [1] tells that the tribe of the Marghi use a very dense part of the forest as a sacred grove, and that the most luxuriant and wide-spreading tree in the grove is considered to typify their god Zumbi, and is worshipped accordingly.

The Barotse buried their dead kings in a grove of beautiful trees surrounded by a high fence, and situated near the village where they had resided. These groves were sacred, no one being allowed to enter them lest the spirits of the dead should be disturbed. They were looked upon as gods, and when any calamity threatened the country they were consulted.

In the North Island of New Zealand, at Mokau Heads, may be seen certain celebrated groves of the *Pomaderris tainui*, which is found only here in the whole of New Zealand. Legend accounts for its existence on this spot in the following manner. The ancestors of the Maoris are said to have originally come from the islands of the Central and Eastern Pacific. They arrived at New Zealand in certain famous canoes, one of which was called the Tainui, and was commanded by Hoturoa. When it entered the Mokau River it was hauled up on skids above high-water mark, and Hoturoa planted three poles to celebrate his taking possession of the land. From these skids and from the poles the grove sprang up and flourished till now. [2]

In the Classic Groves of Greece and Italy the ancient poets found congenial subjects for their songs, and the pages of Homer, Virgil, and others teem with allusions to them. In the early stages of civilisation agriculture was in its infancy, and flocks and herds of sheep and cattle were the principal means of subsistence. All the various operations of a pastoral life were supposed to be presided over by the many and various rustic deities, and the simple people believed in their powers under the names of Pan, Faunus, and others, to bring weal

---

[1] *Travels in Central Africa*, vol. ii. p. 380.
[2] James Cowan, *The Maoris of New Zealand*, 1910, p. 68.

or woe to whatever undertakings they approved or disapproved of. These lesser deities were themselves under the control of the great gods of Olympus, and to these latter many groves were dedicated.

The best known of all the sacred groves of Greece was that of Dodona (sometimes called the Chaonian Forest) in Epirus, consecrated to Zeus or Jupiter, and here a temple to him was raised. It is said that thunderstorms rage more frequently at Dodona than anywhere else in Europe, and it may be that was one reason why the temple was reared in that wood to the God of Thunder. The first temple was situated at the foot of one particular Oak tree, and it was by the rustling of the leaves of this Oak, which moved without being stirred by the wind, that Zeus announced his supreme will to man. Bronze gongs were hung on the Oak trees surrounding the sanctuary, and as the wind swayed them their sonorous tones were probably meant to imitate the thunder, which was often heard rolling in the mountain valleys around. Beech trees also formed part of the grove, and Lucian says that sometimes the oracle was delivered through their medium.

The oracle itself was situated at the foot of Mount Tomarus, and at first the oracles were delivered by an old woman named Pelias, which name means a dove. Herodotus gives the following legend concerning its foundation. Some Phœnician merchants had carried away two Egyptian priestesses of Jupiter from Thebes, one being taken to Lybia where she founded the temple of Jupiter Ammon. The other was conveyed to Greece, and took up her abode in the Dodonian Forest. Here, at the foot of an Oak tree, she caused a temple to Jupiter to be erected, and in after ages many additional edifices and halls were built, and an oracle was founded, known as the Pelasgic Oracle. Hesiod describes it thus : " There is a land Hellopia, rich in fields and meadows, in sheep and broad-hoofed cattle, and many races of mortals inhabit it. At the extreme border is Dodona, walled highly round, chosen by Zeus as his oracle, and honoured by men,

who there receive prophetic rays. Whoever will inquire of
the immortal god must approach with presents and birds of
good omen." [1]

After the temple had been fully established the number of
prophetic priestesses was increased to three, known as Peliades
or Doves, and from this it came to be believed that sacred
doves inhabited the Oak tree at the foot of which the first
temple had been erected, and that these birds themselves
prophesied. This Oak was an Evergreen Oak (*Ilex*), and was
a lofty and beautiful tree, an incredible wonder, as Æschylus
calls it, and it was regarded as the Tree of Life. In it Zeus
himself was supposed to reside, the rustling of the leaves and
the songs of birds denoting his presence there. When the
oracle was to be questioned the leaves rustled, and the priestess
saying, " Thus speaks Zeus," proceeded to interpret the
message. Another source of prophecy was found in the
murmurs of a limpid spring, which gushed, as it were, from
the roots of the tree, and which were interpreted as messages
from the god.

In the year 219 B.C. the temple and all the surrounding
edifices were burned down and utterly destroyed by a band
of Ætolians, and at the time of the birth of Christ the oracle
was practically deserted. Strabo says that only ruins or some
miserable hovels remained, yet Pausanias, writing about the
year A.D. 180, tells that the Sacred Oak still stood, and
Aristides, writing about the same period, seems to infer that
the priestesses still carried on their prophetic rôle. During
the third century, however, an Illyrian robber cut down the
tree, and with its fall the sacred oracle became for ever silent.

There was a temple erected at Delphi to Apollo, and the
oracle in connection with it became famous. Its origin was
as follows : On one occasion some shepherds in the pursuit
of their daily labours discovered a large opening in the ground
from which mephitic vapours arose, and one of the men,
coming under the influence of the vapour, began to foretell

[1] *Frag.* 54, Goettling.

the future. This led to the belief that here was something divine, and pilgrimages with a view to prying into the future began to be made to the spot. Occasionally some of these pilgrims being overcome by the gases, fell into the hole and lost their lives. To avoid these accidents in future a circular metal plate with a hole in the centre was placed over the cavity. On this plate those who wished to be inspired sat. As time wore on it was discovered that Apollo himself was the tutelary deity of this place, and a temple was erected in his honour. The temple was at first composed of Laurel branches, but afterwards one of stone was built, and a Laurel grove grew up around it, as the Laurel was Apollo's own particular tree. The temple would appear to have been a very magnificent edifice, and many historic monuments were placed within it. Two of these, a bronze Palm tree and a gilded image of Athena, are mentioned by Pausanias as being memorials of Athenian valour by land and sea. Priestesses were duly appointed to utter the prophecies, and the opening of their cell was covered with laurel leaves. These priestesses were young girls who were called Pythia in memory of the serpent Pytho, which the god had once killed. They wore laurel crowns, and whoever wished to consult them had to appear before the altar crowned with laurel and chewing laurel leaves. When giving forth the oracle the priestess also chewed the leaves. The idea of this was that it was the god himself who was eaten for inspiration in the same manner as the natives of the South Sea islands believed that by eating their slain enemies they would be inspired by their valour. From this practice the priestesses of Delphi and other Greek diviners were known as Daphnephagi. Plutarch says that every ninth year a magnificent and palatial bower composed of laurel branches was erected in the forecourt of the temple, and the festival known as the Septerion was celebrated.

Herodotus [1] gives particulars regarding the destruction of the Grove of Argus. He tells that when Cleomenes consulted

[1] Cary's Trans., Bk. vi. 78–80.

the oracle at Delphi he was told that he should take Argos. He ordered his Lacedæmonians to fall upon the Argives as they were dining. Many of the latter were slain, and many took refuge in the Grove of Argus, which was then surrounded. Cleomenes, by treachery, induced some of the Argives to come out, and immediately put them to death. As the grove was thick, for some time those within did not realise what was happening, until one of them, by climbing a tree, discovered the foul deeds, and consequently no more would emerge. Cleomenes now set fire to the grove, and on asking one of the Argive deserters to whom the grove belonged, he was told that it belonged to Argus. When he heard this, he uttered a deep groan, and exclaimed : " O prophetic Apollo ! thou hast indeed greatly deceived me in saying that I should take Argos. I conjecture thy prophecy is accomplished." Cleomenes died immediately after this act of sacrilege.

The Grove of the Muses is said to have been situated at the foot of Mount Marandali, one of the summits of Mount Helicon. Pausanias mentions that he saw there the statues of famous poets and musicians. Among these were Hesiod with his lute, Arion on his dolphin, blind Thamyris, and Orpheus singing to the wild beasts.

The Furies were known as the Erinnyes, and on them devolved the bringing to light of secret crimes. There was a grove sacred to them at Kolónos, near Athens, and when Œdipus, who having in ignorance murdered his father and married his mother, became aware of having committed these crimes, he retired to this grove, and there, during a thunderstorm, his life terminated.

It is stated by Pausanias [1] that whoever entered the sanctuary of Zeus in the grove on Mount Lycæus in Arcadia, was believed first of all to lose his shadow and then to die within the year.

Among the mountains of Arcadia was the Grove of Condylea, sacred to Artemis, and the goddess was annually hanged in

[1] viii. 38. 6.

effigy there, consequently going under the name of the Hanged One among the Arcadians.

We learn from Pausanias that in Arcadia there was a grove of various kinds of trees planted on a large mound which was known as the tomb of Kallisto. She had been one of the attendants of Artemis, but falling a victim to the love of Zeus was changed by the offended goddess into a bear.

Legend narrates that Zeus was born of Rhea among the groves of Mount Parrhasion in the mountains of Arcadia, but other spots also claim the honour of having been his birthplace.

Virgil, in Eclogue VIII,[1] says that Mænalus, a mountain in Arcadia sacred to Pan, and now called Roino, clad with Pine trees, " always has a vocal grove and shaking pines ; he ever hears the loves of shepherds, and Pan, the first who suffered not the reeds to be neglected."

Hebe was the handmaiden of the gods. A certain grove composed of Cypresses was sacred to her, and Pausanias mentions having seen the chains of liberated prisoners hanging from the branches of these trees.

In the Grove of Æsculapius at Epidaurus no birth or death was allowed to take place within its sacred bounds, and all sacrifices had to be consumed within it. This grove was wont to be visited by women who desired to have children. Here they slept, and in their dreams they were visited by a serpent. Any children they afterwards bore were believed to have been begotten by this reptile. The serpent was understood to have been Æsculapius himself, as he was said to have often appeared in that form, and live serpents were tended in his various shrines. Among other groves sacred to him was one at Sicyon, and another at Titane. This latter was composed of ancient Cypresses, under the shade of which the sacred serpents roved.

No broken branch was permitted to be removed from the Grove of Hyrnetho, also at Epidaurus.

[1] Trans. by Davidson, p. 24.

In the valley of the Neander was a grove containing a temple dedicated to Pluto and Persephone. It was situated at the mouth of a cave which gave forth mephitic vapours, placed as it was in the midst of a volcanic region. In consequence this cave was regarded as one of the entrances to the infernal regions, and naturally became sacred to the infernal gods. Sick people alone could approach it, and the priests of the temple received revelations as to the treatment of these. It was fatal for anyone in health to draw nigh it.

The first of the labours of Héraklés or Hercules, was to obtain the skin of the Nemeæan lion which lived in the Nemeæan Wood or Grove, and was invulnerable to wounds. Hercules entered the grove and attacked the lion with arrows and his club, but could make no impression on it. He accordingly boldly entered the lion's den, and grasping him by the throat succeeded in suffocating him.

Polydore was the youngest son of Priam and Hecuba, who had been murdered by the King of Thrace at a certain spot. Æneas in the course of his travels arrived at this spot, where he found a grove of Cornel trees and Myrtle trees. Here he was proposing to sacrifice to Venus, and endeavoured to pull up one of the trees for the altar, but to his horror blood welled forth from it, and a voice reached his ears : " Æneas, why dost thou tear an unhappy wretch ? Spare me, now that I am in my grave ; forbear to pollute with guilt thy pious hands : Troy brought me forth no stranger to you ; nor is it from the trunk this blood distils. Ah, fly this barbarous land, fly the avaricious shore ! For Polydore am I : here an iron crop of darts hath overwhelmed me, transfixed, and over me shot up in pointed javelins." The weapons which had slain Polydore had grown up into the trees of the grove. Æneas and his companions renewed funereal ceremonies for Polydore, and, having reared an altar " to his manes, mournfully decked with leaden-coloured wreaths and gloomy cypress," departed from the fatal spot.[1]

[1] Virgil, Æneid, Bk. iii., trans. Davidson and Buckley, 1877.

The Grove of Mykénæ became of note because in it the all-seeing Argos bound Io, in the shape of a white cow, to an Olive tree, and kept watch over her as directed by Hera, who was jealous of her being beloved by Zeus.

There was a grove in Thessaly sacred to Pteleon. He was one of the lovers of Prokris, the wife of Kephales. There was also the Grove of Pergamos, and Pausanias says that a grove at Onchestus, sacred to Poseidon or Neptune, still existed in his time. Protesilaus was one of the warriors of Troy who was killed by Hector during the Trojan war. He was said to have been buried at Eleus, where he had a sacred grove, and where a magnificent shrine was erected. Caphyæ was a sacred grove in Arcadia where a Plane tree was planted by Agamemnon. The Cyprian Grove was the seat of harmony and love as depicted by the poet Claudian ; and the Helicean Grove was dedicated to Neptune.

Many of the Isles of Greece contained sacred groves. Thus in the island of Samos a certain grove was deemed sacred to Hera or Juno, and peacocks were first brought thither from the East and kept in the temple there, where whole flocks of them were fed. From this the tradition grew that the Peacock was the favourite bird of Hera, and that it was a native of that island.

The enchantress Circe lived in a thick weird grove of funereal Willows in the island of Æa, and by her magic arts changed all those who landed on the island into swine. Odysseus, however, by the aid of the plant Moly, escaped this fate. It is related that Jason, during the Argonautic Expedition, passing this island, saw corpses hanging from the tops of the trees.

In the island of Crete grew the Amathusian Grove in which the tomb of Ariadne was said to be situated.

Any person who pastured his cattle or swine in a sacred grove in the island of Chios was liable to be denounced by the first person who saw the act.

There is a doubt as to the situation of the Ortygian Grove,

but it seems to be generally acknowledged that it was on an island, although Tacitus [1] says, speaking of the rights of sanctuaries, that the Ephesians " alleged that ' Diana and Apollo were not, according to the credulity of the vulgar, born at Delos : in their territory flowed the river Cenchri, where also stood the Ortygian Grove : there the teeming Latona, leaning upon an Olive tree, was delivered of these deities ; and thence by their appointment the grove became sacred. Thither Apollo himself, after his slaughter of the Cyclops, retired from the wrath of Jupiter : soon after, the victorious Bacchus pardoned the suppliant Amazons, who sought refuge at the altar : by the concession of Hercules, when he reigned in Lydia, the sanctity of the temple was increased ; nor during the Persian monarchy were its privileges invaded ; they were next maintained by the Macedonians, and then by us.' " In the *Odyssey* we read that Kalypso said to Hermes that " rose-fingered " 'E'ós took Orion, and that " gold-seated " Artemis slew him with her gentle darts in Ortygia.

The island of Cyprus contained a grove sacred to Aphrodite called the Idalian Grove, but the ancient poets who connect it with her worship give no clue as to its exact situation. It is also said that in this island dogs would not venture to follow game into the sacred groves, but stood outside barking.

In the Hesperian Grove in the islands of the west grew the famous golden apples, the quest of which was one of the labours of Hercules. The hundred-headed sleepless serpent Ladon, along with the Hesperides, had charge of the trees in the grove on which these apples grew.

The Ancient Greeks had also several groves in Asia Minor. One of the ancient towns of Lycia there was Candyba, near which was situated the Œnian Grove, which seems to have partaken more of the character of a forest. The site of the above town has been identified with a place called Gendewar, a few miles from the coast to the east of the River Xanthus.

[1] *The Annals*, Oxford trans. 1903, pp. 144–5.

The pine forest which still covers the mountain slopes is believed to be a reafforestation of the Œnian Grove.

In Classic times the Grove of Ares in Colchis, an ancient district of Asia Minor at the eastern end of the Black Sea, became famous because to an Oak tree in it the Golden Fleece was nailed. There it remained until Jason organised the Argonautic Expedition, the object of which was to obtain this fleece. Aided by the enchantress Medea, who had her home in Colchis, Jason entered the grove, overcame all difficulties which he encountered there, and carried away the fleece in triumph.

The Karnasian Grove, or Grove of Carnea, was situated on Mount Ida, near Troy in Asia Minor, and was sacred to Apollo. When the Greeks constructed the famous wooden horse for the siege of Troy they cut down several Cornel trees in this grove to use in its construction. This roused the anger of the god, and the Greeks, to expiate their offence, instituted the feast called the Karneia or Carnia. Pausanias (iv. 33, 4) says that in a Karnasian Grove in Messéné there was a statue of Hermes or Mercury carrying a ram, in allusion to his having on one occasion delivered the citizens of Tanagra, in Bœotia, from a pestilence by carrying a ram round the walls.

As in Greece, so in Italy many groves were found to be dedicated to the various Latin gods and goddesses. Gibbon says that " the superstition of the people was not embittered by any mixture of theological rancour ; nor was it confined by the chains of any speculative system. . . . The thin texture of the Pagan mythology was interwoven with various, but not discordant materials. As soon as it was allowed that sages and heroes, who had lived or who had died for the benefit of their country, were exalted to a state of power and immortality, it was universally confessed that they deserved, if not the adoration, at least the reverence of all mankind. The deities of a thousand groves and a thousand streams possessed in peace their local and respective influence ; nor could the Roman who deprecated the wrath of the Tiber deride the

Egyptian who presented his offering to the beneficent genius of the Nile." [1]

Virgil gives the true poetic touch to those superstitions which gloomy groves impressed upon the early ages in the story of Evander, describing different scenes to his illustrious guest Æneas : " He leads him next to the Tarpeian Rock and the Capitol, now of gold, once rough and horrid with wild bushes. Even then the religious horrors of the place awed the minds of the timorous swains ; even then they revered the wood and rock. This grove, says he, this wood-topped hill, a god inhabits, but what god is uncertain : the Arcadians believe they have seen Jove himself, when often with his right hand he shook the blackening ægis, and roused the clouds of thunder." [2]

The earth itself was considered to be a goddess, and was worshipped as such under the name of Bona Dea. She had a temple on the Aventine Hill at Rome, and there her festival was annually held on the first of May. There was also a grove dedicated to her, situated in the Campagna on the banks of the Tiber, five miles below Rome. This grove was a most peculiarly sacred one, and the trees composing it included Evergreen Oaks and Laurels. Should a rotten branch fall to the ground, should a tree be struck by lightning, or should any damage of any kind occur to one of the trees, expiatory sacrifices of sheep and bulls had to be made. In the case of a tree struck by lightning it was obligatory to dig it up entirely, split the wood and burn it, and then plant another tree in its stead.

The tradition that Romulus and Remus were suckled by a wolf in a dark recess on the side of the Aventine Hill which was shadowed by an overhanging grove, rendered this spot sacred in the eyes of the Romans. Here was formerly celebrated the festival of the Lupercalia in honour of the god Pan, and riotous and lascivious scenes were annually witnessed

[1] *Decline and Fall of the Roman Empire*, ed. of 1847, vol. i. pp. 18–19.
[2] *Æneid*, Bk. viii.

there. After Rome became Christian this festival was celebrated even until the end of the fifth century. In the course of the centuries, that sylvan spot became covered with the stately buildings of the Forum, the seat of justice of Imperial Rome.

Tacitus mentions the *Lucus Asyli*, or the Grove of the Asylum, because Romulus, wishing to gather foreigners into his new State, made a sanctuary there. It was situated between the two rocks of the Capitoline Hill, and now the Piazza del Campidoglio occupies its site. On one of the rocks the temple of Jupiter Capitolinus was built, and on the other that of Feretrian Jove.

The goddess Diana had several groves dedicated to her under her various titles. The modern town of La Riccia, about sixteen miles from Rome, occupies the site of the ancient city of Aricia, which was celebrated for the temple and grove of Diana, the remains of the former still existing on the shores of the Lake of Nemi there, which occupies an extinct crater in the Alban mountains and was called Diana's Mirror. This grove was known as the Grove of Aricia, and also as the Grove of Diana Nemorensis, meaning Diana of the Sylvan Glade. The High Priest of the temple was called *Rex Nemorensis*, the King of the Grove, and was a fugitive slave who always obtained the position by killing his predecessor. Macaulay wrote concerning him :

> " The still glassy lake that sleeps
>   Beneath Aricia's trees—
> Those trees in whose dim shadow
>   The ghastly priest doth reign,
> The priest who slew the slayer,
>   And shall himself be slain."

On the Ides of August a festival called the Nemoralia was celebrated in the grove.

Dr. J. G. Frazer gives the following legend of the origin of the Nemi worship, or worship in a grove, from *nemus*, a grove :

" I begin by setting forth the few facts and legends which

have come down to us on the subject. According to one story the worship of Diana at Nemi was instituted by Orestes, who, after killing Thoas, King of the Tauric Chersonese (the Crimea), fled with his sister to Italy, bringing with him the image of the Tauric Diana hidden in a faggot of sticks. After his death his bones were transported from Aricia to Rome, and buried in front of the temple of Saturn, on the Capitoline slope, beside the temple of Concord. The bloody ritual which legend ascribed to the Tauric Diana is familiar to classical readers ; it is said that every stranger who landed on the shore was sacrificed on her altar. But transported to Italy the rite assumed a milder form. Within the sanctuary at Nemi grew a certain tree of which no branch might be broken. Only a runaway slave was allowed to break off, if he could, one of its boughs. Success in the attempt entitled him to fight the priest in single combat, and if he slew him he reigned in his stead with the title of *King of the Wood* (*Rex Nemorensis*). According to the public opinion of the ancients the fateful branch was that Golden Bough, which, at the Sibyl's bidding, Æneas plucked before he essayed the perilous journey to the world of the dead. The flight of the slave represented, it was said, the flight of Orestes ; his combat with the priest was a reminiscence of the human sacrifices once offered to the Tauric Diana. This rule of succession by the sword was observed down to imperial times ; for amongst his other freaks, Caligula, thinking that the priest of Nemi had held office too long, hired a more stalwart ruffian to slay him ; and a Greek traveller, who visited Italy in the age of the Antonines, remarks that down to his time the priesthood was still the prize of victory in a single combat." [1]

A lesser deity called Virbius was worshipped here along with Diana, and legend says that he was Hippolytos, who had been restored to life by Æsculapius at the instance of the goddess. Hippolytos had been unjustly accused by his step-

[1] *The Golden Bough*, Part I, " The Magic Art and the Evolution of Kings," vol. i. p. 11.

mother of making an attempt on her honour, and his father Theseus cursed him and implored the gods to destroy him. Accordingly, when Hippolytos was driving his chariot, the horses ran away, dashed the chariot in pieces, and dragged Hippolytos, entangled in the reins, along until he was killed. In memory of the circumstance that horses had caused the death of Hippolytos, these animals were not permitted within the sacred grove.

There was a hill called Corne, near Tusculum, on which Pliny [1] says there was a grove of Beech trees sacred to Diana, the foliage of which had all the appearance of being trimmed by art. He adds that Passienus Crispus, the orator, was so attached to one especially fine tree which grew in the grove that he would often embrace it and kiss it, lie down under its shade, and would even water its roots with wine.

Mount Cælius, one of the seven hills of Rome, was at first covered with a grove of Oak trees, the Cælian Grove, and in consequence was called the Mountain of the Oak Grove. Jupiter was here worshipped as the god of the Oak, and not far away was a shrine originally dedicated to the worship of the Oak Nymphs.

Jupiter was worshipped under the name of Jupiter Indiges on the banks of the Numicius, and was said to be Æneas deified. There was a grove dedicated to him there.

Pliny [2] observes that it was well known that at one time Rome was remarkable for the fine forests in its vicinity, and he adds that even at the time he wrote, the name of Jupiter Fagutalis pointed out in what locality a grove of Beech trees (*Fagus*) stood. Festus says that a shrine of Jupiter called the Fagutal was so called from a Beech tree which stood there and was sacred to him.

At Lanuvium, an ancient town near Rome, the modern Civita Lavinia, there was a famous temple dedicated to Juno, and also a grove sacred to her. We are told that a serpent lived within a cave in the grove, and on certain days young

[1] *Nat. Hist.*, xvi. c. 91.   [2] *Ibid.*, Bk. xvi. c. 15.

maidens entered the cave and offered cakes to it. If the maidens were chaste the serpent ate the cakes, but if the reverse, it left them untouched, and ants then came and removed them crumb by crumb, so that the sacred spot might be purified from any sign of the presence of an unchaste maiden.

Lucina appears to have been a manifestation of the goddess Juno, and is said to have received the name from a grove (*lucus*) surrounding her temple at Rome. She was invoked by women in labour, and it has been considered probable that she also obtained her name as bringing children to the *light*.

At the foot of the Palatine Hill in Rome there once existed a grove of Oaks sacred to Vesta.

Beside the Tiber there was a grove sacred to Helernus, and annually, on the 1st of February, a great festival was held within it. Nothing further, however, is known as to the identity of Helernus.

The Egerian Grove was situated near the Capena Gate of Rome. The legend of Egeria is that she was a nymph who was the wife or mistress of the wise King Numa. In the secrecy of this grove, beside a sparkling fountain, he consorted with her, and it was she who inspired him to give the wise laws to the Romans. According to Plutarch she was one of the Oak Nymphs who were believed to preside over every Oak grove. Pregnant women used to sacrifice to her in order that they might have a safe delivery. Another grove sacred to her was in the grove of Diana Nemorensis near Aricia, which see.

Livy writes of the Crotonian Grove, in which, he says, there was a spacious field stored with all sorts of game, and in which the wild beasts were perfectly tame.

There was a grove sacred to Ceres which Erisichthon cut down, or, as Ovid [1] says :

> " And Ceres' grove he ravaged with the axe
> They say, and shamed with iron the ancient glades."

Metam., viii. 741.

Erisichthon was punished by the goddess for this impious deed by an everlasting hunger.

Cicero, in *De Legibus*, speaks of the Grove of Arpinum as containing a famous Oak tree, which, by the flight of an eagle, gave a memorable omen to Marius.

The ancient capital of Latium in Italy was called Laurentum. It was situated about sixteen miles to the south-west of Rome, and derived its name from the surrounding groves of Laurel. Thither the wealthy Roman citizens used to retire at times when they desired seclusion and peace from the eternal turmoil of Rome.

Horace speaks of " the Tiburnian Groves and the orchards watered by ductile rivulets," [1] and describes the pleasant retreat of Tibur, now Tivoli, sixteen miles north-east of Rome, as being the favourite country residence of the Ancient Romans. He writes that " I, a diminutive creature, compose elaborate verses about the grove and the banks of the watery Tibur." [2] Ascribing favour to himself from Melpomene, one of the Muses, he says : " But such waters as flow through the fertile Tibur and the dense leaves of the groves shall make him distinguished for the Ætolian verse." [3]

It is said that the Emperor Vitellius wasted his energies in the Grove of Aricinum and consumed in eating at least six millions of money in about seven months. In fact Tacitus [4] plainly calls him a hog, indulging his gluttony and other vices in the shady recesses of this grove.

There was formerly a flourishing town in Umbria called Hispellum, mentioned by Pliny. It was held in such regard by the Emperor Augustus that he bestowed upon it the Grove and Temple of Clitumnus, though these were at a distance of twelve miles.

Argiletum was a place near Rome where tradesmen kept their shops, and formerly there was a grove there sacred to Argus.

---

[1] Bk. i. Ode 7.   [2] Bk. iv. Ode 2.   [3] Bk. iv. Ode 3.
[4] *The History*, etc., Oxford trans. 1880, p. 158.

Pliny [1] mentions the Grove of Vacuna. She was the Sabine Goddess of Victory, but the Romans made her the goddess of Repose, and husbandmen worshipped her after the harvest had been gathered in when they were *vacui*, or at leisure.

Tradition relates that in a grove of the Sabines consecrated to one Matiena or Matiera, a woodpecker, perched on a wooden pillar, prophesied to the people. This bird was held sacred by the ancient races of Italy, and was considered to be the especial bird of Mars.

Mr. Keightley, in his *Classical Mythology*, mentions several rural deities who were worshipped in their respective groves. Among these was Feronia, who was of Sabine origin and had charge of woods and orchards. At the base of Mount Soracte there was a grove and temple sacred to her, and great markets were held there during the period of her festival. During it her priests walked barefooted over burning coals. Another grove and temple dedicated to her, as well as a fountain, were situated at Anxur.

Furina was a rural goddess who seemed to have been of some importance in the very early days of Rome, and she had a sacred grove beyond the Tiber, in which C. Gracchus was slain, but later on her name became unknown.

The Minturnesian Grove, near the River Liris, was dedicated to the rural goddess Marica. It was deemed so sacred that no stranger was admitted within its precincts, and nothing once brought into it was ever allowed to be taken out again.

The ancient capital of Etruria was called Cære, and later Agylla. It was situated on a small river to the east of Rome. Near the river was a grove sacred to Sylvanus, as Virgil tells us. He says : " Near the cold river of Cære is a spacious grove, sacred all around by the religion of the fathers ; hollow hills on every side have enclosed and encompass the grove with gloomy fir. There is a tradition that to Sylvanus, god of the fields and flocks, the ancient Pelasgi, who were once

[1] *Nat. Hist.*, Bk. iii. c. 17.

the first possessors of the Latin territories, consecrated this grove and a festival-day." [1]

The Grove of Vulcan was usually guarded by dogs.

The Veneti, a nation which lived at the head of the Adriatic, were famous for their breed of horses, and they had a grove sacred to Diomedes. Diomedes of Thrace possessed a brood of very fine mares, and the eighth task of Hercules was to bring them to Eurystheus. He accomplished the task, but the mares tore the keeper he had left in charge of them to pieces. He, however, eventually handed them over to Eurystheus, who turned them loose on Mount Olympos, where they were destroyed by wild beasts. In the above-mentioned grove a white horse was annually sacrificed to Diomedes, and it was said that in it, and in two adjacent groves sacred to Juno and Diana respectively, wild beasts lost their ferocity, and the deer lay down with the wolf. The grove sacred to Diana was the Ætolian Grove, and Strabo said that in it the wolves would follow a man, licking his hands and fawning upon him.

The Avernian Groves, otherwise the Stygian Groves, were the groves which grew in the infernal regions. Virgil [2] depicts Æneas in his descent thither to see his father Anchises, and to learn the fate awaiting him and his descendants the Romans. He had first interviewed the Sibyl of Cumæ, and had begged her to open to him the sacred portals, saying : " Nor hath Hecate in vain given thee charge of the Avernian groves." The Sibyl's answer to the request of Æneas describes the groves in powerful language, and instructs him in what he must do. She said : " Woods cover all the intervening space, and Cocytus gliding with his black winding flood surrounds it. But if your soul be possessed with so strong a passion, so ardent a desire, twice to swim the Stygian lake, twice to visit gloomy Tartarus, and you will needs fondly pursue the desperate enterprise, learn what first is to be done. On a tree of deep shade there lies concealed a bough, with leaves and

---

[1] *Æneid*, Bk. viii. trans. by Davidson.
[2] *Ibid.*, Bk. vi. trans. by Davidson, p. 227.

limber twigs of gold pronounced sacred to infernal Juno : this the whole grove covers, and shades in dark valleys enclose. But to none is it given to enter the hidden recesses of the earth, till from the tree he pluck the bough with its golden locks. Fair Proserpine hath ordained this to be presented to her as her peculiar present. When the first is torn off, a second of gold soon succeeds ; and a twig shoots forth leaves of the same metal. Therefore, search out for it on high with thine eyes, and when found, pluck it with the hand in a proper manner ; for, if the Fates invite you, itself will come away willing and easy ; otherwise you will not be able to master it by any strength, or to lop it off by the stubborn steel. . . . So at length you shall have a view of the Stygian groves, realms inaccessible to the living, she said, and closing her lips, was silent." Æneas, having found the tree and plucked the branch, then descended to Tartarus, accompanied by the Sibyl.

Besides the groves already mentioned in Asia Minor there was the Grove of Daphne, near Antioch in Syria. Daphne was the daughter of the river-god Peneios, who had been changed by her father into a Laurel tree on the spot where the grove afterwards stood, to avoid the importunities of Apollo. The grove was planted by Seleucus, King of Syria, was about ten miles in circumference, and was composed of Laurel and Cypress trees forming avenues. In the centre of the grove he erected a most magnificent temple sacred to Apollo and Diana. Strabo, describing this temple,[1] says that a colossal figure of Apollo almost filled the sanctuary, which was enriched with gold and gems, and was adorned by the skill of the Grecian artists. Apollo was represented as bending, and pouring out from a golden cup a libation upon the earth ; and the ancient rites of Greece were carried on in all their fullness. Several streams flowed out from the mountains around, and these were said to have come from the Castalian fountains in Greece, flowing underground all the way until

[1] I. xvi. p. 1089, ed. Amstel, 1707.

the waters burst out here, oracles being heard in their murmurs. So renowned did the grove and temple become, and so numerous were the pilgrims to it, that in time a village called Daphne sprang up, and therein all sorts of men and women came to reside. In fact the whole place eventually became a pleasure resort, being consecrated to health and joy, to luxury and love. The shady walks and leafy grottoes gratified the senses with harmonious sounds and aromatic perfumes, but Cassius, the commander of the Roman veterans, forbade them to enter this grove, where the sights and sounds were more subduing than the enemy's sword.

In spite of the voluptuous character which the grove attained, for many centuries it continued to attract the veneration of many peoples ; each succeeding Emperor poured out his munificence upon it ; and each generation added new ornaments to the splendour of the temple. With the increasing power of Christianity, however, the rites began to be neglected, and after the body of Babylas, a bishop of Antioch, who had died during the persecution of Decies, had been removed into the centre of the grove, a splendid church was erected over his grave.

But Paganism revived for a time, this church was demolished, and Julian the Apostate endeavoured to renew the ancient rites in the groves of Daphne. He visited the neglected altars and resumed the sacrifices, but saw with mortification and anguish that their reign was over, their sun was going down, and that the mysterious voice had gone forth in Daphne as in the temples of Greece—" Let us go hence." Julian allowed the remains of Babylas to be removed to their former place of interment, which was done in a very zealous manner by the Christians. A most imposing procession accompanied the remains, the multitude chanting lustily the most expressive of the Psalms of David against idols and idolaters. On the evening of the same day the temple was discovered to be in flames ; the statue of Apollo was consumed to ashes, as were also the altars. Julian said this was due to the malice of the

Christians, the latter pointed to it as being the vengeance of God.

On the coast of Æolia, in Asia Minor, there was another grove and temple sacred to Apollo. Being near the town of Grynium it was called Grynium's Grove or the Grynæan Grove. It would seem to have derived the name from *Grynos*, an Oak stump, which suggests the original connection of Apollo with the Oak tree. In this grove grew the Apple tree which was the cause of the dispute between Mopsus and Colchos regarding the number of apples on the tree. Virgil [1] refers to the grove thus : " Here, take these pipes the Muses gave thee, which before [they gave] to the Ascræan sage [Hesiod] ; by which he was wont to draw down the rigid wild Ashes from the mountains. On these let the origin of Grynium's grove be sung by you that there may be no grove in which Apollo may glory more."

Dr. Pococke [2] mentions a grove near Dardanus, not far from Troy, as being sacred to Hector.

Byblus, now Jebail, was an ancient town of Phœnicia, and was the centre of the worship of Adonis. About half-way between Byblus and Baalbec, on the lower slopes of Mount Lebanon, at a place called Aphaca, there was a famous grove and sanctuary of Astarte, the Phœnician Venus or Aphrodite. The site of this sanctuary was recently discovered by modern explorers, and groves of magnificent Walnut trees still over-shadow a small village called Afka.[3] It was on this spot that the legend makes Adonis meet Aphrodite, and here he was slain by the boar. The whole surrounding neighbourhood became sacred to Adonis :

> " Whose annual wound in Lebanon allured
> The Syrian damsels to lament his fate,
> While smooth Adonis from his native rock
> Ran purple to the sea, supposed with blood
> Of Thammuz yearly wounded."

[1] Eclogue vi, Davidson's trans.
[2] " Observations on Palestine, 1737," *Pinkerton's Voyages*, vol. x. p. 704.
[3] Edward Robertson, *Biblical Researches in Palestine* (London, 1867), iii. pp. 603-9.

Dr. J. G. Frazer observes that Jerome (*Epist.* lviii. 3, *Migne Patrologia Latina*, xxii. 581) " tells us that Bethlehem, the traditionary birthplace of the Lord, was shaded by a grove of that still older Syrian Lord, Adonis, and that where the infant Jesus had wept the lover of Venus was bewailed. Though he does not expressly say so, Jerome seems to have thought that the Grove of Adonis had been planted by the heathen after the birth of Christ for the purpose of defiling the sacred spot." [1]

Tasso, in *Gerusalemme Liberata*, canto 13, writes of an enchanted grove which has been identified with a wood near Sichem.

In the Bible, as mentioned previously, there are many references to groves, some of which mean the idol itself under that title.[2]   There are, however, very few groves in Palestine at the present day, whatever there may have been in past ages. It is said that Abraham planted a grove in Beer-sheba (Gen. i. 33), but it is conjectured it ought to read that he planted a tree. Eusebius, in his *Life of Constantine*, mentions the Oaks of Mamre as forming a grove, and says that the Israelites carried on idolatrous practices there, close beside the tomb of Abraham, and that there Constantine built a church.   In Exodus xv. 27, we read that the Israelites " came to Elim, where were twelve wells of water and three score and ten palm trees." The grove most frequently mentioned in Scripture was that one in the valley of Hinnom just outside the walls of Jerusalem.   Here the Ancient Canaanites used to carry out their ghastly rites in honour of their God Baal or Moloch, and the grove was known as the Grove of Moloch. The references in the Old Testament of passing through the fire to Moloch allude to the custom of the Canaanites of burning their children as a sacrifice to that sanguinary deity. The Israelites themselves fell into the same idolatrous practices,

[1] *The Golden Bough*, 3rd ed. 1912, Part IV. " Adonis, Attis, Osiris," vol. i. p. 257.
[2] *Vide ante*, p. 46

the grove being then known as Tophet, which practices were denounced over and over again by the prophets. In course of time this grove became disassociated with these evil customs, and Jerome describes the spot as a pleasant and shady retreat, laid out in gardens which were watered by the rills of cool Siloam.

In Northern and Central Europe we also find a few groves of some importance in ancient times. In Hesse, in Germany, there were two holy groves, the Fridewald and the Spiess; and it is believed that the *Templum Tanfanæ* was the name of a grove which occupied the site of Eresburg, now Ober-Marsberg. In Prussia, the sacred, inviolate Grove of Romowe, where it was sacrilege to break a twig or slay a beast, contained a famous Oak tree, which we shall refer to again.

Tacitus [1] tells us that various races of the north united in the worship of the goddess Hertha, that is, Mother Earth, who was supposed to interfere in the affairs of men and to visit the different nations. He says that in an island of the ocean, generally believed to be Heligoland, though some authorities fixed upon the Isle of Rugen in the Baltic, there grew a sacred and inviolate grove. In it stood a consecrated chariot covered with a veil which only the priest was permitted to touch. In early spring the priest became conscious of the entrance of the goddess into this chariot, which was then drawn through the land by cows, making the season one of peace and joy. Every place which the goddess visited became a scene of festivity; no wars were undertaken; arms were untouched; and peace reigned supreme at home and abroad. When the goddess became satiated with mortal intercourse, the priest conducted the chariot with her in it back to the grove. In a secret lake there, the chariot, the veil, and the goddess herself, underwent ablutions at the hands of slaves, who were forthwith immediately swallowed up by the waters. Tacitus adds that thence proceeded a mysterious

[1] *The History*, etc., Oxford trans., 1880, pp. 332-3.

horror; and a holy ignorance of what that can be which is beheld only by those who are about to perish.

In the Scandinavian countries several important groves are mentioned. The chief of these would seem to have been the Grove of Upsala, which town was the old religious capital of Sweden, and where a celebrated temple still existed up till the end of the eleventh century. The richness of this temple was due to the gold which the Scandinavians gathered during their piratical raids, and in it were placed uncouth representations of their three principal gods, Thor, Odin, and Freya. Every tree in the holy grove surrounding the temple was regarded as divine. What the species of trees were is unknown, but it is said that one was of a mighty size, with wide-spreading branches, was evergreen, and was considered as representing the World Tree Yggdrasil (q.v.). Every ninth year, at the Vernal Equinox, a great festival was held in the grove in honour of the three above-named deities, and the proceedings lasted nine days. Each day six victims, one being a man, the others dogs and horses, were sacrificed, and their bodies were hung from the sacred trees.

Jacob Grim mentions the divine grove Glasir [1] with golden foliage which stood outside Valhalla, and says that in the grove Glasislundr [2] a bird sits in the boughs and demands sacrifices, a temple, and gold-horned cows. He also refers [3] to the great Danish sacrifice at Lêdera, closely resembling that at Upsala, described by Dietmar of Merseburg, which, he says, " was performed in the island which from its even now magnificent beech-woods bore the name of Soelundr, sea-grove, and was the finest grove in all Scandinavia."

There are still dug up in Anglesea, the ancient Mona's Isle, great trunks of Oak, which are the relics of the Holy Groves of the Druids there. Tacitus [4] says that a garrison was established in that island to overawe the vanquished, and destroy the groves dedicated to sanguinary superstitions.

---

[1] *Teut. Myth.*, vol. iv. p. 1310.
[2] Grim, *Teut. Myth.*, vol. i. p. 76.   [3] *Ibid.*
[4] *The History*, etc., Oxford trans. 1880, p. 373.

The Slavs had a sacred grove called Zutibure; and the Esthonians considered it to be an infamous act to pluck even a single leaf in any of their sacred groves. As far as the shade of the grove extended they would not even pick a strawberry, although sometimes they secretly buried their dead in these groves.[1]

The Wotyaks of Russia had a sacred grove at Cura, and the holy groves of Courland were said to have been decorated with Grecian and Spanish gold won during the times of the Tartar invasions.

In the present age Egypt does not appear to be a land very conducive to the growth of groves, yet we find that in the past there were several famous groves in that country, these being more particularly situated in the sacred domains surrounding the temples.

Herodotus [2] tells that there was a temple of Bubastis, this name being the Greek form of the name of the Egyptian goddess Ubasti, to whom the domestic cat was sacred, and who was synonymous with Diana. He says that two canals round the temple were shaded with trees, and that a wall sculptured with figures ran round it, and within the wall was a grove of lofty trees overshadowing the temple in which an image of Ubasti was placed.

In Egypt there were also several groves sacred to Venus.

In the desert of Libya oases are found, each one forming a grove, and, owing to numerous springs, these are very fertile. Some of the more famous of these oases are Khargeh, Farafrah, and Siwah.

Dido, otherwise called Elisa, was the daughter of Belus, King of Tyre, and she was the foundress of the city of Carthage. Virgil tells how she hospitably entertained Æneas after his shipwreck, and in describing the city he says: " In the centre of the city was a grove most delightful in shade, where first the Carthagenians driven by wind and wave dug up the head

[1] Grim, *Teut. Myth.*, vol. ii. p 648 note.
[2] Cary's trans., Bk. ii. p. 138.

of a sprightly courser, an omen which royal Juno showed : for by this [she signified] that the nation was to be renowned for war, brave and victorious through ages.   Here Sidonian Dido built to Juno a stately temple, enriched with gifts, and the presence of the goddess ; whose brazen threshold rose on steps, the beams were bound with brass, and the hinge creaked beneath brazen gates.   In this grove the view of an unexpected scene first abated the fear [of the Trojans] : here Æneas first dared to hope for redress, and to conceive better hopes of his afflicted state." [1]

In Persia we read of a Grove of Eridhu, situated in the Forest of Eridhu, which contained a black Pine tree growing in the centre, traditionally considered as a Tree of Life.

The Rev. W. Wyatt Gill mentions several particular groves in some of the islands of the Pacific Ocean.   He tells us that Rongo, the great Polynesian god of war, was the principal object of worship in Tahiti and some of the neighbouring islands.   The chief seat of his worship was in a sacred grove or maræ at Opoa, on the island of Raiatea, one of the Society Islands, where human sacrifices were constantly offered to this blood-stained deity to obtain his aid in their savage enter-prises.[2]   Mr. Gill adds in a note that this and other similar groves were untouched by man from generation to generation, and consequently a deep and sacred gloom was thrown over the mysteries of the idol-worship, while the trees themselves were accounted sacred, not for their own sake but for that of the place wherein they grew.

Another grove sacred to Rongo was in the island of Man-gaia, one of the Cook Islands, and this grove was called O'Rongo. It was at first on the east side of the island, but was afterwards removed to the western side, and it contained a colossal stone image of the deity.[3]

In the interior of this island was yet another grove, sacred to the spirit of one Motoro.   Mr. Gill relates that Motoro

---

[1] *Æneid*, Bk. i. Davidson's trans., p. 118.
[2] *Myths and Songs from the South Pacific*, p. 14.   [3] *Ibid.*, p. 15.

was the fourth son of Tangiia, the great Raratongan chief, who had been sent to Mangaia to be a god. He was killed by his brothers, but afterwards one of them, actuated by remorse, planted a grove and erected a maræ to him, and in the grove his spirit was supposed to reside. In 1824 the worship of idols here ceased, and a plantation of Plantains took the place of the sacred grove.[1]

[1] *Myths and Songs from the South Pacific*, pp. 25, 26.

CHAPTER V

MYTHICAL DENIZENS OF THE FORESTS AND WOODS

Spirit of the Forest ; Witches ; Fairies ; Demons ; Wood-Spirits ; Wild Huntsman ; Wood-Nymphs.

IN the early ages the Forests and Woods were imbued with a certain degree of mystery, intensified, no doubt, by the deep and solemn shadows which lay hidden within their depths. They were believed to be peopled with crowds of strange beings endowed with superhuman powers and characters, although partaking of human form. These beings were known under various names, and were of different varieties and with different natures. Some possessed benevolent qualities, seeking to do good to mankind, while others were of a malevolent disposition, ever trying to work harm. Among the former may be mentioned the Fairies and other genial spirits, and the latter class comprised Demons of every description. There were also Elves, both good and evil, and Witches, generally malignant. In Scandinavian countries the belief was held that when Lucifer and his angels fell from Heaven those who fell into the woods and forests remained there, becoming known as Wood-Spirits or Wood-Trolls.[1] The Geni, or Spirit of the Forest, is supposed to exist in many different forests throughout the world, where his voice is heard in the rustle of the leaves or the murmur of the breeze. He usually lives in a tree, particularly if it be old and gnarled. In many of the northern countries of Europe an old Pine tree is his favourite abode, and many legends have been grafted upon such trees. The tree which he inhabits is known as the King of the Forest, and he strongly objects to his tree

---

[1] Thorpe, *Northern Mythology*, vol. ii. Introduction, p. xxvi.

being cut down, invariably begging to be permitted to live. He is always depicted as bearing an uprooted Fir tree.

Many tales and legends connected with these denizens of the woods seem to have had their origin in the workings of nature, and the phenomena attendant upon these, and many now well-known diseases of trees, were once attributed to the evil influences which the mythical denizens of the forests exercised upon them. Any tree of curious and abnormal appearance, an old trunk shattered with age or storm, moss-grown or hoary with lichen, would, to the primitive wanderer in the forest, assume a supernatural aspect, especially if seen when the shades of night were falling, or blurred by mists ; and even wreaths of mist, creeping noiselessly along, often assumed shapes which to the eye of fancy took human form. In the forest of Rugaard in Denmark there is said to be a leafless tree which, although it resembles other trees, is nevertheless an Elf who strolls about the forest by night. Dire results would follow any injury to this tree.[1]

Witches mostly frequented those groves or parts of the forest where of old the sacred rites had been carried on and the sacrifices made. On certain festive days they assembled in the sacred wood and engaged in their unholy revels, while the musician, generally the devil himself, sat on a tree. A solitary Thorn tree, never apparently growing any larger, is often seen in a field, and these are considered to be bewitched. They should be carefully avoided at night, as a fiery wheel will come forth, and if a person does not make a hasty retreat he will be destroyed.[2]

The Rev. M. D. Conway says that when Christianity was introduced into Northern Europe the ancient Scandinavian gods became transformed into witches, and that the Ash was their favourite tree.[3] Thus it, in many cases, became a tree of evil, and Dr. George Macdonald has embodied this idea in his romance *Phantastes*. He relates how, in the forest of

[1] Thorpe, *Northern Mythology.*   [2] *Ibid.*
[3] " Mystic Trees and Flowers," *Frazer's Magazine,* November and December 1870.

Fairyland, the Ash was an ogre, or probably the habitation of one. When the witches of Oldenburg were on their way to the revels on Walpurgis Night they were believed to eat up all the buds of the Ash, so that these trees appeared to have none on St. John's Day.

In the days when witchcraft was firmly believed in, it was said that anyone who accidentally found himself beneath an Elder tree was at once overcome by a great horror and became delirious. The Russian belief, however, is that the Elder tree drives away evil spirits out of compassion to humanity.

The Rowan tree was held in the utmost dread by witches on account of the mystic properties which were believed to encompass it. A branch of it, especially if in the form of a cross, put in the churn or cheese-vat, protected the butter and cheese from their evil machinations. No one could be hag-ridden at night who had a branch of it in bed, and old people used to place it on their pillows to keep evil spirits and witches away, while a small piece of it carried on the person was a protection against enchantment. If a branch was brought into the house on Good Friday, no witch could enter. A very ancient song called the " Laidley Worm of Spindleton's Heuglis," alluding to its power over witches, says :

> " Their spells were vain, the boys returned
>   To the Queen in sorrowful mood ;
>   Crying that ' Witches have no power
>   Where there is Rowan-tree wood.' "

Loudon says in the *Arboretum* that " The last line of this stanza leads to the true reading of a stanza in Shakespeare's tragedy of ' Macbeth ' ; the sailor's wife, on the witches requesting some chestnuts, hastily answers, ' A rown-tree, witch ! ' but many of the editions have it, ' Aroint thee, witch ! ' which is evidently a corruption." But Loudon adds : " Nares and Halliwell say ' Aroint thee ' is correct."

When a branch of the tree was hung over a cow's stall or wreathed about her horns, this was effective against the evil eye and other ills, but it was necessary to repeat the prayer—

" From Witches and Wizards, and long-tailed Buzzards,
And creeping things that run in hedge-bottoms,
Good Lord, deliver us ! "

It was once believed that if a man who had been duly baptized touched a witch with a branch of Rowan, she was the one whom the Devil carried off the next time he was seeking a victim.

In Sweden, old women who dwelt in the forest were credited with powers of sorcery, and were believed to have the wolves under their control. Thus they were known as Vargamor or Wolf-crones.[1]

In Indian villages wizards or witches are discovered by the aid of the Sal tree (*Shorea robusta* or *Vatica robusta*). The names of all the women in the village over twelve years of age are written on the bark of branches of the tree. These branches are then steeped in water for four and a half hours. If, after that, one of them withers, the woman whose name is written on it is deemed to be a witch.[2]

The wizards or conjurors, called " Keebet," of the Abipones, a South American tribe of Argentina, were believed to have unparalleled powers over the forces of Nature, as well as over all animals, and even over the spirits of the dead. These powers were imparted to them through diabolical agency, and Mr. Tylor [3] says that Father Dobrizhoffen, in his " Account of the Abipones (1822) " thus described their method of obtaining these powers : " Those who aspire to the office of juggler are said to sit upon an aged Willow, overhanging some lake, and to abstain from food for several days, until they begin to see into futurity."

The Fairies of popular belief are tiny creatures, ever dancing on the greensward in the merry moonlight, and ever

[1] Thorpe, *Northern Mythology.*
[2] *The Hindoos*, London, 1835, vol. ii. 23.
[3] *Primitive Culture* (1871), vol. ii. p. 374.

ready to lend a helping held to embarrassed mortals. Forests were their favourite resorts, and on clear moonlight nights they and the Elves were believed to dance hand in hand around the trees, and the grass being trodden down by their aerial feet, grew up with renewed vigour, and formed green circles known as Fairy rings. They had their abodes in flowers and lived on the honey. Shakespeare and Spencer have immortalized them, and Dr. George Macdonald tells how Anodos entered a garden, and " The whole garden was like a carnival, with tiny, gaily decorated forms, in groups, assemblies, processions, pairs or trios, moving stately on, running about wildly, or sauntering hither or thither. From the cups or bells of tall flowers, as from balconies, some looked down on the masses below, now bursting with laughter, now grave as owls ; but even in their deepest solemnity seeming only to be waiting for the arrival of the next laugh. Some were launched on a little marshy stream at the bottom in boats chosen from the heaps of last year's leaves that lay about, curled and withered. These soon sank with them ; whereupon they swam ashore and got others. Those who took fresh rose-leaves for their boats floated the longest ; but for these they had to fight ; for the fairy of the rose-tree complained bitterly that they were stealing her clothes, and defended her property bravely." [1]

He adds that in the forest " here and there whole mighty trees glowed with an emitted phosphorescent light. You could trace the very course of the great roots in the earth by the faint light that came through, and every vein on every leaf was a streak of pale fire." [2]

Spencer in the Legend of Sir Calidore says :

" But Nymphs and Faeries on the bank did sit
In the wood's shade which did the waters crown " ;

and a little further on he tells how, when Calidore gazed on

---

[1] *Phantastes*, p. 38.   [2] *Ibid.*, p. 48.

the " hundred naked maidens lily white," that danced around the Graces, he wist not

> " Whether it were the train of beauty's queen,
> Or Nymphs or Faeries, or enchanted show
> With which his eyes mote have deluded been."

Milton also wrote of

> " Faery elves
> Whose midnight revels by a forest side,
> Or fountain, some belated peasant sees " ;

and again, he wrote :

> " Of Faery damsels met in forests wide
> By Knights of Logres or of Lyones,
> Lancelot, or Pelleas, or Pellinore."

The Hawthorn tree was in great favour with them, as their trysting-places were believed to be under its shade, and in some parts of Brittany and Ireland it was considered dangerous to pluck even a leaf from old and solitary trees, especially those growing in unfrequented spots on the moorlands.

Each country had its own type of Fairy, but it would appear that the idea was far more fancifully and daintily developed in England than in any other, though the Nymphs and the Dryads of Greece and Italy were closely akin to them.

A race of beings related to the goblin or brownie is the Niägriusar, mentioned in Norwegian lore as peculiar to the Faröe Islands. They are very small, wear red caps, and dwell in the high trees planted round houses. As they are considered to be bringers of luck, care is taken not to fell the trees, especially the very old ones, which they inhabit.[1]

Demons were another class of beings who frequented forests, in many instances, as will be seen, living in trees, particularly one called Norg, who inhabited the hollows of trees, and it is believed that the French word *ogre* gave rise to that name. Germany, among other central European countries, is where the Forest Demon is seen at his best, or at

[1] Thorpe, *Northern Mythology.*

his worst. In Sweden certain trees believed to be inhabited by genii were called Bötra trees.

Resemblances have often been alleged to have been found between human life and the life of trees ; in fact, it has been believed that mankind had origin as a tree, so it is not surprising to find trees credited with inhabitants possessing powers for good or for evil, or that such, in course of time, came to be looked upon as divine, and were worshipped accordingly.

The belief in Wood-Spirits or Forest-Spirits seems to have arisen, as Professor Mannhardt thinks, from the widespread idea that each forest, and even each tree in it, had their own peculiar spirits. Very often the colour of these spirits was green, and their skin was of a mossy texture, while at certain times they were able to appear as veritable men and women. In Germany, and the Scandinavian countries generally, the belief in these wood-spirits was very common and was implicitly held, and their duties were supposed to consist in looking after the forest in general and shielding the trees from injury. For instance, a Wood-Spirit named Pulch dwelt in the Kammerforst who chastised those who stole wood or did injury to the forest trees. Another type of wood-spirit was the Waldgeister, and anciently the forests were supposed to contain these in large numbers, some being of a benevolent disposition and others the reverse. It is said that they alone of all forest-spirits possessed the secret of medicinal plants. One of them was known as the Hylde-moer (Elder-mother), or Hylde-vinde (Elder-queen), as she was believed to reside in the Elder trees, and to avenge all injuries done to her place of abode. Should any person desire to cut down an Elder tree, or take a branch therefrom, he had first to ask permission from the Hylde-moer, otherwise some misfortune would befall him.

The Skogsrå was a female spirit haunting the woods and forests of Sweden. She was young and small, beautifully dressed, and of a friendly disposition, but had claws instead of nails. It was unlucky for hunters to meet her, although she could be propitiated by being offered part of the hunter's catch.[1]

What were known as Wood-Wives frequented the old sacred forests or groves, and apparently it had been they who had formed the court or escort of the ancient gods when they sat enthroned on the trees. These Wood-Wives were principally found in Southern Germany, but varieties of them are mentioned in Northern Germany and in Scandinavia. They were the quarry of the Wild Huntsman (q.v.), but were saved from him if they could reach a tree with a cross on it. In fact, the foresters, when felling trees, used to cut three crosses on a part of the tree. The little Wood-Wives would go and sit in the centre of these, and there they were secure.[2] There is a German superstition which says that on Ash Wednesday the Devil hunts the little Wood-Wife through the forest.[3] These little Wood-Wives are said to approach people when they are baking and ask that a cake might be baked for them ; or else they appear with a little broken wheelbarrow and request that it be mended. They also often appear to the woodcutters asking for food, though frequently they help themselves out of the pot, yet they never fail to give a handsome recompense. This usually takes the form of chips of wood which turn into gold. It is believed that every time the stem of a young tree is twisted till the bark comes off a wood-wife dies.[4]

In Sweden a wood-wife, the Skogsrå mentioned above, is known to be present when a violent whirlwind occurs, and the trees are shaken even to the breaking-point.[5] Some German races worshipped a Wood-Wife between Christmas and Twelfth Day. Occasionally the Wood-Wife was known as the Wish-Wife, and her clothes were believed to be kept in an Oak tree.

A certain type of wood-wife was called Dirne-weibl, very often appearing clad in white, but in one of the forests of

---

[1] Thorpe, *Northern Mythology.*
[2] Keightley, *Fairy Mythology,* p. 231.
[3] Grim, *Teut. Myth.,* vol. iv. p. 1816.
[4] *Ibid.,* vol. ii. pp. 483–4.   [5] *Ibid.,* p. 633.

Bavaria the Dirne-weibl used to appear dressed in a red frock and carrying a basket of fine apples. She would give away these apples, which became changed into money. She often requested people to accompany her, and if they refused she returned into the wood weeping. Children when playing would frighten each other by exclaiming, " Here comes the Dirne-weibl."

Jacob Grim gives the following further information regarding these Wood-Wives. Quoting Buchonia, iv., 2, 94–5, he says that in Schlüchtern wood stand the wild houses and wild table often visited by the wild folk [1] : that because the Wood-Wives wail and cry, there is a saying in Germany when anyone makes an outcry about trifles, " You cry like a wood-wife " (*Uhl. Volksl.*, 149) [2] ; that the holz-frau is shaggy and wild, overgrown with moss (*H. Sachs.*, 1, 273) [3] : and that in Bavaria, on the Finz, the Finz-weibl is spotted, and wears a broad-brimmed hat (*Panz. Beitr.*, 1, 22).[4]   We also learn how, when the poet had missed his way in a wooded wild, he came upon a wailing wife beside the murmuring stream, who imparted advice and information to him.[5]   Again, he tells how, on a May morning, the poet was roused from sleep by a passionate cry. He started up, went into the forest, and climbed over steep rocks until high up he reached a pleasant flowery vale, where, in the dense thicket, he spied a little wight. The latter scolded him soundly and wished to immure him for trampling on his lady's roses. When pacified at last he told him that in a stronghold here Dame Honour with five maidens of her household dwelt.[6]   Another legend narrates that in May-time the poet, when wandering in the depths of the forest, was met by a hairy Wood-Wife who guided him to the tower of Dame Charity, showed him through her chambers, and at last brought him before the high dame herself. After his interview with her she sent him away laden with treasure.[7]

The Moss-Folk or Moss-Women are but variations of the

---

[1] Grim, *Teut. Myth.*, vol. iv. p. 1405.   [2] *Ibid.*, p. 1427.
[3] *Ibid.*   [4] *Ibid.*, vol. iv. p. 1427.   [5] *Ibid.*, vol. ii. p. 894.
[6] *Ibid.*   [7] *Ibid.*, p. 895.

Wood-Wife, and other names for them are Wild-Folk, Forest-Folk, or Wood-Folk. These are considered to be dwarfs, and they live in communities. They are grey and old-looking, and are hideously overgrown with moss, giving them a hairy appearance. Voightland tradition makes the Wild Huntsman appear as one of them. The author of *The Fairy Family* has described them thus :

> " ' A moss-woman ! ' the hay-makers cry,
> And over the fields in terror they fly.
> She is loosely clad from neck to foot
> In a mantle of Moss from the Maple's root,
> And like Lichen grey on its stem that grows
> Is the hair that over her mantle flows.
> Her skin, like the Maple-rind, is hard,
> Brown and ridgy, and furrowed and scarred ;
> And each feature flat, like the bark we see,
> Where a bough has been lopped from the bole of a tree,
> When the newer bark has crept healingly round,
> And laps o'er the edge of the open wound ;
> Her knotty, root-like feet are bare,
> And her height is an ell from heel to hair."

In Tyrol there is a tradition that a spirit called the Salgfräulein, who is dressed all in white, sits under an old Larch tree singing.

Numerous Demons are believed to dwell in the German forests where they often have their abode in trees. A certain demon or goblin of the trees is called Baumesel, or Ass of the Trees ; and another, a forest demon or monster, partaking of the character of a satyr, is called Bockmann, or Man-goat. He is said to frighten little children who go into the forest.

The Askafroa (*Eschenfrau*), or wife of the Ash, was a very evil spirit, and did much damage. To propitiate her it was necessary to make a sacrifice on Ash Wednesday.

There is a certain female Demon, or perhaps more correctly goblin, who is the genius of the Juniper tree and personifies it. She is called Frau Wachholder, and is invoked to make thieves give up their booty. The procedure is as follows : Those

who have suffered the loss repair to a Juniper bush, bend one
of its branches to the ground, keeping it down with a stone
while calling on the thief. The latter is bound to present
himself and give up his prize. They then let go the branch,
and put the stone back in its place.[1]

A Demon called the Katzenveit haunts the forests of the
Fichtelgebirge, and to frighten children people will say,
" Hush, the Katzenveit will come ! " In the forests of the
Harz a similar being, known as the Gübich, roams the woods ;
as does another, called the Rübezal, in the forests of the
Riesengebirge.

In the forests of Franconia there is a Demon known as the
Bilberry-man, who is apt to attack travellers when passing
through the woods. To avert these attacks it is customary
for a person to place an offering of bread and fruit on a
stone before he enters the forest in order to propitiate
the demon.

We hear very little of Fairies in Germany, at least as they
were known in Britain, owing probably to the coarseness of
the Teutonic mentality being unable to appreciate the delicacy
of these ethereal beings. But beings very similar appear to
have been believed in, as it is said that they possessed, along
with the Waldgeister, the secret of medicinal plants, and
from time to time made some of these secrets known to their
favourites among mortals. Elves, however, closely akin to
the Fairy race, were well known, and appear in many tales
and legends. They were said to be the children of witches
by the devil, and could assume at will many various forms,
such as butterflies, caterpillars, and others. The witches
could conjure them into many things ; sometimes into the
stem of a tree in the shape of a caterpillar, and as it bored the
tree, or others ate the foliage, so the hearts of those people
were troubled whom the witches desired to injure. This is
an instance of how natural phenomena came to be regarded
as due to supernatural influences, and Shakespeare, taking

[1] De Gubernatis, *Mythologie des Plantes*, vol. ii. p. 153.

advantage of the belief in these beings, tells in *Tempest* that Prospero reminds Ariel how Sycorax the witch

> " did confine thee,
> By help of her more potent ministers,
> And in her most unmitigable rage
> Into a cloven pine ; within which rift
> Imprison'd, thou didst painfully remain
> A dozen years ; . . . where thou didst vent thy groans,"

and that

> " it was mine art,
> When I arriv'd and heard thee, that made gape
> The pine, and let thee out."

Prospero then lays his commands on Ariel, threatening that

> " If more thou murmur'st, I will rend an oak,
> And peg thee in his knotty entrails, till
> Thou hast howl'd away twelve winters."

These Elves were of a somewhat malicious disposition ; they usually resided underground, but in some cases made the forests their abode, where trees were their homes, and the holes so often found in Oak trunks were supposed to be their means of entrance and exit, while to them were also ascribed the knot-holes found in timber. Grim mentions a tale told in Småland regarding the ancestress of a certain family as being an Elfmaid. It was said that she came into the house through a knot-hole in the wall along with the sunbeams, and married the son of the house. She bore him four children, and then vanished in the same way as she had come.[1]

People were very careful not to offend the Elves, and they studiously refrained from spying upon them, or prying into their doings in their sylvan retreats. Their power was of a nature to be dreaded, and mysterious illnesses affected those to whom they took an ill will, while in many cases death followed an offence against them. As an instance of this latter a German legend mentioned by Mannhardt tells how an

[1] *Teut. Myth.*, vol. ii. p. 461.

old woman tried to uproot a Fir tree in which an Elf dwelt. The Elf was wounded unto death, and at the moment it died the old woman died also. This legend seems to have given rise to the custom, probably yet prevalent in the vast forests of Germany and Russia, of cutting old Fir trees off near the roots instead of uprooting them. The Elves are said to be very much afraid of thunder, and the Esthonians say that during a thunderstorm they burrow several feet under the roots of the trees they inhabit for protection. The Forest Elf or Schrat, like the dwarf in the tale of Rudleib, has a great aversion to a guest who blows hot and cold.[1]

In the songs of Bohemia tremor and terror are personified by two spectral shades called Třas and Strakh. These are pictures as bursting out from the gloom of the forests on to the hordes of the enemy, and are said to clutch them by the throat and squeeze out loud cries of terror.

Very interesting denizens of the forests were the Swan Maidens, of whom Grim says that the Völundarqviða opens with the words : " Maids flew from south through murky wood to the seashore, there they tarried seven years, till they grew homesick : they could resist no longer, and returned to the sombre wood." [2]   In some instances the wicked stepmother changed the maiden into a swan ; and one tale relates how the hero, finding the seven swans, transformed them into maidens again by the aid of woven shirts. Of these shirts, they having been made in a hurry, one lacked a sleeve, and consequently the youngest of the maidens had to be content with a wing instead of an arm. A Slavonic legend tells how a youth was reposing in a forest, lulled with the gentle breeze murmuring in the trees. To him fluttered a snow-white swan which alighted on his breast. Clasping it to his heart, it changed into a lovely maiden, to whom he was united in marriage soon after.[3]

Storms in the forest were once attributed to the furious

---

[1] *Teut. Myth.*, vol. iv. p. 1416.   [2] *Ibid.*, vol. i. pp. 430–1.
[3] S. Baring-Gould, *Curious Myths of the Middle Ages*, 1875, p. 577.

career of the Wild Huntsman, of whom many tales are told under various aspects in different lands. In Germany the legend is very widely spread and seems to have descended from the highest antiquity. The most popular form of the legend is as follows : In Lower Saxony it is told how Hans von Hackelnberg was the Chief Master of the Hounds to the Duke of Brunswick. He was a mighty huntsman, and is said to have died in 1521 as the result of an accident. While on his death-bed he refused to listen to the parson's exhortations regarding his fitness for Heaven, replying to all, " The Lord may keep His Heaven, so He leave me my hunting " ; whereupon the parson said to him, " Hunt then till the Day of Judgment ! " Accordingly, such became his doom, and to this day he hunts when the storm rages in the forest, accompanied by his carriage, horses and hounds. He pursues his wild career through the Thuringerwald, the forest of the Harz, and particularly in the Hackel, a forest situated between Halberstadt, Gröningen, and Derenburg, uttering his wild cry of " Hu-hu ! " His approach is heralded by a distant baying or yelping of hounds, while a night-owl, called by the people Tutosel (i.e. *tut-ursel*, tooting Ursula), flies in front of him. This Ursula, was said to have been a nun who, after her death, joined Hackelnberg and mingled her " Tu-hu " with his " Hu-hu." Travellers, when he passes, fall silently on their faces, and lie terror-stricken listening to the barking of the dogs and the huntsman's weird " Hu-hu."

There are several variations of this legend, one of which says that the huntsman at first lived a holy life in the Sölling Forest near Uslar, but was so much occupied in hunting, and was so fond of the sport, that on his deathbed he prayed God that his share of Heaven might be to be allowed to hunt in the Sölling till the Judgment Day. His wish was granted, and in that forest he fulfils his doom, and often at night the ghastly hunt is heard passing over.[1]

In Westphalia he is known as Hackelbärend, who, when

[1] Grim, *Teut. Myth.*, vol. iii. p. 922.

alive, used to go hunting even on Sundays, for which desecra-
tion he was doomed to hunt in the air both by day and by
night for ever.[1]

There is a story of two young men from Bergkirchen who,
while walking in the forest one evening on the way to see their
sweethearts, heard a wild barking of dogs in the air, and a
voice calling " Hoto hoto ! " Here the hunter was known as
Hackelblock, and, one of the youths having mocked his " Hoto
hoto," Hackelblock set the whole pack of hounds upon him,
and from that time he was heard of never more.[2]

Grim also relates that a Meistersong was made by Michael
Beheim on Eberhart, Count of Wirtenberg, who heard in the
forest a " ' sudden din and uproar vast,' then beholds a spectre,
who tells him the manner of his damnation. When alive he
was a lord that never had his fill of hunting, and at last made
his request unto the Lord to let him hunt till the Judgment
Day ; the prayer was granted, and these 500 years, all but 50,
he has hunted a stag that he never can overtake ; his face is
wrinkled as a sponge." [3]

A story of the Wild Huntsman relates how a peasant had a
tug-of-war with him—the huntsman in the air and the peasant
on the ground. A heavy chain was employed, and each time
the huntsman pulled it up the peasant twisted it round the
stem of an Oak, unloosening it when the former came down
to see why he could not lift the peasant. Three times this
happened, and the peasant went home well rewarded for
having held out against the huntsman, as the latter thought.[4]

Grim quotes a story out of Kuhn's *Nordd. Sag.*, No. 69,
which tells how a man went and stood under a tree in the
forest through which the Wild Huntsman and his retinue rode.
One of the latter, in passing, dealt the man a blow in the
back with his axe, saying, " I will plant my axe in this tree " ;
and from that time onward the man had a hump. He waited
till a year had elapsed, then went and stood under the tree

[1] Grim, *Teut. Myth.*, vol. iii. pp. 920-1.   [2] *Ibid.*, p. 921.
[3] *Ibid.*, p. 931.   [4] *Ibid.*, p. 924.

again. The same person stepped out of the procession and said, " Now I'll take my axe out of the tree " ; and the man was at once relieved of his hump.[1]

Another tale of the Wild Huntsman quoted by Grim is from E. M. Arndt's *Märchen und Jugenderinnerungen*, 1, 401–4, and is as follows : " In Saxony there lived in early times a rich and mighty prince, who loved hunting above all things, and sharply punished in his subjects any breach of the forest laws. Once, when a boy barked a Willow to make himself a whistle, he had his body cut open and his bowels trained round the tree ; a peasant having shot at a stag, he had him fast riveted to the stag. At last he broke his own neck hunting by dashing up against a Beech tree ; and now in his grave he has no rest, but must hunt every night. He rides a white horse whose nostrils shoot out sparks, wears armour, cracks his whip, and is followed by a countless swarm of hounds : his cry is ' Wod, wod, hoho, hallo ! ' He keeps to forests and lonely heaths, avoiding the common highway ; if he happens to come to a cross-road, down he goes horse and all, and only picks himself up when past it ; he hunts and pursues all manner of weird rabble, thieves, robbers, murderers, and witches." [2]

The Forest of Fontainebleau was, and is even yet, of vast extent, many parts of it being practically unexplored, where the wolf and the wild boar still have their lairs in summer. In it *le grand veneur* is still supposed to hunt, and is heard on stormy nights.

The prey of the Wild Huntsman was, as already said, usually the little Wood-Wives, and it is related that a peasant on one occasion, hearing the commotion around, joined in the furious hunt, and was rewarded next morning by finding a quarter of a wood-wife hanging at his stable-door.[3]

In some parts of the forests of the Harz Mountains the Wild Huntsman has been identified with the Wandering Jew.

[1] Grim, *Teut. Myth.*, vol. iv. p. 1588.
[2] *Ibid.*, vol. iii. pp. 927–8.
[3] Keightley, *Fairy Mythology*, p. 231.

There it is said that he was a Jew who had refused to allow Christ to drink out of a horse-trough, but had contemptuously told him to drink from the hoof-marks of a horse in which a little water had gathered. The Jew's doom was to wander restlessly through the world till the Judgment Day.

In the Scandinavian countries very similar beliefs prevail as to the existence of Elves, Witches, Demons, the Wild Huntsman, and others. In Denmark the latter is believed to be the good King Waldemar, who, as a Zealand legend tells, was attracted by the influence of a magic ring, which had been thrown into a marsh, to a fair maiden, and after her death he was said to have sought consolation in hunting in the Forest of Gurre. There he hunts night and day in fulfilment of a wish similar to that of Hackelnberg, that " God may keep His Heaven, so long as I can hunt in Gurre for evermore." His " Ho-ho " and the crack of his whip is heard as he rushes through the forest on a white horse, sometimes with his head under his left arm, and preceded by coal-black hounds with fiery tongues hanging from their mouths.[1]

In a wood called Grünewald, on the island of Möen, a spectral hunter called the Grönjette, or Green Giant, hunts on horse-back, also carrying his head. His prey are the little wood-wives, and he was once seen with a dead wood-wife slung across his horse, when he was said to have exclaimed, " Seven years have I chased her, now in Falster I have slain her." [2]

In Sweden, Odin is looked upon as the Wild Huntsman or spectral hunter. It is said that until very recently, when he was heard riding past in his boisterous career, attended by his ghostly host, the windows of all sick chambers were opened, so that the soul, if it thought fit to depart, might have an opportunity of joining Odin in the furious chase.[3]

In the Scandinavian countries there was a Wood-Wife known as Huldra, who sometimes appeared as young and beautiful, but at other times she was old and ugly ; and some accounts

[1] Grim, *Teut. Myth.*, vol. iii. p. 943.   [2] *Ibid.*, p. 944.
[3] Fiske, *Myths and Mythmakers*, p. 229.

of her say that she was lovely only in front, while behind she was hideous and hollow. She had a tail which she was ever anxious to conceal, and was often heard singing a doleful melody called *huldrslaat*. She was frequently to be seen in the forests as an aged woman clad in grey, marching in front of her flock and carrying a milk-pail.[1]

In Denmark the Forest Demons often hid themselves in old Cherry trees and did harm to those who approached them.[2]

The Elves of Scandinavia, like the Fairies of England, were very fond of dancing in the moonlight in the meadows, and to them were attributed those circles of brilliant green so often seen on the grassy sward. The Elf man is said to have an aged appearance, and to wear a low-crowned hat; but the Elf maidens are young and attractive, though, like Huldra, they are hollow behind. They play on certain stringed instruments, and that so sweetly that young men had to be on their guard lest their hearts should be ravished. A species of Elves in Sweden were known as Grove Damsels, or Grove Folk. These lived in the groves and protected the trees.[3]

The Fairy race has long been looked upon with appreciative eyes in Britain, and particularly so in England. Thomas Hood dedicated his poem " The Plea of the Midsummer Fairies " to Charles Lamb, and in the dedication he wrote : " It is my design in the following poem to celebrate, by an allegory, that immortality which Shakespeare has conferred on the Fairy mythology by his *Midsummer Night's Dream*. But for him those pretty children of our childhood would leave barely their names to our maturer years ; they belong, as the mites upon the plum, to the bloom of fancy—a thing generally too frail and beautiful to withstand the rude handling of time : but the poet has made this most perishable part of the mind's creation equal to the most enduring ; he has so intertwined the elfins with human sympathies, and linked them by so many delightful associations with the productions of

[1] Grim, *Teut. Myth.*, vol. i. p. 271.
[2] De Gubernatis, *Mythologie des Plantes*, vol. ii. p. 57.
[3] Thorpe, *Northern Mythology*.

Nature, that they are as real to the mind's eye as their green magical circles to the outer sense. It would have been a pity for such a race to go extinct, even though they were but as the butterflies that hover about the leaves and blossoms of the visible world."

The spots where the Fairies congregated were of the most rural and romantic character, and they often liked to dance around Oak trees. They were supposed to meet

> " On hill, in dale, forest or mead,
> By paved fountain, or by rushy brook,
> Or on the beached margent of the sea,
> To dance their ringlets to the whistling wind."

Shakespeare tells that Titania's bower was

> " A bank whereon the wild thyme blows,
> Where oxlips and the nodding violet grows,
> Quite over-canopied with lush woodbine,
> With sweet musk-roses, and with eglantine."

One of the Fairies mentioned by Shakespeare is the mischievous Puck, and Mr. Keightley quotes the following passage from an *Essay on the Ignis Fatuus*, by Mr. Allies : " The peasantry of Alfrick and those parts of Worcestershire say that they are sometimes what they call *Poake-ledden*, that is, that they are occasionally waylaid in the night by a mischievous sprite whom they call Poake, who leads them into ditches, bogs, pools, and other such scrapes, and then sets up a loud laugh and leaves them quite bewildered in the lurch." [1] Mr. Keightley says that this proves that in some parts the idea of Puck as a spirit haunting the woods and fields is still retained, and he adds that it is what in Devonshire is called being Pixy-led. He also tells that a Devonshire girl had related that " she once knew a man who, one night, could not find his way out of his own fields, all he could do, until he recollected to *turn his coat* ; and the moment he did so, he heard the Pixies all fly away, up into the trees, and there they

[1] *Fairy Mythology*, p. 317.

sat and laughed. Oh! how they did laugh! But the man then soon found his way out of the field." [1]

The Vale of Avalon, or the " Island Valley of Avilion," of Arthurian romance, was the Fairyland of Celtic tradition, and thither King Arthur was transported after being wounded. There his wounds were healed and he became king of that island. He was also the heir to the Kingdom of Oberon, and all the other haunts of the fairy race in whatever land they were situated. Oberon was the king of the Fairies, and he and his queen Titania are important figures in the Fairy lore of the Middle Ages. Irish romance mentions the Strand of the Yew tree as a trysting-place on earth for Cuchulain and Fand, the Pearl of Beauty and wife of Mananan, the Irish Celtic Sea-god.[2]

Sometimes the Fairies of popular belief may be traced as being descended from some traditionally remembered personage who may or may not have had a real tangible existence. Thus Queen Mab is said to have been originally the queen of a certain early Irish race, her name being Medhb ; while Oberon has been traced to a dwarf named Albe-rich, who was the Court Jester of Dietrich of Bern. Mr. Grant Allen (*Cornhill Magazine*, 1881) suggests that most of the European Fairy traditions had their origin in the early struggles between the Celts and Teutons and the race of small men who had preceded them, these latter, from their diminutive size, having given rise to the legendary tales in which the tiny Fairies figure.

In the beginning of the eighteenth century a writer named Bourne, author of the *Antiquitatis Vulgares*, 1725, gave the following account of the popular belief in Fairies : " According to the description they give of them, who pretend to have seen them, they are in the shape of men exceeding little : they are always clad in green, and frequent the woods and fields. . . . But generally they dance by moonlight, when mortals are asleep, and not capable of seeing them ; as may be observed on the following morning, their dancing places

[1] *Fairy Mythology*, p. 300.
[2] Lewis Spence, *Dictionary of Mediæval Romance*, p. 105.

being very distinguishable : for as they dance hand in hand, and so make a circle in their dance, so next day there will be seen rings and circles on the grass.[1]

Human intercourse with the Fairies often led to the victim vanishing from the sight of his fellow beings for, it may be, centuries, during which period he was entertained in Fairyland, and to him it appeared as though only one night has passed. Thomas the Rhymer was an instance of this in Scotland, and there is a tale regarding the Welsh Fairies as follows : Early one fine summer morning a young man had no sooner left an adjacent farmhouse than he heard a little bird singing most sweetly on a tree near at hand. Enchanted by the song he sat down to listen to it. When it ceased he arose, supposing, as would be thought natural, that only a few minutes had elapsed, but what was his astonishment to see the tree under which he had sat all withered and dead. On returning to the house he saw it changed also, with only an old man, a stranger to him, within it. On asking the old man what he was doing there, the latter angrily asked who it was who dared to insult him in his own house. " In your own house ! Where's my father and mother," said the young man, " whom I left here a few minutes since, while I listened to the most charming music under yon tree, which, when I arose, was withered and leafless, and all things, too, seemed changed ? " " Under the tree ! Music ! What is your name ? " " John," said he. " Poor John," exclaimed the old man, " I heard my grandfather, who was your father, often speak of you, and long did he bewail your absence ; fruitless inquiries were made of you, but old Catti Madlen, of Brechfa, said that you were under the power of Fairies, and would not be released until the last sap of that Sycamore tree was dried up. Embrace, embrace, my dear uncle, your nephew." The old man then attempted to embrace him, but at that moment he crumbled into dust.[2]

[1] Quoted in Keightley's *Fairy Mythology*, p. 297.
[2] Ennemoser's *History of Magic*, vol. ii. p. 489.

Elves in the British Islands were closely akin to the Fairies, and were often confounded with them, but the main difference appears to have been in the generally malicious disposition of the former. One of the beliefs in former days was that the Elves and the Fairies delighted to take a part in the family festive gatherings held at Christmas time, and the origin of the custom of hanging evergreens in houses at that period was that these Elves might take shelter among the leaves from the usual wintry character of the weather. There used to be a pretty saying that in the autumn the little Elves fly away on the brown Oak leaves.

The forests of the Slav countries in general are found to be peopled with mythical beings of a usually malevolent type, though in some instances they have a beneficent character. In the Russian forests what were known as Lieschi, Forest Devils, or Genii of the Forest, were considered to be always present in clumps of trees, and particularly on the tops of Birch trees. These beings were believed to be able to accommodate their stature according to their environment. Thus, when they were wandering in the forest they were as tall as the trees, but when they appeared on the plains they did not exceed the blades of grass in height. Professor Mannhardt tells of the means taken to invoke these Genii. He says that very young Birches are cut down and placed in a circle with the points towards the centre. They then enter the circle and invoke the spirit, which at once appears. Then they step on to the stump of one of the cut trees with their face turned towards the east, and bend their heads so that they look between their legs. While in this position they say : " Uncle Lieschi, ascend thou, not as a grey wolf, not as an ardent fire, but as resembling myself. Then the leaves tremble, and the Lieschi arises under a human form, and agrees to give the service for which he has been invoked, provided they promise him their soul.[1]

There is a Russian proverb to the effect that either an owl or a devil frequents all old trees.

[1] De Gubernatis, *Mythologie des Plantes*, vol. ii. p. 46.

The Czarevitch Ivan is said to have once seen two forest Demons fighting. One was showering blows upon the other with an uprooted Oak tree, while the other was returning the blows with interest with an uprooted Pine tree as his weapon. The fight waged furiously, the Demons exerting all their strength, but how it ended tradition sayeth not.[1]

The intensity of the Russian winter has caused the frost to be regarded as a Demon under the name of Morozko, and frost-cracks and breaks in the trees are attributed to his agency. There is a tale of a maiden who was lost in the forest, when " all at once she heard something. Morozko was crackling in a Fir tree not far off, and he leaped from Fir to Fir and snapped his fingers." [2]

Formerly in Eastern Russia there was a demon who assumed the shape of a mourning widow, and haunted the harvest fields at noon. Should the harvesters fail to fall on their faces when they saw her, she would break their legs and arms. Fortunately there was a remedy in the forest close at hand. There, several sacred trees grew, and by placing some of the bark on the wounds they were at once healed.[3]

The Russians had a belief in certain Wood-Nymphs, or Wood-Maids, called Rusalki, who were very beautiful, with long green hair, and who swung on the branches of trees in the forests. They were usually seen about Whitsuntide, often bathing in lakes and rivers, and at that season the people used to weave garlands for them, and cast them into the waters. Probably some natural growth or parasite of the trees originated this belief.[4]

A fort was founded by the Swedes in 1298 on the banks of the River Neva for protection against the inroads of the Russians, and tradition says that about that period a loud and continuous knocking was heard in the forest near the river. The people wondered greatly what the knocking could mean, until at last a peasant bravely entered the forest in order to

[1] R. Nisbet Bain, *Russian Fairy Tales*, 2nd ed., p. 41.   [2] *Ibid.*, p. 9.
[3] Keightley, *Fairy Mythology*, p. 490.   [4] *Ibid.*, p. 491.

investigate the cause. After he had penetrated some distance he came upon a wood-spirit busily engaged in hewing a stone. On being asked what it meant the spirit replied that " this stone shall be the boundary between the land of the Swedes and Moskovites." [1]

The Tcherkass, a tribe of Circassians, are said to have worshipped a god of woods and hunting, whose name was Mesitch, and who, in his career through the forests, rode a wild boar with golden bristles.[2]

There is a mischievous spirit who lives in the forests of Esthonia called Metsik. Like some of the Fairies and Witches of other countries, he must be propitiated so that he will not injure the cattle. To achieve this, elaborate ceremonies are gone through, in which an image of the spirit figures largely.[3] Even up to the last century the Esthonians believed many trees to be inhabited by powerful Spirits, and in such awe were these held that they did not dare to break off a branch from a tree, nor would they even venture to pluck a flower from the ground on which the shadow of the tree fell.[4] These people have also the belief that when a thunderstorm comes on the Forest Spirits seek refuge from the lightning among the roots of the trees which they inhabit.

A Lithuanian demon was called Kirnis, and was the guardian of the Cherry tree.

A Swedish superstition says that in a case of theft the victim appealed to a Trollman or cunning man, who carved a figure on a young tree. He then muttered potent spells to invoke the aid of the Devil, and finally drove a sharp instrument into the eye of the figure, the belief being that at the same moment a corresponding injury would befall the eye of the thief.

In an epic of Finland called the Kalevala a Nymph is mentioned as having her abode in the Service tree, and she is also understood to protect cattle.

[1] Forsell's *Statistik von Schweden*, p. 1. Quoted by Grim, *Teut. Myth.*, vol. i. p. 487.   [2] Grim, *Teut. Myth.*, vol. i. p. 215.
[3] Dr. J. G. Frazer, *The Golden Bough*, " The Magic Art and the Evolution of Kings," vol. ii. p. 55.   [4] *Ibid.*, p. 43.

Often at night in the forests of Finland a hideous cry is heard, which is alleged to proceed from the Forest Demons who ever haunt the woods.

Among the numerous Gods who presided over the destinies of Finland was a special God of the forest named Tapio, to whom all the wild beasts of the forest belonged, and over which he and his beautiful goddess reigned. To these sylvan deities the hunter had to appeal for permission ere he ventured to hunt or slay any of the forest animals, and oblations were offered to them to induce them to drive the game across the hunter's path. They also protected domestic cattle, both in their stalls and if they should have happened to have strayed into the forest.[1] The Laplanders worshipped a similar Forest God.

In Poland, a female spirit, called a Dziwitza, is very fond of hunting, both in the daytime and on moonlight nights. She appears to be the prototype of the classical huntress Diana or Artemis. She was believed to be a young and lovely princess who roamed the forests accompanied by a most splendid pack of hounds, and she carried a zylba, or kind of javelin. She was in the habit of appearing to people who happened to be in the forest at midday and terrifying them, so it came to be a kind of joke to say to people who had been alone in the Fir woods at noon, " Are you not afraid Dziwitza will come to you ? " [2] Another female wood spirit in Poland was called Boruta, who was said to inhabit Fir trees.[3]

In one of the songs of Bulgaria we read that the mother of Stoïan endeavoured to dissuade that young shepherd from leading his flock through the Forest of the Samodives, who are a kind of Forest Demon, or at least from playing his flute when traversing it, because at the first sound the invoked Samodive would come to wrestle with him. Stoïan disobeyed, and instantly he saw a young man with disordered hair who sought a quarrel with him. The Demon, after three days of battle,

[1] Dr. J. G. Frazer, *The Golden Bough*, " The Magic Art and the Evolution of Kings," vol. ii. pp. 124-5.
[2] Grim, *Teut. Myth.*, vol. iii. p. 933.   [3] *Ibid.*, vol. iv. p. 1425.

invoked his sisters, the tempests, who carried Stoïan over the tops of the trees, beat him, knocked him, tore him to pieces, and destroyed his flock. Another Bulgarian song tells how the forest, without the wind blowing, was uprooted by the mere touch of dragons with long white hair. These pass over, with their wives in chariots of gold, and their children in cradles of gold. Professor de Gubernatis suggests that these dragons with white hair show to us the snowy winter, and their wives are perhaps the days of summer which they carry away, and their children the days of springtime, which they will bring back.[1]

A female being peculiar to Serbian mythology is the Vila, who partakes of the characteristics of both the Fairy and the Elf. These Vilas, represented as Mountain Nymphs, live in the forests on the hills, and love singing and dancing. They are young and beautiful, with long flowing hair, and are usually clad in white. They often mount up into the air, from whence they discharge fatal arrows at men, but they injure none except those who intrude on their revels. There is a Serbian saying— *ustrièlila ga vila*—meaning, the Vila has shot him with her dart. They are often seen sitting on Ash trees singing, and they converse with the stags in the forest. A Serbian song narrates how

" A young deer tracked his way through the lone forest
One lonely day—another came in sadness—
And the third dawn'd, and brought him sighs and sorrow ;
Then he address'd him to the forest Vila :
' Young deer,' she said, ' thou wild one of the forest !
Now tell me what great sorrow has oppress'd thee ;
Why wanderest thou thus in the forest lonely ;
Lonely one day—another day in sadness—
And the third day with sighs and anguish groaning ? '
And thus the young deer to the Vila answered :
' O thou sweet sister ! Vila of the forest !
Me has indeed a heavy grief befallen :
For I once had a fawn, mine own beloved,
And one sad day she sought the running water ;
She entered it, but came not back to bless me.' " [2]

[1] *Mythologie des Plantes*, vol. i. p. 76.
[2] *Servian Ballads*, translated by Bowring. Keightley's *Fairy Mythology*, p. 493.

The Vilas ride through the forests on a seven-year-old stag, which they bridle with snakes, and their cry, echoing through the woods, resembles the sound of the Woodpecker. Should a mother in anger consign her child to the Devil, it is believed that the Vila has a peculiar right to that child. They often appear dancing gaily round a Cherry tree, and a Serbian ballad begins :

> " Cherry ! dearest Cherry !
> Higher lift thy branches,
> Under which the Vilas
> Dance their magic roundels." [1]

The cumulus clouds of a summer day are supposed to be castles which the Vila builds in the air, and there her daughter Munya, or the lightning, plays with her brothers, the two thunders.

The Vila is a skilful physician, curing wounds for a high fee, but if offended she will poison her patient.

In Rumania a Forest Fairy named Muma Padura goes into the forest to seek for, and to help, children who have strayed thither and lost themselves.

The Wild Huntsman is found also in Carinthia, where the peasant places a wooden bowl full of meat on a tree in front of his house so as to propitiate the wind, that it may do him no harm.

The maidens of Franconia still go to a certain tree on St. Thomas's Day, and knock on its trunk three times. They then listen intently to hear the spirit which dwells within the tree tell them by means of answering knocks what kind of husbands they will have.

In the sunny lands of Greece and Italy, where the woods and groves waved perpetually green beneath the azure heavens, and the calm lakes reflected the summer skies in their pellucid depths, each grove, each tree, each river, each lake, and even

---

[1] *Servian Ballads*, translated by Bowring. Keightley's *Fairy Mythology*, pp. 491–2.

each pool, was regarded by the ancients as being the home of supernatural beings, who bore different names and possessed different qualities and attributes. The early inhabitants of Italy do not appear to have had the same facility for invention which characterised the Greeks, and consequently they adopted the ancient deities of Greece, but called them by other names. Thus the Mythology of Italy is very similar to that of Greece, but lacks the true poetic touch which was a feature of the latter. The most powerful of these mythical beings came in course of time to be worshipped as the principal gods, and there were many lower beings to whom a certain meed of reverence was paid, while to them was also attributed a human form. Among the latter were Nymphs, and it was believed that to them was given the guardianship of the woods and of the trees.

These Nymphs were of divine origin, and Homer tells that when Zeus, after the return of Achilles to the battle, called a council of the gods,

> " Not one was absent, not a rural power,
> That haunts the verdant gloom, or rosy bower ;
> Each fair-haired Dryad of the shady wood,
> Each azure sister of the silver flood." [1]

The Nymphs which we have particularly to deal with here were imagined by the Greeks as beautiful female forms. They were the Wood-Nymphs or Dryads, and a variety of them known as Tree-Nymphs or Hamadryads. There were also particular kinds of Tree-Nymphs who frequented fruit trees and watched over gardens. These were called Meliades, or Melian Nymphs, and they were also known as Flock-Nymphs, because they took flocks of sheep under their protection. They were also known in Italy, and Keightley [2] relates a legend to the effect that in the early ages, when the people of Italy were in the pastoral stage, a number of Flock-Nymphs

---

[1] *Iliad*, Pope's trans., xx. 11–14.
[2] *Classical Mythology*, p. 213.

were once seen by some shepherds dancing at a place in Messapia called the Sacred Rocks. The shepherds, having left their flocks to gaze on them, offended the Nymphs by saying they could excel them in dancing. After much argument a dancing contest was begun, but the light and graceful movements of the Nymphs could not be equalled by the clumsy efforts of the youthful shepherds, who, of course, were vanquished. The Nymphs then cried out to them, " O youths ! you have been contending with the Epimelian Nymphs, therefore you shall be punished." At these words the shepherds became trees forming a grove round the temple of the Nymphs. To this day, says Nikander, a voice as of lamentation is heard at night to issue from that grove, and the place is called the place of the Nymphs and the Youths.

One of the Homeric hymns relates that, after Dionysos or Bacchus was born, his father handed him over to the care of the Nymphs, by whom he was brought up in a shady grotto in the valley of Nysa. After he grew up he was reckoned as one of the immortals, being the god of wine, was crowned with Laurel and Ivy, and whithersoever he went he was closely attended by a train of Nymphs singing and dancing in joyous abandonment. Dionysos himself loved a Nymph named Staphyle.

Other varieties of Nymphs were the *Oriades*, or Mountain-Nymphs, which haunted the mountains ; the *Napœæ*, or Dale-Nymphs, frequenting the valleys ; those which frequented the meadows, known as *Leimoniades*, or Mead-Nymphs, and which appear to have approximated more to the Fairy type ; the *Naiades*, or Water-Nymphs, found by rivers, brooks and fountains ; and the Lake-Nymphs, or *Limniades*, haunting the lakes and pools.

Some of the Nymphs were distinguished among others, and among them the following may be mentioned : When speaking or calling out loudly in the woods or fields the ancients would often hear, as we do, their voice repeated once or several times, and this phenomenon was seized upon by them as a pivot round which to weave one of their prettiest legends. The echo became personified, and was regarded as a Nymph called Echo, who was beloved by the God Pan. She, however, would have none of him, as she had fallen deeply in love with a youth named Narcissus. But the latter was so intensely enamoured of his own image, becoming eventually the flower which bears his name, that he rejected her advances, and fled whenever he saw her approaching. Deeply chagrined at the coldness of the youth, Echo retired into solitary places, where her unrequited love gradually consumed her away until there was nothing left of her but her voice, and she may still be heard speaking far away among the hills and woods. Other explanations of the echo are that it is the voice of Faunus speaking in the woods, or that it proceeds from a Wood Elf who mocks the speaker.

The God Apollo had many loves among the Nymphs, of whom Dryopé was one. The Hamadryads had become very fond of her, and taught her to dance and sing. Apollo saw her when thus engaged, and conceived such a strong affection for her that she bore him a son called Amphissos, who, when he grew up, erected a temple to his father. Dryopé appeared at the temple one day, when the Hamadryads carried her away, causing a Poplar tree to spring up in her stead. The legend then tells how Amphissos, out of gratitude to the Nymphs for their goodness to his mother, erected a temple to them and instituted sports in their honour. At the latter, however, no woman was permitted to be present, because, as was said when Dryopé was carried away, two maidens had told the people, upon which the angry Nymphs had turned them both into Fir trees.

Cyrene, the daughter of the River-God Peneus, was another of the Nymphs loved by Apollo, to whom she bore a son named Aristæus. To the latter was ascribed the invention of the art of bee-keeping. Virgil (*Georgics*, iv.) tells how Aristæus, being in love with Eurydice, the wife of Orpheus, had relentlessly pursued her, and how the Napœan Nymphs, her companions, had destroyed all his bees. He appealed to his mother, Cyrene, for assistance, when she told him to " suppliant bear offerings, beseeching peace, and venerate the gentle wood-nymphs ; for at your supplications they will grant forgiveness, and mitigate their wrath." He carried out all her instructions, sacrificed cattle in the grove, and at last, on the ninth day, " they beheld a sudden prodigy, and wonderful to relate, bees through all the belly hum amidst the decomposed bowels of the cattle ; pour forth with the fermenting juices from the burst sides, and in immense clouds roll along ; then swarm together on the top of a tree, and hang down in a cluster from the bending boughs." [1]

Among the loves of the God Pan was the Water-Nymph or Naiad called Syrinx. She was a Nymph of Arcadia, and Pan pursued her till she reached the River Ladon, on the banks of which she implored her sister Nymphs to enable her to cross it. Pan, as he thought, had grasped her, but instead, found his arms filled with reeds, into which she had been changed. Hearing the breeze, as it passed through these reeds, make a low musical sound, the god plucked seven of them and formed his pipes, which he named Syrinx, or popularly Pan-pipes.

Far in the western ocean was the island of the Hesperides, who were three celebrated Nymphs, the daughters of Hesperus. To them was given the guardianship of the garden or grove wherein grew the golden apples which Juno had given to Jupiter on their nuptial day.

Pausanias (v. 15, 3) mentions that at Olympia, where an Olive tree grew, from the branches of which the victors' crowns were formed, an altar dedicated to the Nymphs of the Fair Crowns had been erected.

Certain young and lovely Nymphs who dwelt in forests and groves were known as Dryads, and they were the companions and attendants of the huntress goddess Artemis. In the

---

[1] *Virgil*, trans. by Davidson, Bohn's Cl. Lib., p. 101.

Orlando Furioso it is said that Rinaldo saw one in the Enchanted
Forest where

> " An aged oak beside him cleft and rent,
> And from his fertile hollow womb forth went
> (Clad in rare weeds and strange habiliment)
> A full-grown Nymph."

It was considered unlucky to see the Dryads or to keep
company with them, and Ovid, in the Fourth Book of the
Fastes, warned Pales " not to see the Dryads or Diana bathing,
or Faunus, when wandering through the fields at midday."

As distinguished from the Dryads, who, though having
their abodes in trees and groves, were free to move about,
was another class of beings known as Hamadryads, or purely
Tree-Nymphs, who dwelt in trees, were believed to be part
of the tree, and whose existence was closely bound up with
that of the tree. In fact it was believed that the Hamadryad
was female only to the waist, her lower extremities forming
part of the trunks and roots of trees, much in the same way
as the Mermaid was female to the waist, the rest of her being
a fish's tail. These Hamadryad trees were also said to grow
only in remote and secluded spots, where men were unlikely
to discover them. They seem, however, to have been pretty
well known in other parts, as there are frequent allusions to
them by the ancient poets. When their tree withers and dies
the Hamadryads also cease to be, and when their tree happens
to be cut down, a cry of anguish escapes them as the axe
descends.

Homer, in the hymn to Aphrodite has a very full description
of them. The goddess is represented, when she informs
Anchises of her pregnancy, and how she is ashamed of its
being known to the gods, as saying of the unborn child :

> " But him, when first he sees the sun's clear light,
> The Nymphs shall rear, the mountain-haunting Nymphs
> Deep-bosomed, who on this mountain great
> And holy dwell, who neither goddesses
> Nor women are. Their life is long ; they eat

> Ambrosial food, and with the deathless frame
> The beauteous dance. With them, in the recess
> Of lovely caves, well-spying Argos-slayer
> And the Sileni mix in love. Straight pines
> Or oaks high-headed spring with them upon
> The earth man-feeding, soon as they are born ;
> Trees fair and flourishing ; on the high hills
> Lofty they stand ; the Deathless' sacred grove
> Men call them, and with iron never cut.
> But when the fate of death is drawing near,
> First wither on the earth the beauteous trees,
> The bark around them wastes, the branches fall,
> And the Nymph's soul, at the same moment leaves
> The sun's fair light." [1]

Mr. Keightley quotes the following two legends. In the *Argonautica* of Apollonios Rhodios (ii. 475) Phineus explains that the poverty of Peræbios was due to a crime committed by his father,

> " for one time, cutting trees
> Alone among the hills, he spurned the prayer
> Of the Hamadryas Nymph, who, weeping sore,
> With earnest words besought him not to cut
> The trunk of an oak-tree, which, with herself
> Coeval, had endured for many a year.
> But, in the pride of youth, he foolishly
> Cut it ; and to him and his race the Nymph
> Gave ever after a lot profitless." [2]

Also the following tale from Charon of Lampsakos : " A man, named Rhœkos, happening to see an oak just ready to fall to the ground, ordered his slaves to prop it up. The Nymph, who had been on the point of perishing with the tree, came to him and expressed her gratitude to him for having saved her life, and at the same time desired him to ask what reward he would. Rhœkos then requested her to permit him to be her lover, and the Nymph acceded to his desire. She at the same time charged him strictly to avoid the society of every other woman, and told him that a bee should be her messenger. One time the bee happened to

---

[1] Keightley's *Classical Mythology*, 4th ed., pp. 210–11.
[2] *Ibid.*, p. 211.

come to Rhœkos as he was playing at draughts, and he made a rough reply. This so incensed the Nymph that she deprived him of sight." [1]

Ovid writes in a similar strain thus :—

" Within the grove of Ceres tower'd an oak
Huge in the bulk and strength of centuries ;
Itself a grove : and up its massy trunk
Midway, fresh wreaths and floral offerings hung
Votive : oft under it the Dryads whirl'd
In festive dances, and with linked hands
Clipt its dark bole, which filled the utmost grasp
Of nymphs thrice five ! As far the encircling wood
Was under it, as the uncropt herbage lay
Beneath that wood. Yet the Thessalian foe
His axe withheld not.
    As he swung oblique
Its fatal edge—shudder'd the sacred tree
And moan'd ; each leaf, each acorn, at the stroke
Grew pallid :—chill damp started on each bough ;
And when that impious hand the wounded trunk
Smote deep, blood flow'd from forth its cloven rind,
As when a noble steer, a victim, drops
At the altars, and swift gushing purple life
His neck distains.
    All in deep stupor gaz'd !
When, issuing from beneath the riven oak,
This voice resounded ;—' I, the nymph most dear
To Ceres, bleed within her sacred tree ;
And dying I foretell a direful doom
For thy fell deed impending : thus I find
In death my solace.'
    Yet the criminal
His work still urges ; till the umbrageous mass,
Tottering from countless blows, and dragg'd by ropes,
Falls, crashing, crushing half the subject grove." [2]

Arcadia, with its woods and mountains, was the favourite haunt, along with the Dryads, of the rustic god Pan. Pan was said to have been the son of Hermes or Mercury by a Nymph of Arcadia. One of the ancient writers (Servius) described him as being formed in the likeness of Nature,

[1] Keightley's *Classical Mythology*, p. 211.
[2] *Metam.*, Bk. viii. 11.

inasmuch as he had horns to resemble the rays of the sun and the horns of the moon ; that his face was ruddy in imitation of the ether ; that he wore a spotted fawn-skin resembling the stars in the sky ; that his lower limbs were hairy because of trees and wild beasts ; that he had feet resembling those of the goat to show the stability of the earth ; that his pipe had seven reeds in accordance with the harmony of Heaven, which was said to contain seven sounds ; that his pastoral staff bore a crook in reference to the year which curves back on itself ; and, finally, that he was the God of all Nature.[1]

The occupations of Pan were many and various ; whether he was roaming on the mountains, pursuing game in the valleys, or playing on his pipes in the groves, which music was often heard by travellers through the woods. The Arcadians called him the Lord of the Woods. Often loud and incomprehensible noises were heard among the mountains which gave to the timid a kind of superstitious terror, and these being ascribed to Pan, gave rise to apprehensions which are now known as panic.

Pan had many amours among the Nymphs, who, however, invariably fled from his ill-favoured appearance, and in many cases they were saved from him by being transformed into trees.

A legend mentioned by Nikander tells of a shepherd named Terambos who possessed many flocks, and who was much loved by Pan and also by the Nymphs, the latter assisting him in looking after his flocks. Pan, on one occasion, warned him that a severe winter was coming, and advised him to drive his flocks down into the plains. Terambos derided this advice, but the prophecy was too truly fulfilled, all the flocks being destroyed, and he himself was changed by the Nymphs into a Cockchafer.

Pan has been looked upon as one of the Satyrs, who were rough and shaggy beings, goat-like, and of a somewhat

[1] Keightley's *Classical Mythology*, p. 203.

demoniacal character. They were closely connected with Dionysos, and formed part of his Bacchanalian train. Fauns were the Italian counterpart of the Greek Satyrs, and an altar to Pan was erected in the grove below the Palatine Hill, where it was said Romulus and Remus were suckled by the wolf.

H. Usener, in his *Italische Mythen*, p. 198, speaks of two malignant female Wood-Spirits, named respectively Strudeli, which appears to mean a witch, and Strätteli, meaning a nightmare. It is believed, particularly on the shores of the Lake of Lucerne, that these have an adverse influence on the fruit-bearing trees ; so, in order to frighten them away, a certain ceremony is carried out on Twelfth Night. On that night the boys of the village walk in a procession making hideous noises with horns, cowbells, and other sonorous articles, believing that if sufficient noise is not made the fruit crop will be very scanty in the ensuing year.

A Wood-Spirit named Picus, believed to have been a son of Saturn, was said to have assisted the wolf in nursing the babes Romulus and Remus. Another legend says that Picus was a mighty hunter, and one day went to the chase arrayed in purple garments and wearing a golden collar. When so engaged he met the enchantress Circe in a wood, who fell in love with him. He, however, spurned her, whereupon she changed him into a Woodpecker, whose plumage is purple with a ring of yellow feathers round its neck.

In Sicily several curious superstitions have gathered around the Fig tree, because it is there believed to have been the tree on which Judas hanged himself, and never to have flowered since. It is, therefore, thought to be a tree of ill-omen. Each leaf, it is said, harbours an Evil Spirit or Devil, and, in addition, certain bloodthirsty Spirits or Demons, called Fauni Ficarii, frequent its neighbourhood. At Avola it is considered to be imprudent to rest in the shade of a Fig tree during the warm hours of the summer days. To whoever cares to run the risk will appear a female dressed as a nun, and holding a knife in her hand. She will ask him to say whether he will take the knife by the point or by the handle. If he says by the point he will be at once killed, but if he says by the handle, he will be successful in all he undertakes. In fact, in this island it is believed to be unsafe to sleep under any tree on the Eve of St. John, as on that night, which is the shortest night of the year, the Spirits and Demons of the trees leave their sylvan abodes and enter the first object they see, which might well be the sleeper. Similarly, the Albanians believe certain trees to be haunted by Devils, which they name Aërico, and which particularly haunt the Cherry tree when it becomes old and barren. The very shadow of these trees is believed to be evil, and to cause swellings and pains in the hands and feet. The peasants who live on the slopes of Mount Etna avoid sleeping under the trees, particularly on St. John's Night, lest they should be beset by the Devil. If, however, it happens that they have occasion to sleep there, they must first cut a branch from off the tree, or, as they say, *sagnari l'arvulu*, i.e. bleed the tree.[1]

In Ancient Chaldea there were seven Evil Spirits or Demons known as Maskims, and against these in particular the White Cedar was considered to be an infallible protection, though it was useful against all other Evil Spirits and spells. Ancient Chaldean writings revealed that " The White Cedar is the tree which breaks the Maskims' noxious might." One of the hymns to the sun commences : " O Sun, I have called unto thee in the bright heavens. In the shadow of the Cedar art thou " ; meaning that the sun causes the Cedar to cast a shadow, which is as holy as the tree itself.[2]

In Arabia certain Demons known as Jinns frequent waste and desert places, as well as the neighbourhood of trees and groves, and particularly the dense, untrodden thickets which generally occupy the bottom of the valleys. Some of these do good, others do evil, being in this respect similar to the Peries and Deevs of the Persians. There is an Arab legend of two men who lived a generation before Mohammed. They

---

[1] De Gubernatis, *Mythologie des Plantes*, vol. i. p. 111.
[2] Zenaïde A. Ragozin, *Chaldea from the Earliest Time to the Rise of Assyria*, p. 171.

had set fire to a wild and tangled thicket, intending to bring the ground under cultivation. The legend says that the Jinns flew away in the form of white serpents uttering doleful cries the while, and as the two men died soon after, it was believed that these Demons had slain them " because they had set fire to their dwelling-place." [1]

A malignant Demon or Deev called Siltim haunts the forests of Persia, appearing in human form and doing injury to man. Moore, in *Lalla Rookh*, says of the enchantress Namouna :

> " All spells and talismans she knew,
>   From the great Mantra, which around
> The Air's sublimer spirits drew,
>   To the gold gems of Afric, bound
> Upon the wandering Arab's arm,
> To keep him from the Siltim's harm."

What may be looked upon as the Fairies of Persia are known as Peries, whose food is perfume ; while the Demons bear the name of Deevs. Between these two sets of spirits there is constant warfare, in which, according to Persian legend, the Peries invariably get the worst of it. It is said that the Deevs, when they capture any of the Peries, enclose them in iron cages, which they hang from the tops of the highest trees. Here they are visited by their companions, who bring them the choicest perfumes for their nourishment, and these perfumes also repel. the Deevs, to whom fragrant odours are obnoxious.[2] Mr. Keightley mentions a Persian romance which relates how a merchant's son of a city in Hindostan, assuming the dress of a wandering dervish, went away from his native place. After travelling for some time he was overcome with fatigue, and rested at the foot of a tree beside a pool. While resting, and as the sun was setting, four doves alighted from a tree on the edge of the pool, and were at once transformed into Peries. They disrobed and commenced to bathe. He quickly took possession of their garments and concealed them

---

[1] Dr. W. Robertson Smith, *The Religion of the Semites.*
[2] Keightley's *Fairy Mythology*, p. 16.

in a hollow tree, behind which he retired. When the Peries had finished bathing they were much distressed at the disappearance of their clothes, and looked for them everywhere in vain. At length they discovered the young man, and conjectured that he had taken them, whereupon they implored him to restore them. He consented on the condition that one of them should become his wife. This was agreed to, and he took his bride home, but he carefully concealed her Peri-raiment so that she would be unable to leave him. After the lapse of ten years he again had occasion to travel, and left the Peri in charge of an old woman, to whom he had revealed the secret of his wife's real nature, and also showed her where he had concealed the Peri-raiment. During his absence the Peri cajoled the old woman to bring her her garments, that, as she said, " I may wear them for an instant, and show thee my native beauty." No sooner, however, had she them on, than she called out " Farewell," and, ascending to the sky, vanished from sight.[1]

In India certain spirits known as Vanadevâtas are supposed to preside over the trees in which they make their home, and many of the Buddhist legends refer to their intervention in human life. In some districts Wood-Spirits are believed to dwell in the summits of trees, and should these trees be cut down they will take revenge on the aggressor. There are white female Spirits called Sankchinnis which inhabit trees, at the feet of which at midnight they may often be seen standing. A Brahmin's wife was once attacked by one who shut her up in a cavity in the trunk of the tree.

In the early days of Buddhism there was much controversy as to whether trees had souls or not, and it was finally decided that they had not, though at the same time it was admitted that certain Spirits called Dewas, or Genii of the trees, did reside in the trunks of trees and spoke from within them.[2]

Some trees, such as the Sâl Tree, Pîpal Tree, and Mahua

[1] Keightley's *Fairy Mythology*, pp. 20–1.
[2] Edward B. Tylor, *Primitive Culture*, p. 429.

Tree, are the abodes of Evil Spirits, and to propitiate them offerings are made to the trees, and no one will venture to climb them. Some large and very old trees in Travancore are inhabited by Demons and are held sacred. It would be considered very dangerous to cut these down.[1] An Indian legend refers to a Banyan tree, which was the abode of numerous spirits who were said to wring the necks of all persons who approached their tree during the night.[2]

The nomadic tribe of the Bhîls believe in a forest giant called Mhowah or Mhaoah, who provides them with wood, bread, and the water of life ; while in the Neilgherry Hills a Forest Spirit or kind of Faun, known as Betikhân, resides, who hunts the wild beasts and is greatly revered.

There are certain Demons or Devils known as Pishashas, which are held in dread all over India. When women and others move about the forest travelling from village to village, they believe these Demons to be everywhere around them, and they endeavour to propitiate them with all sorts of articles laid here and there in crevices, sacred stones, and hollow trees. Pregnant women, especially in Malabar, when travelling, carry a scrap of iron, or a few leaves or twigs of the Neem tree, to scare away the Demons which are always lurking in the woods or groves they must pass on their way. Two Demons, or monsters, known respectively as Chûtâs or Bhûtûs, and Piçaćâs, have their abodes in the trees of the forest. There is a goddess called Sarna Burhi, or the Woman of the Grove, known in Bengal, to whom is dedicated a sacred grove called the Sarna, in which she is supposed to dwell. This grove is a remnant of the primeval Sal forest. Some of the aboriginal races of India believe that the spirits of the dead haunt the forests and have their abodes in the trees, and the leaves of some particular trees are used as charms against them.

Certain kinds of Elves and Nymphs would appear to have had existence in India. In a legend it is recorded that a youth

[1] Dr. J. G. Frazer, *The Golden Bough*, " The Magic Art and the Evolution of Kings," vol. ii. p. 42.
[2] R. Folkard, *Plant Lore, Legends and Lyrics*, p. 79.

named Satyavant, while endeavouring to cut down a tree, mortally wounded the Elf who inhabited the tree, and as her life ebbed away so likewise did his.

" In the Buddhist legend," says Professor de Gubernatis, " where the imprisoned sages in the centre of the ocean throw up fire and storm against the trees which threaten to cover all the earth these trees have a double character—creator and destroyer ; it is a form of the myth of the Deluge. The indignation of the sages is unlimited, so the god Soma interposes. The sages then collect themselves, and dream, like Manu in the Brahman legend, of repeopling the earth, by uniting themselves with Mârishâ, who is the daughter of a nymph, i.e. of the moisture deposited by a nymph on the leaves of the trees."

The Wild Huntsman of Germany has his counterpart in India, as one of the Vedic hymns addressed to the Storm Gods known as Maruts or Rudras says : " They shake with their strength all beings, even the strongest on earth and in heaven. . . . Mighty you are, powerful, of wonderful splendour, firmly rooted like mountains, (yet) lightly gliding along ; you chew up forests like elephants."

The Padams of Assam think that if a child has strayed and been lost, it has been stolen by the Forest Spirits. To force the Spirits to give up the child they commence to fell the trees, until the Spirits, fearing that no tree will be left for them, return the child, which is usually found lying in the fork of a tree.[1] The Miris of Assam dread offending the Forest Spirits by felling their trees to obtain new patches of ground for cultivation, and accordingly they use the ground they have already cleared as long as it is possible to grow crops on it.[2]

In Burmah and Siam the trees are believed to be inhabited by Spirits, and the natives of both countries are afraid to cut down any tree lest they incur the wrath of the Spirits domiciled there. In fact the En tribes of Upper Burmah say that if a

[1] E. F. Dalton, *Descriptive Ethnology of Bengal*, p. 25.
[2] Dr. J. G. Frazer, *The Golden Bough*, "Spirits of the Corn and of the Wild," vol. i. p. 123.

tree is felled a man dies. In Burmah some of these Spirits are known as Kaluks, to whom, before cutting down a tree, the Burmese offer prayers. They say they always know a Spirit or Demon to be in the trees whenever the leaves tremble without any visible cause.

The general name in Burmah for Tree Spirits is Nats, and of these there are four different kinds. Three of these live in different parts of the tree. Thus the Akakasoh dwells in the topmost branches of the tree ; the Shekkasoh dwells in the trunk ; while the Boomasoh has his abode among the roots. The fourth is a Wood-Spirit or Demon called Hmin, who ranges at large throughout the forest, and seems to be the Fever or Ague Demon, as it is said that he violently shakes all those whom he meets. As in many other tropical countries, when fever or ague attacks one in the jungle, it is believed to be the work of this Demon, or of another called Phi, and certain ceremonies are gone through to exorcise it. One is that the victim must place an offering beside the tree he last rested under, from the branches of which the malaria fiend had descended upon him.

The Siamese consider the Tree Spirits to be a kind of Nymph, whom they style Mothers of Trees. When they cut down a tree and build a boat from its wood they believe that these Spirits enter into it, and sacrifices are accordingly made to the boat itself.

The Samoyeds of Siberia say that little Elves haunt the woods and streams, and these again are ruled by a Great Spirit, the Forest Spirit and the River Spirit respectively.

Ancient Japanese beliefs gave souls to trees, and the grotesque and gnarled trunks of many an ancient tree in the forests of Japan may even yet in some cases appear as menacing Spirits to the wanderer in the shades. The Japanese wood-cutter had an unspeakable dread when he found himself belated in the gloom of the wood, and he saw a Spectre or Demon in every contorted trunk. Many legends of Japan speak of Cedars having centuries of age, which are still so vital

that when the axe falls on them drops of blood often ooze
out from the cuts.

After Korea regained its independence from Japan, the
event was celebrated by the king proceeding in state to a dark
Pine wood wherein was situated the altar of the Spirits of the
Land, the most sacred altar in Korea, and there taking an oath
before the spirits of his ancestors to inaugurate certain reforms.[1]

In Korea the belief in malignant Demons is very widespread,
and every old and gnarled tree is supposed to be the residence
of one of them. Mrs. Bishop says that near Seoul heaps of
stones sacred to Demons are placed under large trees, and
that tall posts with ruddy carved human faces are placed on
each side of the road with straw ropes stretched across, the
idea being to prevent the ingress of malignant Spirits.[2]   It is
believed that if a person dies of the pestilence, or by the road
side, their spirit takes up its abode in a tree ; and certain
ancient and contorted trees are looked upon as the residences
of the spirits of those people who have died before attaining
sixty years of age, and it also seems to be believed that they
had died owing to the evil influence exercised by the Evil
Spirit of the tree.[3]   In Korean belief every shady tree harbours
a Demon, and shrines to them are erected under the shadow
of large trees. These Demons are exorcised by certain blind
wizards, who are called Pan-su, and parts of the ceremony are
performed by the aid of two magic wands, one of Oak or Pine,
and the other a special one made from the eastern branch
of a Peach tree.[4]

There is a famous altar-piece in a monastery at Yu-chöm-sa,
which represents the upturned roots of a tree, among which
fifty-three idols appear. Below them are carved three fearful-
looking dragons. Mrs. Bishop says the legend of this altar-
piece is that fifty-three priests came from India to introduce
Buddhism, and when they reached this spot they sat down
under a great tree beside a well. Three dragons emerged

[1] Mrs. Bishop, *Korea and Her Neighbours*, vol. ii. p. 31–2.
[2] *Ibid.*, vol. i. p. 83.   [3] *Ibid.*, pp. 106–7.
[4] *Ibid.*, vol. ii. pp. 229 *et seq.*

from the well and attacked the priests, and also invoked a mighty wind, which tore up the tree, leaving the roots exposed. Each priest then placed an image of Buddha on each root, which thus became an altar. In the end the dragons were defeated, thrown into the well, and great stones were placed on the top of it. The priests then built a temple over the well and founded the monastery.[1]

The Chinese believe in a species of being which they call Shinseën, which haunt the forests and the mountains. They appear to be an inoffensive race, dwelling in a state of peaceful beatitude, but yet exercising a certain benign influence over the affairs of humanity. Occasionally they may be seen in the shape of old men with long beards, while in other cases they appear as fair young maidens sauntering at ease amid the moonlit forest glades.

The natives of the Malay Peninsula and of the Malay Archipelago have an implicit belief in all sorts of Forest Spirits and Forest Demons. Such is their awe and reverence for the forest that no native will dare to enter it alone, but must always have a companion. To him the forest is the abode of evil and supernatural beings who are ever on the outlook to do him injury, and in consequence, before entering the forest, he repeats the following invocation to avert their wrath :

> " Peace unto ye all !
> I come as a friend, not as an enemy.
> I come to seek my living, not to make war.
> May no harm come to me, nor mine,
> To my wife, my children, or my home,
> Because I intend no harm, nor evil,
> I ask that I may come, and go, in peace."

The farther they penetrate into the forest they become all the more assiduous in their incantations.

The general name for these Spirits of the Forest is Hantu Hutan, and they are equally dreaded with the tiger and other wild beasts. There are different varieties of them, the names

---

[1] Mrs. Bishop, *Korea and Her Neighbours*, vol. ii. p. 170-1.

of some being Jin Tanah, or Spirits of the Earth, having power over the forest and all its inhabitants ; Gergasi, great tusked giants or ogres, no doubt originating in the elephant or some remote ancestor of his ; and Orang Bunyi, or Voice-Folk, " spirits whom all may hear but none may see." [1] These latter invisible supernatural people inhabit the forest, and in one place there is a cave which is supposed to be their home. Their voice is said to be very similar to the human voice, and they are often heard calling to each other in the forest depths, which may easily be mistaken for the tones of a human voice in distress. Tales are often told of those who under this impression have answered the call and proceeded towards the voice, but having once done so, they could not retrace their steps. The unfortunate one is lured ever farther on into the dark recesses, until at last the Voice-Folk become visible to him, and his doom is to become one of them and invisible to man, only his voice betokening his presence.[2]

There is a Demon named Bota who frequents a district on the Perak river, and who causes travellers to see visions of wondrous palaces and ravishingly beautiful females, which give promise of all sorts of entrancing delights. However, when the dawn appears, the unhappy traveller finds himself faint and in a dying condition in some gloomy thicket, with all the promised joys vanished.[3]

In Perak there is a very fine and large tree called the Toallong, the sap of which is poisonous and produces intense irritation if it touches the skin. Curious hollow excrescences are found on the trunks of many of these trees at the point where a branch has been broken off. These excrescences are considered by the Malays to be the abodes of the Tree-Spirits, and nothing will induce them to cut down such a tree, because they say the Spirits will be much offended, and the man who cuts one down will die within a year.[4]

---

[1] George Maxwell, *In Malay Forests*, 1911, pp. 9–11.
[2] *Ibid.*, pp. 267–8.   [3] *Ibid.*, pp. 146–7.
[4] Dr. J. G. Frazer, *The Golden Bough*, " The Magic Art and the Evolution of Kings," vol. ii. p. 41.

Mr. Maxwell (*In Malay Forests*) gives an interesting account of the old pagan religion which has now been superseded by Mohammedanism, and tells how the *pawangs* or sorcerers, in their office as priests, fulfil their duties. He particularly mentions the method pursued during a deer drive in the Malay forests, in which ropes, called *sidins*, with many nooses are used. These are stretched in long lines through the forest from tree to tree under the superintendence of the *pawang*. The latter carefully selects the trees and invokes the Forest Spirits thus :

> " Hail ! all hail !
> Mother to the earth !
> Father to the sky !
> Brother to the water !
> I crave permission to enter on your domain,
> And to tie my nooses to this tree."

Numerous incantations are uttered to propitiate the Evil Spirits, also prayers to the various trees to which the ropes are tied, and likewise instructions to the deer to pass along the right line. This being done, if all goes well, several deer are captured. Various other ceremonies are gone through at the end to propitiate the Forest Spirits which are thought to be waiting to avenge the death of the deer.

When a Malay desires to become invulnerable he retires to the innermost recesses of the forest and there spends three days in solitude. Should he, on the third day, dream that a beautiful Spirit has come and spoken to him, his desire is considered to be fulfilled.[1]

Some of the most interesting Spirits which haunt the forests of the Malay Peninsula are those which preside over the Camphor trees in the extensive Camphor forests of that region. The natives believe that unless they propitiate these Spirits they will be unable to obtain any camphor. The form which this propitiation takes is that of employing a special kind of language when engaged in the camphor search, which usually

[1] Edward B. Tylor, *Primitive Culture*, 1871, vol ii. p. 375.

occupies them for three or four months. The language used is a mixture of the ancient obsolete dialects with Malayan words perverted from their original meaning. This language is known as the *bassa kapor*, or Camphor language. Thus the camphor is never referred to by its proper name, but by words meaning " the thing that smells." A similar language is used in the Camphor forests of Borneo and Sumatra, and other islands of the Malay Archipelago, and is used at other times than on the occasions of camphor gathering. The natives usually feel very uncomfortable when wandering through these great primeval forests, for they know that if they are unfortunate enough to offend the Forest Spirits by using words which are offensive to them some evil will assuredly ensue. Thus, if fine weather is desired to be continued, the word " rain " must not be uttered, as if it is the Rain Spirit will hear it, and, thinking he is wanted, will put in an appearance. Indeed, in some parts which are liable to heavy storms the word must never in any circumstances be mentioned, otherwise a hurricane will be the result. A similar kind of language is used among the Chams and Orang-Glaï of Indo-China when they are searching for Eagle wood ; and the aborigines of Malacca must do the same when searching for the Gaharu tree, or *Lignum aloes*. This tree possesses a Guardian Spirit called Hantu Gaharu, who must have a human victim in exchange for the tree, Mr. A. D. F. Hervey says that when a man has found one of these trees and dreams that Hantu Gaharu demands a victim, he endeavours to find someone asleep and smears his forehead with lime. The Spirit, seeing this, takes the soul of the sleeper away ; in other words, the victim dies, and the dreamer gets his Aloes wood.[1]

Tree-Demons properly speaking are called Hantu Kayu, and are found in every species of tree, some trees being particularly noted for the malignancy of the Demons which inhabit them, and these afflict mankind with all manner of diseases.

A Spectral Huntsman, very similar to the Wild Huntsman

[1] *Indian Notes and Queries* (December, 1886), p. 45, § 154.

of Germany and other countries, ranges the Malay Forests. He travels with a pack of ghostly dogs, and whenever he is seen sickness or death is sure to follow. Certain night-flying birds, whose note is loud and peculiar, are believed to be his attendants. When their weird cry is heard the peasants run out making a clatter with a knife on a wooden platter, and cry, " Great-grandfather, bring us their hearts." The huntsman believes they are his own followers asking a share of his bag ; so he passes on, leaving them unharmed, and the tumult of the wild hunt gradually dies away.[1]

The forests of the various islands of the Malay Archipelago are similarly haunted by Spirits and Demons. In some of the Eastern Islands the natives, before felling a sacred tree, drive nails of gold or silver into its trunk to warn the Spirit to leave before its abode is hewn down.[2] In Borneo and Sumatra certain trees are believed to be inherited by Spirits and must on no account be cut down ; while in Sumatra in particular old and venerable trees are considered to be the actual frame of the Spirit. In some parts of Borneo these Spirits are looked upon as the souls of the dead. The Dyaks of Borneo believe the forests to be full of Goblins who are ever at enmity with them, and who assume various weird shapes at will. If a Dyak has been walking solitary in the forest, he considers it probable that one of these Goblins has stolen his soul, although he is not conscious of the loss. To guard himself, however, before he leaves the forest, he makes a point of asking that his soul be returned to him, after which he goes away with a lightened heart. Among the Looboos of Sumatra the wandering spirits of the dead, known as Soemangots, are held in particular dread. There are several methods employed to avoid their unwelcome attentions. Should a man have lost his way in the forest he knows that this is due to one of these Evil Spirits who had been following him and casting spells upon him. To throw the Spirit off the track, he splits a rattan

---

[1] W. W. Skeat, *Malay Magic*, p. 112.
[2] Dr. J. G. Frazer, *The Golden Bough*, " The Magic Art and the Evolution of Kings," vol. ii. p. 36.

and creeps through the opening. This done, the rattan immediately closes, and the Spirit is considered to be baffled in its pursuit.[1]

The Pelew Islanders assert that the Tree Spirits will remain in the wood with which they have built their houses unless they have been previously expelled, and accordingly when they are felling a tree certain incantations are used to induce the Spirit of that tree to leave it, and to take up its abode in another. Similarly, in the Philippine Islands and in Borneo the Spirit is requested to leave a tree about to be felled. In the latter island the Dyaks strike an axe into a tree, demanding a sign from the Spirit. The axe is left all night in the tree, and if in the morning it is still there, this is a sign that the Spirit has left. If, however, the axe is found lying on the ground, that shows that the Spirit has cast it out, and the tree must on no account be interfered with.[2]

In the Island of Siao, one of a tiny group, certain Spirits are believed to dwell in the woods, and in massive trees standing apart. This Spirit is said to have an enormous head, a massive body, and long arms and legs. It appears when the moon is full, and must be propitiated by offerings of food set in the spots which they haunt.[3]

The natives of the Island of Nias, to the west of Sumatra, say that when a tree dies the Spirit which inhabited it becomes a Demon. This Demon will kill a Cocoanut palm by merely resting on it, and can kill children by sitting on a post of the house in which they live. Other trees, when still living and uninjured, are said to be the ordinary homes of Demons, but if they be injured or felled, the Demon then becomes free to roam about and cause much harm. Consequently these trees are carefully guarded.[4]

The Island of Celebes contains many powerful Spirits and Demons, and it is stated that the Demons inhabiting many of the largest trees have human forms—the higher the tree the

[1] Dr. J. G. Frazer, *The Golden Bough*, " The Magic Art and the Evolution of Kings," vol. ii. pp. 182–3.
[2] *Ibid.*, p. 37.   [3] *Ibid.*, p. 33.   [4] *Ibid.*, pp. 33–4.

more powerful the Demon. If it is necessary to fell such a tree the Demon is duly informed of the fact, and is requested to leave the tree, provisions being provided for his sustenance on his journey hence while he looks for another home. In some instances a small ladder is placed against the tree to enable the Demon to descend safely, while some tribes build a little hut for him to inhabit after he has left his tree.[1]

In Java, likewise, great umbrageous trees are believed to be the abodes of Spirits.

A German missionary, writing regarding the Papuan tribe of the Bukaua in what was formerly German New Guinea, says : " Of forest spirits the number is infinite ; for it is above all in the mysterious darkness, the tangled wildernesses of the virgin forest, that the spirits love to dwell. They hold their meetings in what are called evil places. They are never bent on good. Especially at nightfall the native fancies he hears the voice of the spirits in the hum and chirping of the insects in the forest. They lure hunting dogs from the trail. They make wild boars rabid ; in the form of snakes they make inroads into human dwellings ; they drive men crazy or into fits ; they play roguish tricks of all sorts." [2]

In the western part of British New Guinea female Demons of a very dangerous character inhabit large trees which are never felled. The natives of the districts surrounding Geelvink Bay see in the mists which often hover on the tops of the high trees, a Spirit or a God which they call Narbrooi. The Spirit draws out the soul of those whom he loves and bears it away to the mist-enshrouded tree-tops. Therefore when a man falls ill one of his friends goes to those trees to endeavour to recover the soul. He makes a peculiar sound to attract the attention of the Spirit, and then, sitting down, lights a cigar. As the smoke curls up from it, Narbrooi appears in the midst, young and elegant, and in answer to

[2] Dr. J. G. Frazer, *The Golden Bough*, " The Magic Art and the Evolution of Kings," vol. ii. p. 35.

[1] Stefan Lehner, " Bukaua " in R. Neuhauss's *Deutsch Neu-Guinea*, iii. (Berlin, 1911), pp. 414–16.

inquiries, says whether the soul is with him or not. If it is, on receiving an offering, Narbrooi returns it. It is then conveyed in a straw bag back to the sufferer, and the bag emptied over him. Often, however, Narbrooi does not keep his word, but takes away the soul again, in which case the sufferer likely dies.[1]

The Kei Islands, to the south-west of Papua, are the abode of multitudes of Evil Spirits, who inhabit every tree and are most vindictive. Even speaking when passing their abode brings down their wrath on the offender's head, who must appease them by an offering, or drive them away by the offensive smell of burnt hair or horn.[2]

It is in Africa that the superstitious belief in Forest Demons and Evil Spirits of all kinds reaches its greatest development, and the belief in these beings is general among all the tribes of that dark continent. The Rev. John H. Weeks tells that the Boloki of the Upper Congo believe themselves to be surrounded by Spirits which continually endeavour to thwart them and do them harm at every hour of the day and night. They believe the rivers and the creeks to be crowded with the Spirits of their ancestors, as well as the forest and the bush. These are ever seeking to do injury to travellers when overtaken by night. Mr. Weeks remarks he had never met a man among them daring enough to go at night through the forest that divided Monsembe from the upper villages, even though a large reward was offered. They invariably replied : " There are too many spirits in the bush and forest." [3]

Sacred trees, which are reverenced as being the abode of a divinity, are found in every part of the great continent. Every Bambaras village on the Upper Niger has usually a Tamarind tree in which the fetish resides ; great and mischievous Spirits reside in mighty Baobabs on the Tanga coast of East Africa ; among the Galla tribes of East Africa a certain

[1] Dr. J. G. Frazer, *The Golden Bough*, " Taboo and the Perils of the Soul," pp. 60-1.

[2] *Ibid.*, "The Scapegoat," p. 112.

[3] *Among Congo Cannibals*, London, 1913, p. 261.

tree is consecrated by a priest and so becomes holy, and is usually the abode of Jinns. No one may break a branch of such a tree, nor dare anyone even approach it or tread on its shadow. The natives of Guinea know that good and evil Spirits lurk in every ancient hollow tree, every grove, every cave, etc., and when passing such places they leave an offering of some kind of trifle, even though it be but a leaf.[1]

In Senegambia a long-haired Tree-Demon is believed to send diseases to the natives.

The Bongos and the Niam-Niams consider their forests to be weird and mysterious places, the haunts of dreadful supernatural beings, very malignant, and when the natives pass through these woods they think they hear in the rustle of the foliage the mysterious conversation of these Demons as they conspire against them. Those which frequent the vast forest proper are called Bitâbohs or Hitâbohs, while others of a more sylvan type and of a gentler character, haunting the groves and more open spaces, are known as Rangas. The latter seem to include nocturnal owls, as well as a small red-eyed monkey called the Ndorr. This latter hides in the daytime in the hollows of trees, issuing forth only at night. Bats also are included, one species of which flies about from tree to tree in broad daylight. To escape the influence of these Evil Spirits the Bongos use certain magic roots. All the old people, principally the women, are accused of having relations, more or less strict, with the Spirits. These people, the Bongos tell you, are seen wandering in the glades with no other object than that of looking for the magic roots. Apparently they sleep quietly in their huts, but in reality they consult Evil Spirits in order to learn the way to destroy their neighbour.[2]

Among the Basoga of Central Africa a Spirit called Kakua Kambuzi is thought to have the tall spreading Incense-tree under its protection, and Sir Harry Johnson says that if a man was discovered to have had improper relations with a virgin,

[1] J. L. Wilson, *West Africa*, pp. 218, 388.
[2] De Gubernatis, *Mythologie des Plantes*, vol i. p. 73.

the erring couple were sent at night to Kaluba's village, where they were tied to a certain Incense-tree and left. Next morning, when found by the people of the neighbourhood, they were released and allowed to settle near the tree of the protecting Spirit.[1]

One of the largest and tallest trees of the West African forests between the River Senegal and the River Niger is the Silk-cotton tree, which is looked upon as the abode of a God or Spirit called Huntin. Only some, however, of these trees are honoured by having him as a resident, such being surrounded by a girdle of Palm leaves, and are thus exempted from all injury. Sacrifices of fowls, and sometimes of human beings, are made to this God, and if it is necessary to fell such a tree an offering of fowls and palm oil must first be made to propitiate the Spirit.

Probably this Huntin is a member of the class of Forest Spirits known to the Tschwi of the West African coast as Sasabonsum, which also have the Silk-cotton trees as their abodes. Miss Mary H. Kingsley gives the following account of this Spirit which she obtained from the Tschwi themselves : " He lives in the forest, in or under those great silk-cotton trees around the roots of which the earth is red. This coloured earth identifies a silk-cotton tree as being the residence of a Sasabonsum, as its colour is held to arise from the blood it wipes off him as he goes down to his underworld home after a night's carnage. All silk-cotton trees are suspected because they are held to be the roosts for Duppies. But the red earth ones are feared with a great fear, and no one makes a path by them or a camp near them at night.

" Sasabonsum is a friend of witches. He is of enormous size and of a red colour. He wears his hair straight, and he waylays unprotected wayfarers in the forest at night, and in all districts except that of Apollonia he eats them. Round Apollonia he only sucks their blood. Natives of this district after meeting him have crawled home and given an account

[1] *The Uganda Protectorate*, London, 1902, vol. ii. pp. 718 *et seq.*

of his appearance, and then expired." As Sasabonsum is a friend of witches he is able to give the power of becoming witches to those who may so desire it. To achieve this the person takes a certain object, and in the forest depths performs various incantations over it, when it becomes a suhman or tutelary deity which he reverences and makes offerings to. Possessed of this he is able to do many things, and particularly to bring about the death of other people. Miss Kingsley tells us, further, that Sasabonsum is married, his wife, or rather his female form, being called Shamantin, and adds : " She is far less malignant than the male form. Her name comes from Srahman—ghost or spirit ; the termination *tin* is an abbreviation of *tsintsin*—tall. She is of immense height, and white ; perhaps this idea is derived from the white stem of the silk-cotton tree, wherein she invariably abides. Her method of dealing with the solitary wayfarer is no doubt inconvenient to him, but it is kinder than her husband's ways, for she does not kill and eat him, as Sasabonsum does, but merely detains him some months while she teaches him all about the forest : what herbs are good to eat, or to cure disease ; where the game come to drink, and what they say to each other, and so forth." [1]

Another class of Spirits is called Ombwiri, who appear to be of the nature of Dryads, and to whom trifles are offered when passing the tree of their abode.

In West Africa there are often seen heaps of branches lying in the forests of the Fan country, the reason for these being that each traveller through the forest adds a leafy branch to the heap, by doing which it is believed that the Demons inhabiting the trees will not allow them to fall on the traveller, nor their roots trip him up.

Paul du Chaillu, in his extensive travels in Equatorial Africa, mentions a Forest Demon, Nburu by name, for whose accommodation small houses are built in the forest. His bed,

[1] *Travels in West Africa, Congo Français, Corisco and Cameroons*, pp. 509–12.

of dry leaves covered with a mat, was on the ground, and his pillow consisted of a smooth round piece of wood.[1]

For long the pigmies of Central Africa had been regarded but as mythical creatures inhabiting the forests of that mighty continent. The records of Ancient Egypt, however, speak of them as being really existent. The tombs of the Sixth Dynasty bear record of them. Thus, there is one telling how the Pharaoh Assa spoke of having seen a pigmy brought from the land of Punt, now known as Somaliland, and five reigns later there is the record telling how the Pharaoh Mer-en-Ra sent a servant to bring a pigmy from the land of Punt by the lake Punt. Homer mentions them when he wrote of the annual warfare between the cranes and the pigmies; and Herodotus says he had heard from the registrar of Minerva's treasury at Sais in Egypt of certain young Nasamonians, a Libyan tribe, who, while exploring in the south, had been captured by certain diminutive men, and carried away to their city. Sir Henry M. Stanley, in his journey across Africa, proved that these pigmies had a very real existence by discovering them in the solitudes of the vast Central African forest. He says they are between three and four feet high, and adds : " That little body of his represented the oldest types of primeval man, descended from the outcasts of the earliest ages, the Ishmaels of the primitive race, for ever shunning the haunts of the workers, deprived of the joy and delight of the home hearths, eternally exiled by their vice, to live the life of human beasts in morass and fen and jungle wild. Think of it ! Twenty-six centuries ago his ancestors captured the five young Nasamonian explorers, and made merry with them at their villages on the banks of the Niger." [2]

When Australia was first discovered it was found that the aborigines believed that every thicket and grove was densely populated with Evil Spirits ; Demons whistled in the Bush, and stooped from the trees with outstretched arms to seize

---

[1] *In African Forest and Jungle*, p. 31.
[2] *In Darkest Africa*, vol. ii. p. 40.

the wanderer. A curious form of the belief in Tree Spirits is found among the Warramunga tribe of Central Australia. They believe in reincarnation, and that the souls of the dead while waiting rebirth take up their abode in certain trees. Thus their women will not strike one of these trees with an axe, fearing that the blow will dislodge one of these Spirits which will find its way into her body, and there await rebirth.[1]

The natives of Tasmania also had a firm belief in Evil Demons which resided in hollow trees, while others of a less malignant nature had some resemblance to the Elves of other lands.

The Rainbow had been looked upon as a Demon by some primitive nations, and among the Maoris of New Zealand the myth describing the warfare of the Tempest against the Forest makes the Rainbow, as representing the Tempest, place his mouth close to Tane-mahuta (*q.v.*), and blow till the trunk is broken and the branches strew the ground.

The Maoris had likewise a belief in Fairies of a kind, and Mr. Cowan [2] gives the following fairy tale called *Te Rii and the Enchanted Forest*, as it was narrated to him. The narrator, Te Rii, said : " Friend, the *Patu-paiarehe* (Fairies) are still a numerous people in this land, and their dwellings are the great bunches and bushes of *Kiekie* and *Kowharawhara* (Fairy Flax) which you see growing in the forks of the forest trees. They live ever in the forest, and you may pass their homes a hundred times and never see them, yet they are still there, as I myself well know, for I have seen them in the night, and heard them singing their fairy songs." On a ridge of hills near the Waitara River the narrator said " the bush there is full of birds, and it is a grand place for the fruit of the *Kiekie*, but there is a peculiar thing about the Kiekie there— the fruit is quite red inside, instead of being white, as it is elsewhere. This is because it is the food of the fairies ; and if we go there for that fruit we shall have to propitiate them with a *karakia* (invocation), else things may perhaps not go

[1] Spenser and Gillen, *Northern Tribes of Central Australia.*
[2] *The Maoris of New Zealand*, 1910, pp. 204-7.

well with us. Immediately a stranger, a Maori, or a *pakeha* of this outer world, enters these *tapu* forests, his presence is detected by the fairies, and they will sometimes play strange tricks on him. He will perhaps hear a strange wild woman's voice calling, thin and high, our Maori cry of welcome to visitors :

" Haere-mai e te manuhiri tuarangi,"

and so on, but when he follows in the direction whence the invitation came, he will find no one—it was the phantom voice of the *Patu-paiarehe*."

Te Rii then related how he went into the forest and killed a wild pig, after which he wandered on and on, finally finding himself back at the place where he had killed the pig. He was lost, but set off again, and once more found himself at the same place. Here he lay down and slept. In the morning he saw, lying on the ground, a stick which moved. It was an enchanted stick, and Te Rii, continuing his story, said : " Anyhow, I took hold of the stick. As soon as I grasped it I felt it move and draw me away. I did not let go, though I knew there was wizardry in it, but it was daylight now, and I did not feel as much fear as in the black night. I retained hold of one end of the stick, and it drew me on and away ; the fairies had hold of the other end, though I could see no one. I left my pig lying on the ground ; the stick would not wait for me to take it, and I thought it best to leave it there as a peace-offering to the spirits of the bush. The stick led me down out of the forest and set me on the homeward path, and then it vanished. And as I left the forest of enchantment I heard a voice call after me, a thin voice from the shadows of the bush—' Go, and beware ! Do not come into these forests of ours again.' "

In the islands of the Pacific Ocean, Tree Spirits and Tree Demons are also met with. In some parts Fairies are likewise known, the Fairyland of these regions being known as Kupolu. The Fairies themselves, both male and female, are called

Tapairu. The Tapairu, or peerless ones properly speaking, are the four daughters of the female demon Miru, who is ugly and deformed, resides in the lower regions, and cooks human spirits in her oven. Her four daughters are of an unsurpassed beauty, and often ascend to the upper world at sunset. After arranging their lovely tresses in the moonbeams they deign to take part in the dance performed by mortals in honour of their brother, by name Tautiti, this particular dance being known by his name. These Fairies, however, will only dance on a floor of fresh banana leaves, which are not in the least injured by their dainty steps. In the eastern islands of the Pacific, Tapairu, or Fairest of the Fair, is a favourite name for girls.[1]

In the Tonga Islands certain particular trees are believed to be inhabited by Spirits, and the natives lay offerings at the feet of these.[2]

One of the gods formerly worshipped in Fiji was known as Roko Suka, and his representative on these islands was said to be the land crab, as that creature is rarely seen there. Whenever one appeared, the priest, an old man, was at once told that the God had favoured them with a visit, whereupon a string of new cocoanuts was at once presented to him, as any neglect might cause him to bring disasters upon the people.[3] The natives are greatly afraid of ghosts, especially the ghosts of the dead. These are supposed to plant a tree called the Tarawau, which bears an intensely bitter fruit.[4]

A certain Ironwood tree (*Casuarina*), which had been planted in a valley in Fiji by the Tongans, was believed to be the impersonation of an Evil Spirit named Vaotere. A man named Oārangi heard that its wood was very useful in other lands, and resolved to cut it down. Accompanied by four friends he set out on this errand. When they came to the tree

[1] Rev. W. Wyatt Gill, M.A., *Myths and Songs from the South Pacific*, 1876, pp. 256–7.
[2] S. S. Farmer, *Tonga*, p. 127.
[3] Thomas Williams, *Fiji and the Fijians*, 3rd ed., 1870, p. 186.
[4] *Ibid.*, p. 203.

they found that it had four gigantic roots, which they proceeded to cut, but after each root had in turn been nearly severed, when they returned to complete the work, the roots were as intact as ever. Each man then applied himself to one root, and in due course at dawn the mighty tree fell with a crash. Then they resolved to return home and complete the work next day. Two of them, however, died on the way, and next day, when Oārangi and his two surviving friends returned, they found the tree standing as erect as ever, but, significant omen, the whole was of a blood-red colour, as if resenting the treatment it had received. The three then proceeded home, the two remaining friends of Oārangi likewise dying on the way. Still hopeful, however, Oārangi, accompanied by a number of other friends, returned one day, but failed to find the tree. The Rev. W. Wyatt Gill tells the rest of the legend thus : " Oārangi had done his utmost, but had been foiled by the malicious demon of the iron-wood tree, and soon after died. But was there no one who could overcome Vaotere and render the wood of the tree useful to mankind ? Ono came from the land whence this tree was originally derived, and had in his possession a remarkable iron-wood spade, named Rua-i-paku = *the-hole-where-it-must-fall*, given to him by his father Ruatea, ere he set out on his voyagings, for any dangerous emergency. This talisman was very valuable as a club. Armed with Rua-i-paku he resolved to do battle with the demon Vaotere. Upon reaching the shady valley of Angaruaau, he carefully surveyed the coveted tree, and began his operations by digging up the earth about the roots, being careful, however, to avoid injuring any of the main ones. Day after day, entirely unassisted, the brave Ono persevered in his arduous task in pursuing the roots in all their deviations over the valley and hill-side. Upon their becoming small and unimportant, although exceedingly numerous, he fearlessly chopped them with his famous spade. The chips flew in all directions, over hill and vale, under his mighty blows. After many days' toil all the surface roots were bared

and severed at their extremities, so that the tree began to
totter. The tap-root alone remained. Ono dug to a great
depth into the red soil, and then, at a blow, divided it. At
this critical moment, the head and horrid visage of the Evil
Spirit Vaotere became visible, distorted with rage at being
again disturbed. His open jaws, filled with terrible teeth,
prepared to make an end of the impious Ono, who, perceiving
his danger, with one well-directed blow of his spade-club
luckily succeeded in splitting the skull of Vaotere.

"The victorious Ono now leisurely removed the four great
gnarled roots, which were, in sooth, the arms of the fierce
Vaotere, and afterwards divided the enormous trunk—the
bleeding body of the demon—into three unequal portions :
one to furnish a quantity of long spears, another to be split
into *araâ*, or 'skull-cleavers'; the third to furnish *aro*, or
wooden swords. All this was accompanied by the versatile
qualities of Rua-i-paku, which was used first as a spade, then
as a club, and now as an axe.

"The thousand chips from the small roots of this wonderful
tree falling everywhere over hill and valley and sea-shore,
originated the Iron-wood trees now covering the island : but,
happily, Vaotere can no more injure mankind." [1]

Many songs were formerly sung relating to the exploits of
this Ono, and a fragment of one in connection with the above
says :

> "'The iron-wood tree of Vaotere is felled :
> It lies low on the earth.
> Once it stood erect; now it is prostrate,
> Turn the log over and over,
> The tree thus laid low.
> Formerly it was the glory of the valley,
> Once it stood erect; now it is prostrate.'" [2]

The New World possessed Forest Spirits and Forest Demons
very similar to those which infested the forests of the Old
World. Dr. Robert Brown, speaking of the vast forests of

---

[1] *Myths and Songs from the South Pacific*, pp. 81–6.   [2] *Ibid.*

North America, says that " to the Indians these dark primeval forests are the home of all things fearful and to be avoided. There they lie, wave after wave of forest and forest—clothed hill, oak and alder and pine, and the bright autumnal yellow-leaved maple, full of bear and of beaver and of elk, and, if the scared Indian hunter is to be credited, worse things still —Cyclopean Smolenkos, one-eyed jointless fiends, who run along the mountain-sides swifter than the black-tailed deer— Pans, and dryads, and hamadryads, gods of the woods and the groves and of the waterfalls and the running streams ;— all these haunt the country out of sight of the salt water, for (evidence uncontrovertible !) had not Kĕkĕān's father's brother's friend seen them when he was seeking his medicine, or Maquilla's grandfather's cousin, Wiccaninish, heard a hunter of elk tell it to the wondering lodge at Kalooish's great salmon feast at Shesha ? ' Laugh as you like, chief of King George,' an Indian said once to me, when pressing him to join me in exploring a portion of the great forest, ' but as long as there are salmon in the Stalow, and deer in Swuchas, you will not get me to go with you there.' " [1]

The forests of Belle Isle, an island situated near Newfoundland, are still as wild and desolate as they were four hundred years ago. This island, and a neighbouring one called Quirpon, were, in early days, known as the Isles of Demons, from the marvellous tales which the early explorers brought home regarding them. The forests were supposed to be infested with demons, and the terror-stricken mariners who sailed past their shores heard the hideous shrieks and outcries which announced the celebration of some infernal orgy. So strong was the belief in these Demons that maps were drawn of the islands, showing their infernal inhabitants to be adorned with the usual accessories of Devils, such as tails and horns. This somewhat resembles the account given of Mount Atlas by Pliny, who, after referring to the wooded character of the landward side, writes that when travellers approach it, especially

[1] *The Races of Mankind*, vol. i.

during the night, the mountain " gleams with fires innumerable lighted up ; it is then the scene of the gambols of the Ægipans and the Satyr crew, while it re-echoes with the notes of the flute and the pipe, and the clash of drums and cymbals."

Many of the North American tribes believed tall old trees to be the homes of Spirits who cried out when the tree was cut down or fell through the natural effect of wind or floods. An example of this belief may be found in Washington Matthew's *Ethnography and Philology of the Hidatsa Indians* (1877, p. 48 *et seq.*). These Hidatsa Indians believed that the Cotton-wood tree, one of the giant trees of the Upper Missouri valley, had an intelligence or spirit of its own, and that it could aid the Indians under certain conditions. They believe that when the Missouri, sweeping down in flood, uproots some tree on its banks, the spirit of that tree calls out. Consequently they will not fell such trees, but will only use those that have fallen naturally, and some of the older Indians declared that many of the misfortunes which befel their people were due to some of the trees having been cut down.

An Elf, resembling the Puck of England, named Mikamwes, was believed to frolic in the moonlight in the glades of the vast forests of North America. Fairies also, called Mamagwasewug, frequented the Canadian forests, and were every whit as mischievous and lovable as their European relatives.

The Indians of the Far West, before entering the defiles of the Black Mountains of Nebraska, hang offerings on the trees to propitiate the Spirits, and so ensure good weather and good hunting.

Nor is the Wild Huntsman absent from North America. Among the Iroquois Indians he is known as Heno the Thunder. He rides on the clouds, and splits the forest trees with his thunder-bolts. When he gathers the clouds together he pours out the warm rain, and so becomes the God of Agriculture, and the Indians call him Grandfather.[1]

[1] Edward B. Tylor, *Primitive Culture*, vol. ii. p. 277.

The Forests of Central America likewise have their weird beings. Dr. Robert Brown quotes the following : " Living in dark and gloomy forests of which they do not know the extent, the ideas of the Indians naturally turn towards the mysterious and wonderful, and for want of any known inhabitants they people these unexplored tracts with fabulous monsters. The heads of several dark and shady creeks, blocked up by a mass of fallen trees and bamboos, is regarded as the abode of the great *wowlos* (a huge species of serpent). On paddling some distance up these creeks presently a rumbling as of thunder is heard at the head, and, strange to say, the stream immediately begins to flow upward with irresistible force ; a fierce wind tears through the trees, and the unhappy victims are carried without hope of rescue to the terrible jaws that await them." There is another fierce monster called the Wihwin, resembling a horse, which, although its native place is the sea, takes up its residence for the summer in the mountains, and roams through the forests at night in search of victims.[1]

In these forests, and also in the West Indian islands, the natives had a legend of a bird-headed woman who was very beautiful and sang most divinely. She frequented the depths of the forests, and by her song men were irresistibly lured towards her, when she seized upon them and destroyed them. On dark moonless nights she was said to roam around the native villages, and was held in the utmost dread.

Among the Caribs of the West Indian islands the belief is that when men die the souls of some frequent the seashore, where they upset boats, and others enter the forests, where they become Evil Spirits.[2]

In some parts of South America there is a belief in a Good and an Evil Spirit called respectively Mauari and Saraua ; as also the Spirits of the Waters and of the Forest, known as the two Gamainhas.[3]

[1] *Races of Mankind*, vol. i. p. 252.
[2] Edward B. Tylor, *Primitive Culture*, vol. ii. p. 102.
[3] *Ibid.*, p. 226.

In the Forests of Brazil a lame Demon leads the hunter astray.   In these forests, as in all other forests, many unaccountable sounds are often heard.   Mr. Henry W. Bates says that sometimes a sound is heard as if a hollow tree had been struck with an iron bar, or it may be that a piercing cry resounds through the forest.   These, he says, the natives attribute to a Demon, or wild man, of the woods, who is known as the Curupira, or Curupuri.   This being is variously described in different localities.   In some parts he is said to be a kind of orang-utang, covered with long shaggy hair and living in trees. In other parts he is described as having cloven feet and a bright red face.   He is believed to be married and has children, and the whole family often come to the native plantations to steal the crops.   Mr. Bates says that a native made a charm for him to protect him against this Demon.   He plaited a young Palm leaf, then formed it into a ring, and hung it to a branch in the track the travellers were to pursue.[1]

Another kind of Forest Demon, or rather Hobgoblin, is called the Caypór.   He, however, is neither an object of worship nor of fear, except perhaps to children.   He is said to be a bulky, misshapen monster, his skin is red, and he has long shaggy red hair which hangs half-way down his back.[2]

The belief in these two demons has evidently had its origin in tales of the wild animals of the Brazilian Forests, clearly some of the monkey tribe, which tales, highly embellished, have been handed down from generation to generation.

Among the aborigines of Brazil the souls of the dead are believed to be constantly plotting evil against the living, who live in constant dread of them.   They are known as Bopi, and every few days a terrified native hastens home in a frenzy to report that he has seen a spook lurking in the jungle, and instantly the whole community is wildly excited.   These ghosts of the dead are usually seen just as soon as the shades of night are beginning to fall.[3]

[1] *The Naturalist on the Amazons*, pp. 34–35.
[2] *Ibid.*, p. 263.
[3] William Azel Cook, *Through the Wilderness of Brazil*, p. 409.

One part of the mouth of the Amazon is said to be haunted by the ghost of a Pajé, or Indian wizard, who, as the Indian canoe-men believe, requires to be propitiated to enable them to have a safe return from their voyages into the interior. To do this they must deposit some article on the spot, and the trees are usually seen to be hung with rags, shirts, straw hats, bunches of fruit, and so forth.[1]

---

[1] Henry W. Bates, *The Naturalist on the Amazons*, pp. 118–19.

CHAPTER VI

TREES

Trees in General ; Shadow of Trees ; Trees as the Origin of Mankind ;
Worship of Trees ; Transformations into Trees ; Trees Preside over
Marriages ; Trees Planted at Births ; Arboreal Tribes ; Burial on
Trees ; Funereal Trees ; Elsbeer Tree ; Christmas Tree ; Genealo-
gical Tree ; Devil Trees ; Guardian Trees ; Abode Tree ; Speaking
Trees ; Life Tree ; Bull Oaks.

Trees in General

The remark of Ruskin, " What a great thought of God was
that when He thought a tree ! " epitomises the tree in all its
various aspects, considering its utility from every point of
view, whether as contributing to the shelter of mankind by
its timber, or by its foliage, from the bitter blasts or from the
torrid heat ; or ministering to his æsthetic emotions by the
beauty of the leaves and flowers ; or providing for his sustenance by the luscious fruits and nourishing juices. The Ancient
Greeks called the Oak the " Mother Tree," because their
mythology avers that after Jupiter had slain the giants, the
Oak sprang up from the body of one of them called Rhoecus.
This tree the Greeks looked upon as the first tree which grew
upon earth and which provided nourishment to men by its
acorns. According to Galen, the Arcadians continued to
feed on acorns when all the Greeks were using cereals. In
fact, primitive man seems to have nourished himself largely
on acorns and nuts of various kinds, which diet was in no
way detrimental to him, as they being

> " Fed with the oaken mast,
> The aged trees themselves in age surpassed."

To the imagination of early man a tree, being the largest of
plants, must have presented a marvellous and bewildering
aspect. In some countries he would see it bare and withered-

looking during winter, but as soon as the first breath of spring was wafted over the land a wondrous transformation would commence. Gradually the leaves would unfold, day after day becoming larger and of a more vivid green, until, in the height of summer, a verdant canopy would overshadow all the forest, and man in his nakedness would feel grateful for the welcome shade afforded from the overpowering rays of the sun. To the tree he would assign a supernatural intelligence, and would regard it as a sentient being. As the summer wore on and the autumn days drew nigh, the kaleidoscopic changes in the leaf colouring would anew rivet his attention, and as the days passed the fall of the leaves would fill him with a presentiment of evil, which would be realised by the trees becoming again bare and apparently lifeless, leaving him shelterless against the biting blasts of winter. As year after year passed with the same continual changefulness, trees, or perhaps one outstanding tree on account of its size and age, would come to be regarded with an especial reverence, and primitive imagination would people it with all sorts of beings, such as Gods, Nymphs, and Demons. A curious fact found among the Khasia tribe of Eastern Bengal is that the words meaning tree and house are practically the same, which would appear to indicate that in primeval times the ancestors of that tribe had their habitations in hollow trees.

In this prosaic age too little is thought about trees and the romance connected with them. Their sweet music, as the summer breezes play gently through their foliage, gives a certain peace to existence to the loiterers among the woodlands, and to the imaginative mind the tree appears to have many moods which one can understand and sympathise with. As Dr. Kitto remarked : " The tree seems to have stood among and to have witnessed the ever-changing panorama of human life, and we know that it has been itself an object of notice, and has ministered some pleasure in past ages to eyes long quenched in dust." [1] Writers in all ages have used trees by

[1] *The Lost Senses—Deafness*, p. 57.

way of illustration, and Homer frequently embellishes his subjects with references to them. In the poems of Ossian the following beautiful passage occurs in Malvina's lamentation for Oscar : " I was a lovely tree in thy presence, Oscar, with all my branches round me ; but thy death came like a blast from the desert, and laid my green head low ; the spring returned with its showers, but no green leaf of mine arose." Again, when old and weary, blind, and almost destitute of friends, Ossian compares himself to a tree that is withered and decayed : " But Ossian is a tree that is withered ; its branches are blasted and bare ; no green leaf covers its boughs : from its trunk no young shoot is seen to spring ; the breeze whistles in its grey moss ; the blast shakes its head of age ; the storm will soon overturn it, and strew all its dry branches with thee, O Dermid, and with all the rest of the mighty dead, in the green winding vale of Cona."

In very remote conceptions of mythology there appears to have been no distinction drawn between the trees growing on the earth and those which imagination conceived as growing in the sky. As soon, however, as the ambrosia, the divine life-giving fluid, fell upon the earth, the trees there took on a different character from the sky trees, and seeded and multiplied, but since that time, unlike the latter, their life, like the life of man, has been limited in duration.

The Ancient Persians considered the tree to be the emblem of human existence owing to the changes which it undergoes during the various seasons, and it was also regarded as a type of immortality owing to its lengthened period of life. A number of venerable and umbrageous trees were believed to be inhabited by Celestial Spirits. These were looked upon as peculiarly sacred trees, and the Great Spirit Ormuzd, speaking to Zoroaster, said : " Go, O Zoroaster, to the living trees, and let thy mouth speak before them these words : I pray to the pure trees, the creatures of Ormuzd." The Magians were obliged by the precepts of their religion to cultivate the soil, and they considered it a most meritorious act to plant a tree.

A tree has often been conceived of as a kind of republic, or an agglomeration of isolated beings, and De Candolle opined the forest giants to be so many aggregates of individuals, or buds, annually succeeding on the stem which represents a living soul. An analogy has been drawn between coral and a tree, the coral insect constructing the coral branches in a somewhat similar way to the individuals of the tree constructing the boughs. This is not so far-fetched as might appear, when we remember that each leaf may be looked upon as a separate being possessing mouths for respiration, and so helping to nourish the whole bulk of the tree. Edward Gibbon speaks of the City of Rome under the allegory of a tree. He says : " Amidst the arms of the Lombards and under the despotism of the Greeks, we again inquire into the fate of Rome, which had reached, about the close of the sixth century, the lowest period of her depression. By the removal of the seat of empire, and the successive loss of the provinces, the sources of public and private opulence were exhausted ; the lofty tree, under whose shade the nations of the earth had reposed, was deprived of its leaves and branches and the sapless trunk was left to wither on the ground."

The primitive races of mankind believed that trees possessed souls, and Captain Cook said that the natives of Tahiti believe that the souls of trees at death ascend to the divinity with whom they at first mix, and thereafter each one passes into the particular mansion allotted to it. The Ancient Greek philosophers also attributed intellect and sense to trees.

Naturally, when a soul was given to a tree, it was likewise endowed with the power of speech. This speech is often in a mysterious, emblematical, or silent language, which, how-ever, often makes itself heard, it may be in the creaking of the branches, or in the leaf rustling in the breeze. Many trees have even taken human speech, as in the Cornel tree, in which Polydorus spoke, or in the Juniper tree mentioned by an author of the seventeenth century named Loccenius, which was indignant, and cried out when it was pulled up.

In Burmah the temples were surrounded with trees because
the first holy men dwelt in the forest and worshipped under
the shade of the trees, and thus each succeeding incarnation
of the Buddha had a connection with some particular tree.

The Scandinavian god Odin had human victims regularly
offered to him, and these were put to death by being hung on
a tree and stabbed with a spear. One of his titles was " God
of the Hanged," or " Lord of the Gallows," and the *Hamaval*
tells how, when young, he was sacrificed to himself in the
same way, and represents him as saying :

> " I know that I hung on the windy tree
> For nine whole nights,
> Wounded with the spear, dedicated to Odin,
> Myself to myself."

His mysterious wisdom came to him during the period of
this ordeal.

In some countries it is believed that trees suffer from the
evil eye as well as men, so much so that if one looks with evil
intent upon a tree, that tree is considered to be cursed. Professor de Gubernatis [1] mentions several instances of this.
He says that several trees are indebted for their evil reputation
to the curse of some divine personage, and many were cursed
by the Virgin Mary during the Flight into Egypt. A Bulgarian
song mentions the cursing of three trees by her, and adds
that she afterwards went to a convent and there confessed her
outburst of temper. In India, if a native marries a widow, as
this kind of union is usually attended by fatal consequences,
he hurls his curse on an expiatory tree, which absorbs all the
future evils and at the same time perishes. Schweinfurth,
during his travels in Central Africa, found this superstition
prevalent among the Nubians, and tells how the inhabitants
of a certain village showed him the branch of a colossal tree
(*Ficus lutea*) which had fallen simply because a warrior, in
passing it, had cast on it the evil eye. There was a belief
once current in Ireland that if one confides a dream he has

[1] *Mythologie des Plantes*, vol. i. pp. 113–14.

had to a tree, that tree at once loses its leaves and withers, and this because dreams were considered to be the work of the Devil.

SHADOW OF TREES

There was a curious early primitive belief that a tree could be injured through its shadow, which was considered to be sensitive. Dudley Kidd tells us that if a Kaffir witch doctor required the leaves of a tree for his brews, as the shadow of the tree will feel the touch of his feet, he " takes care to run up quickly, and to avoid touching the shadow lest it should inform the tree of the danger and so give the tree time to withdraw the medicinal properties from its extremities into the safety of the inaccessible trunk." [1]

A myth among some East African tribes has a strong resemblance to the story of the Tower of Babel, only in this case men wished to reach the moon, and sought to accomplish their object by placing one tree on the top of another until the whole fell down.[2]

In Nigeria a human victim, usually a leper, was always offered to Obumo, the God of Thunder. The victim was first wrapped in Palm leaves, and was then tied to the top of a high tree.[3]

To trees and parts of trees have been attributed many marvels. It is narrated in the *Travels of Gaspare Balbi* to India in 1582 that the sea threw up on the shore an enormous tree. When it was measured it was found that its length was precisely that which was required for the pillars of the church which was being constructed in honour of St. John the Baptist.

When a Maori of New Zealand desired a tree for the purpose of making a canoe, he would select his tree and cut a strip of bark from off it. The tree then became *taboo*, and no one would so much as touch it.

Should a West African native of the Ashira tribe intend going on a trading expedition he first rubs himself all over

[1] *Savage Childhood*, p. 71.   [2] Dr. J. G. Frazer.   [3] *Ibid.*

with the juice of the Oloumi tree, which he believes will render him very acute at driving the best bargain.

An episode similar to the concealment of King Charles II. in the Royal Oak is recorded of one of the kings of Tezcuco, in Mexico. When, in the year 1418, the Tepanecs killed the King of the Tezcucans, his son and heir, the young Prince Nezahualcoyotl, who was then fifteen years of age, saw his father murdered before his eyes, he himself being concealed among the friendly branches of a tree which overshadowed the spot.[1]

When Cortez took possession of Tobasco he gave three cuts with his sword on a large Ceiba tree which grew in the place, and proclaimed aloud that he took possession of the city in the name and on behalf of the Catholic sovereigns, and would maintain and defend the same with sword and buckler against all who should gainsay it.[2]

TREES AS THE ORIGIN OF MANKIND

The origin of mankind from plants seems to be a myth of ancient Aryan origin, and Hesiod, when treating of the ages of the world, speaks of five succeeding races of mankind, and he tells that the Third, or Brazen Race of men were formed by Zeus out of Ash trees. This race, he says, delighted in war. Although they ate no corn yet they had prodigious strength, while all things they used were composed of brass, " for black iron was not yet. Their end was their slaughter by each other, and, leaving no fame behind them, they went down to the " mouldy house of cold Aïdes."

Virgil,[3] speaking of King Evander, the founder of the Roman glory, causes him to say : " These groves the native Fauns and Nymphs possessed, and a race of men sprung from the trunks of trees and stubborn oak ; who had neither laws nor refinement ; knew neither to yoke the steer, nor to gather

[1] W. H. Prescott, *History of the Conquest of Mexico,* ed. 1844, vol. i. p. 146.
[2] *Ibid.,* p. 253.   [3] *Æneid* Bk. viii.

wealth, nor to use their acquisitions with moderation ; but the branches, and hunting, a rough source of sustenance, supplied them with food.

In Italy it is said that a man comes from a *ceppo*, i.e. trunk, stump, etc. ; or from *stipite*, i.e. a stem.

In the Phrygian cosmogony, according to Pausanias (vii. 17, 11), an Almond tree was considered as the father of all things probably from its lilac blossoms appearing before the leaves, and thus being the earliest heralds of the spring.

Almost all the Semitic and Aryan races inherit the tradition of mankind having originated from a tree, and Schoebel, conjecturing the probable origin of this belief, wrote, in *Le mythe de la femme et du serpent*, that : " In the tree man saw such a resemblance to himself that he thought he had come from the earth like, and under the form of, a tree."

The prophet Isaiah (xi. 1) allegorically depicted human beings as trees when he wrote that out of the stem of Jesse should come forth a rod and from his roots a branch, and this gave rise to an artistic myth which depicted the Virgin Mary coming out from the waist of a tree which was planted in the navel of the personage who was the founder of the family ; and sometimes she is compared to a flowering stem from Paradise.

Many of the ancient races conceived the clouds as being parts of a mighty universal tree, and as from clouds descended the rain, the ambrosia, or the life-giving fluid, vegetation became looked upon as symbolical of life and generation. Thus man, in course of time, connected his origin with these cloud-trees, which became materialised into actual trees.

Scandinavian mythology tells how the dwarfs fashioned two figures out of trees. These figures were found by Odin and his brothers, who endowed them with life and under-standing. They named them Askr and Embla, and they were the first human beings.

Among the Scandinavian races the goddess Holda, who combined the form of a lovely woman with the trunk of a tree, was believed to have been the creator of mankind. A legend of Hesse describes her as being a beautiful woman in front, while behind she resembles a hollow tree.

The Oak and the Ash have both been looked upon as progenitors of mankind. The Greeks had a tradition that a mighty cosmogonic or cloud-ash produced the first race of men through the Meliai or Nymphs of the Ash, who were regarded as cloud-goddesses. They also looked upon the Oak as having produced the first men, and Oak trees were called the first mothers. The Romans also shared this belief, and Juvenal, in his Sixth Satire, speaks of mankind as born of the opening Oak which, mother-like, fed man with her own acorns ; while Ovid says that man's first food was " acorns dropping from the tree of Jove." Even yet in some parts of Germany the belief is current, especially among children, that babies are brought by the doctor from out some ancient hollow tree or stump.

The Genealogical tree is said to commemorate the descent of man from the trunk of a tree, and Dante imagined the human family under the form of this tree.[1]

The Persian or Iranian tradition of the creation of man is that originally the first human pair grew up as a double tree with the fingers of each folded over the ears of the other. When this tree had attained maturity it was separated into two by the decree of Ormuzd, who endowed each half with a separate existence and a human soul, as a man and a woman, with the gift of knowledge.

Some Indian tribes believe that men originated from trees. Thus M. Rousselet, speaking of the Cassia tree, known in India under the name of Mhowah, as supplying all the native wants, says : " We are therefore not surprised to learn that in the Windhyas and Aravalis the inhabitants look upon it as equal to the divinity. It is from it that the Gounds, Bhîls, Mhairs, and Minao derive their existence."

Regarding this ancient belief in the human race having been originally descended from trees there is a tale, found through-

[1] Nork, *Mythologie der Volkssagen und Volkmärchen.*

out Asia, of four travellers who spent a night in a forest and agreed that one of them should keep watch by turns while the others slept. The first who kept watch was a carpenter, and to while away the time he carved out the shape of a beautiful woman from the trunk of a tree lying near at hand. When the second, a tailor, saw the figure, he clothed it. The third, when his turn came, being a jeweller, decked out the image with jewels. The fourth was a holy man, and he was so impressed by the sight of the lovely image that he invoked all his magic powers and endowed the image with life. When the rest awoke each claimed the lovely being as his wife because they all had a hand in shaping her. The dispute waxed furious, and the authorities of the neighbouring village were appealed to to solve the problem as to which of the four the hand of the disputed bride should belong. This they were unable to do, and finally the case was submitted to a higher court. The whole court went out to the cemetery, where prayers were offered for a decision from on high. During this time the woman was leaning against a tree, when suddenly it opened, and the woman, entering it, was seen no more. As she vanished, a voice from the heavens was heard, saying : " To its origin shall every created thing return." [1]

A Central Indian race called the Khatties believe that they originated in the following manner : At the time when the five sons of Pandou, the heroes of whom the Mahâbhârata has sung the exploits, were reduced to being simply guardians of their cattle, Karna, their illegitimate brother, thought he would deprive them of this last resource. Recognizing that he would be unable to employ the warriors—that is, the nobles —in such a dishonourable enterprise, Karna struck the earth with his wand ; the wand opened immediately, and from it came a man called Khat, a word meaning " engendered from wood." Karna employed him in the theft of the cattle, by guaranteeing in the name of the Gods that a similar action

[1] W. R. S. Ralston, " Forest and Field Myths," in *The Contemporary Review*, vol. xxxi, February 1878.

would never be considered as a crime either in him or in any of his descendants. On account of this accommodating tradition the Khatties always bless the memory of Karna.[1]

The Kabyles of North Africa believe that the men who lead the tribes are formed from the Ash tree.

Meyer tells us that the aborigines of Encounter Bay, in Australia, say that the first man was formed from the gum of a Wattle tree. He then entered into a young woman and was properly born.

This belief is also found widespread in America, where trees were worshipped as an emblem of life. A myth of the Yurucases of Bolivia relates that when all mankind had been destroyed by fire, the god Tiri opened a tree and from it drew forth all the various tribes. When a sufficient number had come forth he closed up the tree. But these people were weak and ignorant, so a virgin prayed to Ulé, who was the most beautiful tree of the forest, or rather, the tree contained Ulé, who came forth and embraced the Virgin, and from their union the culture hero sprang who taught the people the arts of life.[2]

The Quiches of Central America had certain divine beings whom they called Givers of Life. These first made men from clay, who, however, were weak and watery, and they were destroyed by water. They next made men from wood, and women from the pith of trees. These peopled the earth with wooden mannikins, but this race, being still considered unsatisfactory, was destroyed. Some other experimental races were made, until finally men were formed from white and yellow maize, and these were the progenitors of the present races of mankind.

In the legends of the Bakairi Caribs of the Antilles, in the West Indies, the mythical twin heroes Keri and Kame brought the original animals from the hollow trunk of a tree.

A North American legend or epic tells the adventures of

[1] De Gubernatis, *Mythologie des Plantes*, vol. i. p. 43.
[2] David G. Brinton, *Myths of the New World*.

a mythical being called Kuloskap, or Glooscap, who on one occasion took his bow and arrows and shot at an Ash tree. From the hole made by the arrowmen came forth the first of the human race.

Among the South American tribes of Guiana a great creator is acknowledged. They say that all created things came from a branch of a Silk-cotton tree which had been cut down by the Creator, but that the white man had sprung from the chips of a particularly useless tree. Another belief was that all plants grew from one tree in the centre of which was a huge pool of water inhabited by fish. A reminiscence of the Deluge is that a monkey let loose this water, which thus drowned the world. The classical myth of Deucalion and Pyrrha, who repeopled the earth by throwing stones behind them, finds its counterpart among the Tamanca tribes of the Orinoco, who say that the only survivors of the Deluge, a man and a woman, repopulated the world by throwing the stones of the Ita Palm (*Mauritia*) over their heads, which at once became human beings.

WORSHIP OF TREES

If, as might be said, man's first ideal was the life of the tree, naturally his first worship would be that of the tree, and in many countries trees were held in the utmost reverence, which, in some cases, has survived down to the present day.

Modern research has thrown much new light on the mythological origin of Tree Gods and Tree Spirits, more particularly as regards the mythology of Ancient Greece. Professor Rendel Harris [1] remarks that the Gods of Olympos are fading away into the earlier forms from which they were evolved. The most primitive and simple of religious beliefs among both northern and southern races connected the object with the divinity, and when the Ancients declared the Oak sacred to Zeus, they identified the tree with the god—in other words, the

[1] *The Ascent of Olympos* (1917), p. 1.

tree itself was the god, and in very primitive times was worshipped as such.   This hypothesis is still further elaborated
by the fact that the Oak is the tree most often struck by lightning, and thus Zeus, being also the God of Thunder, or the
Thunder itself, dwelt in, or rather had his being in, an Oak
tree.   Professor Harris puts it thus : " The Thunder-god
goes back into the Thunder-man, or into the Thunder-bird
or Thunder-tree ; Zeus takes the stately form in vegetable
life of the Oak-tree, or if he must be flesh and blood, he
comes back as a Red-headed Woodpecker."   The parasites of
the Oak, such as Mistletoe and Ivy, would evidently partake
of the attributes of the tree and would thus be the thunder also.
In the case of the Ivy a new and subordinate Thunder God
would become evolved under the name of Dionysos, and
Professor Harris says : " Dionysos is the ivy ; in the first
instance he is ivy, nothing more or less " [1]; and again : " The
tree is the thunder and makes all its parasites and its denizens
thunder also." [2]

The God of Thunder among the Finns was Ukko (or Oak),
and the Mountain Ash or Rowan, under the name of Rauni,
was considered to be his wife.   The red berries of this tree
were very sacred, and apparently it was on account of them
that the tree derived its sanctity, as the following passage from
the Kalevala would indicate :

> " In the yard there grows a rowan,
> Thou with reverend care should'st tend it.
> Holy is the tree there growing,
> Holy likewise are its branches,
> On its boughs the leaves are holy,
> And its berries yet more holy." [3]

From the redness of its berries it was known as Thor's tree.

When Christianity began to take a hold on the nations the
priests endeavoured to do away with this ancient worship of

---

[1] *The Ascent of Olympos* (1917), pp. 4–5.   [2] *Ibid.*, p. 8.
[3] *Kalevala*, transl. Kirby, xxii. 221–6.   Quoted in *The Ascent of Olympos.*
Professor Rendel Harris, pp. 10–11.

trees, looking upon it as a diabolical invention. It was, however, so deeply ingrained in the human heart that in many cases it was utilised by the Church for its own ends by blessing the most ancient and venerated trees, and by erecting Christian altars and placing crucifixes and images of the Virgin near to those trees under which in ancient times the people had sacrificed to the heathen divinities. It is related of St. Martin that he once demolished a temple unopposed, but when he endeavoured to cut down a sacred Fir tree near it the people prevented him. Round the Cross itself a legend was woven by which it was recognised as having been formed from a tree lineally descended from the Tree of Adam (*q.v.*). Among the Jews tree-worship appears to have been pretty widespread at one time. The Asherah, to which frequent reference is made in the Old Testament, was often simply a grove, but frequently it was an image such as an artificial tree, and as such is often seen on Assyrian inscriptions or sculptures, tree-worship having been very common in Assyria. The worship of the Asherah seems to have been entirely local, and the prophets protested vehemently against it. At Temnos Aphrodite was worshipped in the shape of a growing Myrtle tree which might be considered as an image.

Dr. James Fergusson mentions a curious instance of tree-worship in India which he had witnessed himself. He says : " While residing in Tessore, I observed at one time considerable crowds passing near the factory I then had charge of. As it might be merely an ordinary fair they were going to attend, I took no notice ; but as the crowd grew daily larger and assumed a more religious character I inquired, and was told that a god had appeared in a tree at a place about six miles off. Next morning I rode over, and found a large space cleared in a village I knew well, in the centre of which stood an old decayed date tree, hung with garlands and offerings. Around it houses were erected for the attendant Brahmins, and a great deal of business was going on in offerings and Pûjâ. On my inquiring how the god manifested his presence, I was informed that soon after the sun rose in the morning the tree raised its head to welcome him, and bowed it down again when he departed. As this was a miracle easily tested, I returned at noon and found it was so! After a little study and investigation the mystery did not seem difficult of explanation. The tree had originally grown across the principal pathway through the village, but at last hung so low that, in order to enable people to pass under it, it had been turned aside and fastened parallel to the road. In the operation the bundle of fibres which composed the root had become twisted like the strands of a rope. When the morning sun struck on the upper surface of these, they contracted in drying, and hence a tendency to untwist, which raised the head of the tree. With the evening dews they relaxed, and the head of the tree declined, thus proving to the man of science, as to the credulous Hindu, that it was due to the direct action of the Sun God." [1]

The mysterious processes connected with the life and growth of trees from the tiny seedlings developing in the course of centuries into the hoary giants of the forests, led primitive man to people these trees with all kinds of supernatural beings, and even, as already said (*vide* p. 152), to endow them with separate souls of their own, and this belief, with various modifications, was found in all countries. In many parts of the Egyptian desert, and at a considerable distance from the Nile, may be seen Sycomore fig trees (*Ficus sycomorus*) of luxuriant growth, green and flourishing among the sand. The truth is that the water of the river has infiltrated through to them, and it may be said that they stand with their feet in the river though apparently far removed from it. These trees are considered to be divine, and to be animated by the goddesses within them. These goddesses or spirits sometimes manifest themselves, and Professor Maspero says that at such times the head, or even the whole body, would emerge from the trunk of the tree, after a time re-entering it, being reabsorbed, or, as the Egyptian expression has it, the trunk *ate* it again. The

[1] *Tree and Serpent Worship*, 2nd ed., 1873, p. 80.

chief goddesses who dwelt in these trees were Hâthor, Nout, Selkît, and Nît, as well as other less-important divinities. These thus shrouded their divinity in trees and so became Tree Goddesses. Many of these trees yield a fluid which in some instances is limpid and in others milk-like. It was thus believed that these divinities provided nourishment and refreshment for their devotees on earth, and many of the Ancient Egyptian monuments depict the goddess as bending over the earth pouring out the water of the Nile from a vase, which represents the annual inundation, and milk issuing from one of her breasts. The Sycomore Fig is one of those trees which produces a milky fluid. It was from it, in this case clearly a mythical tree, that the goddess provided sustenance for man. The Ancient Egyptians believed that the souls of the dead had a long and arduous journey before they reached the Islands of the Blest. The Book of the Dead gave them full instructions, which, if they obeyed them to the letter, enabled them to reach the goal without fail. Professor Maspero, describing the journey of the soul, says: " On leaving the tomb he turned his back on the valley, and staff in hand climbed the hills which bounded it on the west, plunging boldly into the desert, where some bird, or even a kindly insect such as a praying mantis, a grasshopper, or a butterfly, served as his guide. Soon he came to one of the Sycomores which grow in the sand far away from the Nile, and are accounted magic trees by the *fellahîn.* Out of the foliage a goddess—Nûît, Hâthor, or Nît—half-emerged, and offered him a dish of fruit, loaves of bread, and jar of water. By accepting these gifts he becomes the guest of the goddess, and could never more retrace his steps without special permission. Beyond the Sycomore were lands of terror, infested by serpents and ferocious beasts, intersected by ponds and marshes where gigantic monkeys cast their nets." Having successfully eluded all these and other perils, he at last reached the Islands of the Blest, where perpetual bliss was his lot.[1]

[1] *The Dawn of Civilisation,* 1894, pp. 183–5.

In some instances the original form of the Tree Spirit was the actual tree, and this may have been the idea of the Karok Indians of California. Mr. S. Powers mentions that when an Indian has occasion to cut branches from off a sacred tree he takes care to leave the topmost branch and two side branches, causing them to resemble a man's head with two outstretched arms beneath. He is usually in great distress when cutting the wood and weeps copiously, but cannot say for what reason, unless it be that by his grief he hopes to mitigate the wrath of the spirit whose branches he has cut off.[1]

The God of Vegetation under the different names of Adonis (in Syria), Attis (in Phrygia), and Osiris (in Egypt) was considered to be a Tree Spirit, and as such was charged with the duty of watching over the crops, stimulating their growth, and averting all evil influences from them until they attained to maturity. The mythological conceptions of this god under these three names are embodied in the legend which narrates how the god is destroyed by the boar or the bear of winter, and is resuscitated with the breath of spring.

In the very early days of Egypt, Osiris was undoubtedly a Tree Spirit, and, as the legend says, his dead body was enclosed in a tree. Many of the Ancient Egyptian monuments, particularly some in the Hall of Osiris at Denderah, depict it so. Dr. J. G. Frazer mentions a ceremony showing Osiris in this character as described by Firmicus Maternus (*De errore profanarum religionum*, 27). This states that a Pine tree was cut down and the centre hollowed out. An image of Osiris was made from this wood, which was then buried like a corpse in the hollow of the tree. Dr. Frazer observes that it is hard to imagine how the conception of a tree as tenanted by a personal being could be more plainly expressed, and adds that this image was kept for a year and then burned, as was similarly done in Phrygia with an image of Attis attached to a Pine tree.[2]

---

[1] *Tribes of California* (1877), p. 25.
[2] *The Golden Bough*, Part IV, "Adonis, Attis, Osiris," vol. ii. pp. 107 *et seq.*

At Grbalj, in Dalmatia, spirits inhabited only certain particular trees, and if one of these trees was felled, the perpetrator of the deed either died on the spot or became an invalid for the rest of his life.

There was a Plane tree at Bythnia which was said to have grown from the tomb of Amycus, and his spirit had entered into it. He is said to have been one who fought with all strangers, and it was believed that if any part of this tree, such as a bough, was taken on board a ship, constant quarrelling ensued until his malign influence was got rid of by throwing the branch away. This bears a close resemblance to the legend of the piece of Oak from the grove of Dodona placed by Minerva in the prow of the Argo.

A similar tale is mentioned by Mr. W. R. S. Ralston. He says there is a Czech story of a nymph who appeared by day among men but always went back to her Willow by night. She married a mortal, bore him children, and lived happily with him, till at length he cut down her Willow tree ; that moment his wife died. Out of the Willow was made a cradle, which had the power of instantly lulling to sleep the babe she had left behind her ; and when the babe became a child it was able to hold converse with its dead mother by means of a pipe cut from the twigs growing on the stump which once had been that mother's home.[1]

In Croatia witches were formerly buried under old trees in the forest, and it was believed that their souls passed into these trees.

In some districts of Austria forest trees are said to have souls and to feel injuries done to them.

Up to little over a century ago the Esthonians reverenced certain holy trees in the Island of Dago, and under them sacrifices were offered on St. George's Day for the well-being of their horses. No one ventured to break a bough, and even the fallen boughs were left to decay on the ground.

---

[1] " Forest and Field Myths," in *The Contemporary Review*, vol. xxxi, February 1878.

Among the Samoyedes of Siberia any curiously contorted tree was adopted as an idol and worshipped as containing a divinity.

Throughout Africa the belief in spirits is universal. In Nigeria many trees are said to be inhabited by the spirits of the dead, and Mr. C. H. Partridge says that in every village of the Indem tribe there is a large tree into which the souls of the villagers enter at death. These trees are held to be sacred and are not cut down.[1] Mr. Partridge also mentions that this big tree is considered by the natives of other villages to be "their life," and if anyone injures it he will become ill, or may even die, unless he pays a fine to the chief.[2]

Some Abyssinian tribes believe that a tree groans while it is being felled, implying that a curse will rest upon the woodman, consequently he endeavours to explain to the tree that it was not he, but an elephant or a rhinoceros which caused it to fall.

Sometimes the tree is considered to be the god himself, as for instance, the tree Walleechu (q.v.). In the religious system of Dahomey the second most important gods, the first being serpents, are considered to be tall and beautiful trees, the most revered of these being the Cotton tree (*Bombax*), and the Poison tree. Prayers are offered up to those trees, especially in times of sickness, and offerings are made to them.

The aboriginal races of India, the Kolarians and the Dravidians, worshipped spirits, particularly the spirits of their ancestors, and demons. Each family had its tutelary spirit, and these were supposed to dwell in very large and ancient trees. On the outskirts of almost every village may be seen a gigantic tree, which is regarded, not only as a temple or shrine but as the centre of the village life as far as its widespread shade extends. Sacrifices are offered to the resident spirits of these trees, and votive offerings are hung on the branches.

[1] *Cross River Natives* (London, 1905), p. 272.
[2] *Ibid.*, pp. 5, 194, 205.

These trees appear to have been a survival of the ancient practice of the Kolarians of leaving one solitary tree standing, as a refuge for the dispossessed spirits when clearings were made in the jungle.

Mr. W. W. Hunter tells us that the whole of the inhabitants of the capital of Beerbhoom go once a year to a certain shrine in the jungle where a ghost dwells in a Bela tree. The shrine consists of three trees—the Bela tree, a Kachmula tree, and a Saura tree. Mr. Hunter adds that, though these trees are only about seventy years old, the shrine is said to be of the greatest antiquity, and tradition alleges that the three trees never grow thicker or taller, but remain the same for ever.[1]

In the north-west of India the Chili tree (*Juniperus excelsa*) was the abode of a Tree Spirit who caused women to bear children, and flocks and herds to multiply.

It is believed among the Tibetans that whenever a Lama is born all withered trees and other plants surrounding his birthplace put forth green leaves, this being the sign that a holy child is born.

Mynher J. J. M. de Groot, in his work on the *Religious System of China*, says that in China the Tree Spirits are usually shaped like human beings, or appear in the likeness of bulls, serpents, or other creatures. He tells how sometimes when a tree is being felled the Tree Spirit has been seen to rush out in the semblance of a blue bull, and adds that even yet the Chinese belief in dangerous Tree Spirits is very strong. In Southern Fuhkien people are deterred from felling large trees or cutting off heavy branches lest the spirit of the tree become angry and cause disease and other calamities. The Green Banyan, or Ching, which is the largest tree found in that district of China, is particularly respected. In Amoy there is a strong aversion to planting trees, because it is thought that as soon as the stems are as thick as a man's neck the planter will probably be throttled by the indwelling spirit. Mynher de Groot

---

[1] *Annals of Rural Bengal* (London, 1868), p. 131.

thinks that this may account for the almost total neglect of forestry in that part of China.

Some of the tribes of Borneo, in common with other races, when they are making clearings in the forest, leave a few trees standing, so that the ejected spirits may have some places in which they can take refuge. The Dyaks will never cut down an old tree, as they attribute souls to trees ; and in like manner the Buddhists of Siam refuse to break even the branch of a tree, as they believe that everything possesses a soul. The Tasem tree (*Antiaris toxicaria*) of Central Borneo is believed to possess a soul. This is the Poison tree with the juice of which arrows are poisoned. Its spirit is very fractious, but if suitable offerings are made to it it shows its pleasure by endowing the wood with a particularly pleasant perfume.[1]

In many countries trees are supposed to utter cries of pain, and even to bleed when they are cut down or wounded in any way, and in some cases the chief of the tribe and his family die as the result of such a sacrilege.

William Ellis [2] relates how a great gambler, Kaneakama by name, had, in the reign of Kamaraua, a king of ancient days, staked and lost all he possessed except one pig, which, being dedicated to his god, he durst on no account stake. That night he dreamed that his god appeared to him and told him to stake his pig next day, when he would be successful. He did so, and dedicated a great part of his gains to his god. That night in his dreams the god appeared again to him and told him to tell the king that a clump of trees would be found growing in a particular spot, and that if he cut down one of them and made an image from it, he (the god) would reside in the image and impart his power to it, and that Kaneakama should be his priest. The king, hearing of this, sent a number of men to cut down one of the trees of the clump, which clump had been miraculously caused by the gods to grow up in a single night and into which they entered. The gods gave

---

[1] A. W. Nieuwenhuis, *In Centraal-Borneo* (Leyden, 1900), vol. i. p. 146.
[2] *Polynesium Researches*, 2nd ed., 1832, vol. iv.

a sign which tree was to be cut down. When the men were working with their stone axes, chips of the wood, striking one or two of them, killed them instantly. This terrified the others, and they ceased to work. Kaneakama, however, persuaded them to resume their labours, which they did, first covering themselves with native cloth and the leaves of the Ti plant, and instead of axes they used their long daggers or *pahoas*, with which they also carved out the image. From that circumstance the idol obtained the name of Karaí-pahoa, meaning dagger-cut or carved. The carving was very curious. The arms of the idol were extended with the fingers spread out. The head was covered with human hair, and the large mouth was armed with rows of sharks' teeth. The wood of the tree was very poisonous, and it was said that anyone drinking water in which the wood had been steeped would die within twenty-four hours.

Among many nations not only are trees said to possess souls of their own, but the souls of the dead are believed to take refuge in trees and so become Tree Spirits. Mr. H. Ward tells us that on the River Congo it is believed by some of the tribes that a sick man's soul, having left his body, wanders aimlessly about, and it is necessary to capture it and restore it to the owner. This is done by the witch doctor, who, after various incantations, announces that he has succeeded in charming the soul into a branch of a tree. This branch is then broken off and conveyed to the side of the sick man, who is placed in an upright position beside it. After further incantations have been performed, the soul is then believed to have re-entered its owner's body.[1]

A variation of this belief is found in Melanesia, where the spirits or ghosts of ancestors are supposed to be the cause of illnesses, and various methods are adopted to drive them back to their graves, a vicarious sacrifice often being made. Mr. R. H. Codrington mentions that in the island of San Cristoval this sacrifice takes the shape of a pig or of a fish. The natives

---

[1] *Five Years with the Congo Cannibals* (London, 1890), pp. 53 *et seq.*

believe that a malignant demon called Tapia has taken a sick
man's soul and imprisoned it within a Banyan tree, so some
person who is on confidential terms with Tapia offers a pig
or a fish to him, saying : " This is for you to eat in place of
that man ; eat this, don't kill him." Tapia accepts the offering,
releases the soul, and the man recovers. Other similar cases
are found in the island of Amboyna and the Babar Islands,
where a branch of a tree, or even a leaf, may be the recipient
of a man's soul which had been taken by demons, and
which, by various incantations, may be restored to its
owner.[1]

Demons often reside in trees, and in the Roman Catholic
countries of Europe small crucifixes, or images of the Virgin
Mary, may frequently be seen in the forests, either placed on
the trunks or suspended from the branches of the trees.
Professor de Gubernatis says that these images are thought to
drive away from the tree the demons which hide under the
bark, but that, nevertheless, it is to the tree itself which is
given sanctity and adoration. Behind them still lies the
awe, the " holy horror," which Lucain breathed in the forests
of ancient Gaul, and the demons which are driven away are
the ancient gods, the old forces of Nature.[2]

In Chaldea, evil spirits or genii were much dreaded, especially
during the night, when the belated traveller was liable to have
one pounce out upon him from a hedge or from behind a tree.
The gods of Chaldea often inhabited trees among other objects—
the Tree of Eridhu (q.v.), which pronounced oracles, being one.
A Chaldean legend, the meaning of which is still obscure, is
depicted on an intaglio. The scene shows a goddess, pursued
by a demon with a double face, taking refuge under a tree.
The tree bends down as if to protect her, and while the demon
is endeavouring to break down the tree, a god comes out from
the trunk and hands a stone-headed mace to the goddess with
which to protect herself against her foe.[3]

[1] *The Melanesians*, pp. 138 et seq.
[2] *Mythologie des Plantes*, vol. i. p. 273.
[3] Maspero, *The Dawn of Civilisation*, pp. 681-2.

Even at the present day in Palestine the Carob tree and the Fig tree, or Sycomore fig, are believed to be inhabited by devils, the former in particular as the reddish colour of its wood suggests blood. The Tamarisk tree, on the other hand, is usually considered to be inhabited by a saint or *wely*.[1]

The worship of ancestors is very widespread in some countries, trees or animals being considered as the residences of the ancestral spirits. Thus several of the tribes of Central Australia believe that the human soul passes through endless reincarnations, and that men and women are simply their own ancestors reborn. Between each incarnation the soul exists in some natural object, in many cases in a tree. In South Australia the tribe of the Dieyerie consider some large sacred trees to be transformations of their fathers, and hence they take the utmost care of these trees.[2]

In the Philippine Islands the natives refrain from felling certain large and stately trees, which they consider to be the homes of the spirits of their ancestors. The spirit speaks in the rustling of the leaves, and anyone passing such a tree begs pardon of the spirit for disturbing it. Each village of the Ignorrotes, in the district of Lepanto, has a sacred tree in which the ancestral spirits live, and offerings are made to it. If it is injured, some misfortune falls on the village, but if it were unfortunately cut down the whole village would perish. In Bontoc, a province of Luzon, large trees are left standing in which the ancestral spirits reside, and these spirits are further honoured by food being placed under the trees for their use.[3]

The natives of the north-west coast of Papua think that the spirits or souls of their ancestors live in the branches of trees. On these they hang strips of white or red cloth, seven or a multiple of seven in number, and also baskets of food, as offerings to the spirits.[4]

[1] W. Robertson Smith, LL.D., *The Religion of the Semites*, 1901.
[2] S. Gason, " The Dieyerie Tribe," *Native Tribes of South Australia,* p 280.
[3] Dr. J. G. Frazer, *The Golden Bough.*   [4] *Ibid.*

Mrs. Bishop tells that in Korea the souls of women who die in childbed take up their abode in trees.[1]

From time immemorial the Chinese have planted trees, particularly the Cypress and the Pine, on graves, in order to strengthen the souls of the deceased and save the body from decay. These special trees being considered fuller of vitality than others, are consequently often identified with the spirits of the dead.[2]

A sacred tree stands at the entrance of every Miao-Kia village and in this tree is believed to reside the soul of the first ancestor of the villagers which presides over their destinies.

TRANSFORMATIONS INTO TREES

Seeing that at a very ancient period the belief was held that mankind originated from trees, it is not surprising to find the converse belief that men and women were often transformed into trees, and this was equivalent to translation to the company of the gods. Classical Mythology abounds in fables of this kind, several of which have already been mentioned.

A devoted couple named Philemon and Baucis were one day sitting outside their home when two men approached asking hospitality, and saying that every other house in the town had spurned them. This hospitality was cordially given. Next morning the two men, who really were the gods Zeus and Hermes, took them to the top of a hill, from whence they witnessed the destruction of the town by a flood, their own house being alone left standing but transformed into a magnificent temple. On the gods asking them to express their desires they asked that they might be appointed to officiate as priests in that temple, and to be united in death. Their prayer was granted, and one day, long after, when they were standing outside the temple, they were suddenly transformed, the one into an Oak tree, and the other into a Lime tree.

When Phaeton, unwarrantably driving the chariot of the

[1] *Korea and Her Neighbours*, London, 1898, vol. i. p. 106.
[2] J. J. M. de Groot, *Religious System of China*.

sun, was hurled from his seat by the indignant Zeus, he fell into the River Eridanos. His sisters, the Heliades, who were standing on the river banks, witnessed his downfall, and, as they bitterly lamented, were changed into Poplar trees. Their tears are still said to flow and to become amber as soon as they fall into the water of the river.

Pluto or Hadés, it is said, dearly loved the O'Keanis Leuké, and on her death he caused the White Poplar to spring up on the Elysian Plain.

There were once two beautiful youths named respectively Cyparissos and Hyacinthus, who were much loved by Apollo. On one occasion the former accidentally killed a favourite stag, and being so grieved he pined away until the god in pity changed him into a Cypress tree. Another legend regarding the origin of the Cypress is that these trees, before they became trees, had been the daughters of Eteocles. Being carried away by the goddesses in a series of whirlwinds, after revolving in endless circles they at length fell into a pond. Gaea pitied them and changed them into Cypress trees. Yet a third legend tells how Sylvanus had loved a child named Cyparissus and changed him into a Cypress tree. Rapin tells the tale in the following verse :

> " A lovely fawn there was—Sylvanus' joy,
> Nor less the fav'rite of the sportive boy,
> Which on soft grass was in a secret shade,
> Beneath a tree's thick branches cooly laid ;
> A luckless dart rash Cyparissus threw,
> And undesignedly the darling slew.
> But soon he to his grief the error found,
> Lamenting, when too late, the fatal wound :
> Nor yet Sylvanus spared the guiltless child,
> But the mischance with bitter words reviled,
> This struck so deep in his relenting breast,
> With grief and shame, and indignation prest,
> That tired of life he melted down in tears,
> From whence th' impregnate earth a Cypress rears ;
> Ensigns of sorrow these at first were born,
> Now their fair race the rural scenes adorn." [1]

[1] *Les Plaisirs du Gentilhomme Champêtre*, 1583.

The nymph Pitys was loved both by Pan and Boreas. She favoured the former, whereupon the latter, in a fit of jealousy, blew her over a cliff, and at that spot a Pine tree sprang up which became the favourite tree of Pan. Writing of this Professor Max Müller says : " If there was anywhere in Greece a sea-shore covered with pine-forests, like the coast of Dorset, any Greek poet who had ears to hear the sweet and plaintive converse of the wind and trembling pine-trees, and eyes to see the havoc wrought by a fierce north-easter, would tell his children of the wonders of the forest, and of poor Pitys, the pine-tree wooed by Pan, the gentle wind, and struck down by jealous Boreas, the north wind." [1]

The Pine tree was sometimes called the Tree of Cybele. This goddess, also known as Rhea, the mother of the gods, was deeply in love with a Phrygian shepherd named Atys. She made him vow that he would always live in chastity, but he broke this vow by having an amour with a nymph named Sangaris. Through remorse he endeavoured to slay himself, and Cybele then transformed him into a Pine tree, which she cherished ever afterwards and mourned her faithless lover under its shade. Jupiter, to please her, decreed that the Pine should remain evergreen. Ovid refers to the legend thus :

> " To Rhea grateful still the Pine remains,
> For Atys still some favour she retains ;
> He once in human shape her breast had warmed,
> And now is cherished to a tree transformed."

A Rumanian song tells of two lovers who died of love and were buried in the same grave. One became a Pine tree and the other a vine, and so the lovers continued to embrace each other.

Servius mentions an ancient tradition giving the origin of the Almond tree. There was once a beautiful Thracian queen named Phyllis, who loved Demophoon, the son of Theseus and Phaedra, and married him. Demophoon, soon after his marriage, was recalled to Athens on account of the

---

[1] *Chips from a German Workshop*, ed. 1895, vol. iv. p. 274.

death of his father. Promising faithfully to return very soon to his bride, he failed to do so, and Phyllis, dying of grief at his apparent desertion, was transformed into an Almond tree, which the Greeks called *Phylla*. Some time after, Demophoon returned, and, learning of the fate of Phyllis, he ran to the tree, which he clasped in an agony of remorse. At that moment the tree suddenly burst forth into leaves and blossomed, as an evident token that the love of Phyllis was unchangeable.

Another classical legend tells that when Io, the daughter of King Midas, lost her lover Atys, violets sprang from his blood, and from his body an Almond tree uprose which bore bitter almonds as a symbol of grief.

The origin of the Myrrh tree was as follows. Myrrha was the daughter of Cinyras and had offended Aphrodite. The goddess in revenge inspired her with a passion for her own father, which she succeeded in gratifying unknown to him. When Cinyras found out what he had done, he pursued his daughter with a drawn sword in order to slay her. Just as he had almost reached her she prayed to the gods to render her invisible. They in pity changed her into a Myrrh tree, the precious odoriferous resin being produced by her tears. Dryden wrote:

> " And still she weeps, nor sheds
>   her tears in vain,
>   For still the precious drops her
>   name retain."

In due time Adonis was born from this tree.

Daphne was a nymph, being the daughter of the river god Peneios. She loved the chase, scorning all other loves. Apollo, however, having seen her, fell vehemently in love with her. She fled before him, while he, pursuing, urged his rank, his power, and his possessions. When she reached the banks of her father's stream she stretched forth her hands, imploring him to protect her. He heard, and, covering her with bark and leaves, she gradually became changed into a Laurel tree. The legend adds that she continued speaking until the encrusting bark had crept up to her mouth, and Apollo, coming up, clasped the tree in his arms, and vowed that ever afterwards it should be his favourite tree.

The Lotos tree or Lote tree (*Zizyphus Lotus*) was fabled to have been originally a daughter of Neptune called Lotis, who, being importuned by Priapus, begged the assistance of the gods, and was by them transformed into the tree bearing her name.[1] The legend further tells that Dryope, passing this tree one day with her sister Iole, plucked some of the fruit and was at once changed into a second Lotos tree. Ovid relates how Iole recounted her sister's fate to Alcmena thus :

> " But lo ! I saw (as near her side I stood)
> The violated blossoms drop with blood ;
> Upon the tree I cast a frightful look,
> The trembling tree with sudden horror shook,
> Lotis, the nymph (if rural tales be true)
> As from Priapus' lawless lust she flew,
> Forsook her form ; and, fixing here, became
> A flow'ry plant, which still preserves her name.
>
> This change unknown, astonished at the sight,
> My trembling sister strove to urge her flight ;
> Yet first the pardon of the nymph implored,
> And those offended sylvan powers adored :
> But when she backward would have fled, she found
> Her stiffening feet were rooted to the ground."

R. Rapin, in his poem entitled *De Hortorum Cultura*, gives the following to account for the origin of the Alder along with that of the Willow, both preferring to grow in most situations :

> " Of watery race Alders and Willows spread
> O'er silver brooks their melancholy shade,
> Which heretofore (thus tales have been believed)
> Were two poor men, who by their fishing lived ;
> Till on a day when Pales' feast was held,
> And all the town with pious mirth was filled,
> This impious pair alone her rites despised,
> Pursued their care, till she their crime chastised :
> While from the banks they gazed upon the flood,
> The angry goddess fixed them where they stood,
> Transformed to sets, and just examples made
> To such as slight devotion for their trade.

[1] Loudon, p. 178.

> At length, well watered by the bounteous stream,
> They gained a root, and spreading trees became ;
> Yet pale their leaves, as conscious how they fell,
> Which croaking frogs with vile reproaches tell."

The creation of the Fig tree has been attributed to Bacchus, who is sometimes seen crowned with its leaves, and the first figs of the season were very frequently offered to him. There are two classical legends, however, of which one says that Syceus when being pursued by Zeus was changed by Rhea into a Fig tree ; and the other tells how the Fig tree was born from the love of Oxyle for a hamadryad.

The *Orlando Furioso* of Ariosto speaks of the Myrtle tree to which Ruggiero tied his hippogriff, which pulled at the tree till it remonstrated, and in melancholy tones announced that it was Astolfo, enchanted by the wicked Alcina.

Dion, King of Laconia, once gave hospitality to Apollo, and as a reward for this his three daughters received the gift of prophecy, on condition that they never misused it, nor pried into matters in which they had no concern. This condition was broken by the youngest, called Carya, with whom Bacchus fell in love. Her sisters were jealous, where-upon the god changed them into stones, and Carya herself into a Walnut tree. In consequence the ancients thought that the nut promoted the powers of love.

The Ancient Greek legend of the origin of the Frankincense tree relates how Clytia, the daughter of Oceanus, was beloved by the sun-god, but he deserted her for Leukothea, the daughter of Orchamus, the King of the East. The god visited the latter in the shape of her mother, and Clytia, in a fit of jealousy, betrayed her to Orchamus. Orchamus in anger buried his daughter alive, and the god then changed her into the Frank-incense tree, while the sorrowful Clytia became a Sunflower.[1]

Professor de Gubernatis says that in a popular Bulgarian song an unhappy lover thus complains : " I, I have become a green Maple ; you, near me, a slender Fir ; and the woodmen

---

[1] Keightley's *Classical Mythology*, p. 53.

came, the woodmen with sharp-edged axes, they cut down the green Maple, then the slender Fir, cut them into white boards, make beds of us, they will place us near each other, and thus, my dear, we will be together." [1]

Professor de Gubernatis also quotes a tale from the *Urano-graphic chinoise* (Schlegel) p. 679, which tells how a Chinese husband and wife were transformed into Cedar trees to eternalise their love. It is said that Hanpang, who was secretary to King Kang in the days of the Soungs, had a young and beautiful wife called Ho, whom he tenderly loved. The king, being desirous of her, threw her husband into prison, where he died of grief. His wife, to escape the odious pursuit of the king, threw herself from a high terrace. After her death a letter addressed to the king was found in her girdle. In the letter she asked him, as a last favour, to bury her in the same tomb as her husband. The king was very angry, and gave orders that they should be interred separately. The will of Heaven, however, was not long of being revealed. During the night two Cedars grew from the two tombs, and in ten days they became so tall that they were able to interlace their branches and roots, although separate from one another. The people, therefore, called these Cedars " The Trees of Faithful Love." [2]

Rapin gives the following as the origin of the Pomegranate tree. A young girl of Scythia, who was anxious to know her fortune, consulted the diviners. They told her that she was destined one day to wear a crown. This so elated her that she easily fell a victim to Bacchus, who in return for her favours, promised to give her a crown. He soon, however, wearied of her, whereupon she pined away and died. In a fit of remorse the god transformed her into a Pomegranate tree, and in order to fulfil his promise he placed a crown on the Pomegranate fruit in the form of the calyx on its summit.[3] This worthless crown was the reason why Queen Anne of Austria adopted a Pomegranate as her device, with the motto,

[1] *Mythologie des Plantes*, vol. i. p. 161.
[2] *Ibid.*, vol. ii. pp. 53–4.
[3] *Les Plaisirs du Gentilhomme Champêtre*, 1583.

" My worth is not in my crown." [1] In the island of St. Vincent there is a French conundrum which asks, " *Quelle est la reine qui port son royaume dans son sein ?* "

Oppien tells of a man who, having lost his wife, became enamoured of his own daughter, whose name was Side, which means a pomegranate. To avoid his persecution she killed herself, and the gods then transformed her into a Pomegranate tree. At the same time her father was changed into a sparrow-hawk, and it is said that that bird will never alight upon a Pomegranate tree but constantly avoids it. [2]

There is a tale which relates how a girl had been transformed into a tree by her angry mother. A musician happening to pass the tree, cut a branch from it to form a violin bow, and was horrified to see blood issuing from the cut. Nevertheless, he made the bow and played on his violin with it before the mother. Heart-rending wails mingled with the music, so that the mother deeply repented of her evil act.

Among some of the Indian tribes of British Columbia the belief prevails that men are transformed into trees, and that the creaking of the branches in the wind is their voice.

The Bushmen of South Africa fancy that at the time when a girl should be kept in strict seclusion a glance from her eye will at once change men into trees that talk. [3]

A New Zealand legend given by Mr. Cowan in connection with a semi-deified wizard or high priest of the Arawa tribe called Ngatoro-i-rangi, mentions the Ti-Palms of the Kaingaroa Plains : " Some of these Ti it was said were originally women, and were changed by enchantment into trees, which forever kept moving about among the plains in the strange days of old, so that the traveller might set his course towards them but never reach them." One of them, however, could be readily approached. The Maoris say that when the wizard was passing this spot he plucked a hair from his head, muttered

---

[1] Reid's *Hist. Bot.*, i. p. 150.
[2] Referred to by De Gubernatis, *Mythologie des Plantes*, vol. ii. p. 167.
[3] W. H. J. Bleek, *A Brief Account of Bushman Folklore*, London, 1875, p. 14.

a charm over it, and threw it down. Immediately a Ti-Palm sprang up which became a shrine in after years where pious Maoris were accustomed to propitiate the genii of the plains.[1]

Trees Preside over Marriages

Considering a tree in its character as anthropogonic, it presides over marriages, and there are often found trees which represent the betrothed and afterwards the young married couple. Thus, in several German and Slav countries one or two trees are planted before the house of the newly wedded pair, or carried in front of them, as a token of the happiness which is desired for them.

A superstition is prevalent in Prussia according to which, if a lover desires his sweetheart always to love him, he puts three of her hairs into a fissure of a tree which represents himself. The belief is that the hairs and the love of the maiden grow along with the tree.[2]

Dr. Mannhardt tells us that according to Strakerjan there is a very curious custom which exists near Oldenburg. Among the inhabitants of that district, when a youthful bridegroom leaves the paternal home to go to a strange village, he embroiders the corner of the bed linen which he takes with him with flowers, and a tree on the top, among the branches of which cocks are seen. At the sides of the trunk of the tree the initials of the family name and the bridegroom's baptismal name are also embroidered. In like manner the bride embroiders a tree on her chemise with the initials of her own name and those of her husband's name.[3]

There is a certain marriage custom in India which consists in making the bride and bridegroom walk several times round a tree. Among some of the hill tribes of India, before the actual marriage takes place, the bride is tied to a Mahwá tree, having first touched it with red lead and clasped it in her arms.

[1] *The Maoris of New Zealand*, 1910, p. 99.
[2] De Gubernatis, *Mythologie des Plantes*, vol. i. p. 253. Footnote.
[3] *Baumkultus der Germanen*, p. 46.

A similar ceremony is enacted by the bridegroom with a
Mango tree. The idea of this appears to be that the repro-
ductive power of the trees may be communicated to the newly
married pair.[1]

TREES PLANTED AT THE BIRTH OF A CHILD

Following out the train of ideas whence originated the belief
that mankind had his origin from trees, or that he was often
transformed into trees, it can clearly be understood how an
intimate and close analogy could be drawn between the life
of a man and the life of a tree. Man, in fact, has always
assumed a kind of inevitable relationship between the one and
the other, and this may be seen from the many legends which
tell how trees shed drops of blood, groan, speak, or become
withered on the death of persons of whom they were the
symbolic representatives. In connection with this there still
exists a kind of half-superstitious custom with a poetic strain
in it. Many families in Great Britain, France, Germany,
Italy, and other countries retain the custom of planting a
young tree for good luck when a child, particularly an heir, is
born. This tree grows with the child, and as its destiny is to
increase and to multiply itself, so a similar destiny is desired
for the child. This symbolic tree is most carefully tended,
but should the tree perish from any cause it is considered that
the life of the being it represents is in the utmost jeopardy.
A Poplar tree was planted at the birth of Virgil.

In many of the islands of the Pacific Ocean, at the birth of a
child a Cocoanut palm is planted, of which the number of
joints is thought to indicate the number of years promised to
the newly born.

Among some tribes of North American Indians the custom
of planting trees at birth, or soon after, is also found. The
parent chooses a small tree which grows along with the child,

[1] Dr. J. G. Frazer, *The Golden Bough*, "The Magic Art and the
Evolution of Kings," 1911, vol. ii. p. 57.

and in future years its appearance is believed to foreshow the welfare of the person, whether well or ill, alive or dead. Various legends have been founded on this custom.

Dr. Walsh tells us that the Turks, on the birth of a son, plant a Platanus, as they do a Cypress on the death of one. He adds that in the court of the seraglio there is a venerable Plane tree, which, tradition says, was planted by Mahomet II. after the taking of Constantinople, to commemorate the birth of his son Bajazet II., and that the trunk of that tree was fifty feet in circumference.

ARBOREAL TRIBES

In some parts of the world several tribes may be described as arboreal, from their habit of living on trees. The Guaranos of the delta of the Orinoco, owing to the annual overflowing of that river, are forced to form their huts above the flood level. This they do by fixing them on the Ita palms (*Mauritia*), from which tree they likewise derive numerous articles of food.

In Papua, as we are told by Mr. H. Wilfrid Walker, there are found in the villages many curious tree-houses situated high up among the branches of very large trees. Some of them were eighty feet from the ground, and they had broad ladders reaching up to them, and Mr. Walker says they looked very curious and picturesque. These ladders were made of long rattans from various climbing palms, and were twisted in such a way as to support the pieces of wood which formed the steps. Mr. Walker remarks that these tree-houses were built partly as look-out houses from which to discern the approach of an enemy, and partly as vantage-points from which the natives could hurl down spears on their opponents below when attacked.[1]

While these arboreal men have an actual existence, the

---

[1] *Wanderings Among South Sea Savages, and in Borneo and the Philippines.*

Maoris of New Zealand have various legends of a tree-dwelling people called Nuku-mai-toré, which their ancestors seem to have brought with them from the islands of Borneo and Sumatra, the home of the Orang-utang. These tales speak of that people as of small stature and always chattering, and they were said to have lived in the great bunches of long-leaved Astelias and grasses which grew in the forks of trees.[1] This is clearly a remembrance of the Orang-utang of their original home.

BURIAL ON TREES

Many races of mankind, instead of interring their dead, place the bodies on trees, which custom in some instances probably bore a mythical relation to placing them on the Tree of Life. Thus among some Indian tribes of North-West America the dead bodies are placed in boxes, which are slung by cedar-bark cords from the branches of trees. Frequently these cords give way, and then the bones strew the ground beneath.

One of the forest tribes of Madagascar called the Tanala wrap up their dead in mats, and then place the body in a large box, which is simply part of a hollow tree. The box is then carried into the depths of the forest and left there.

In Australia also, among the natives, the dead bodies are placed on trees, and this practice, Mr. J. G. Eyre says, may have been designed to facilitate rebirth, because the souls of the dead are considered to reside in trees awaiting an opportunity to be reborn. Among some tribes, however, the bodies of very old people are placed in the ground, but those of children and young people are laid on platforms among the branches of trees.[2] As regards children in particular, Messrs. Spencer and Gillen tell us that this is done in the hope that " before very long its spirit may come back and enter the

[1] James Cowan, *The Maoris of New Zealand*, p. 40.
[2] *Journals of Expeditions of Discovery into Central Australia*, London, 1845, vol. ii. p. 345.

body of a woman—in all probability that of its former mother." [1]

John Evelyn says that he had read that some nations were wont to bury, not malefactors only, but their departed friends, and those whom they most esteemed, upon trees, as so much nearer to heaven and dedicated to God ; believing it far more honourable than to be buried in the earth.[2] Evelyn probably read about this practice in the travels of Sir John Maundevile. When describing his travels in India, Sir John speaks of an island that is called Caffolos, and says that " Men of that Contree, whan here Frendes ben seke, thei hangen hem upon Trees ; and seyn, that it is bettre, the Briddes [birds] that ben angeles of God, eten hem, than the foule wormes of the Erthe." [3] To this description Sir John appends the sketch of a tree with a man hanging from it.

FUNEREAL TREES

There are many trees of a somewhat forbidding aspect, and others which give off unwholesome emanations, some of which are found to be fatal to life. These trees have been called funereal trees, and a Neapolitan physician of the sixteenth century tells us that it is to sombre and dark trees that a fatal power is preferably attributed. The most widely believed in tree of this nature was the famous Upas tree, although its evil qualities have been much exaggerated.

What may be looked upon as a Funereal tree, or possibly the reverse, according to the standpoint from which it is viewed, is found in a tale told by Chaucer taken from Cicero's *De Oratore*. It is as follows : " Valerius tells us that a man named Paletinus one day burst into a flood of tears ; and, calling his son and his neighbours around him, said : ' Alas, alas ! I have now growing in my garden a fatal tree, on which my first poor wife hung herself, then my second, and

[1] *Northern Tribes of Central Australia*, p. 506.
[2] *Sylva*, 4th ed. reprint, vol. ii. p. 234.
[3] *The Voiage and Travaile*, ed. by J. O. Halliwell, 1883, p, 194.

after that my third. Have I not therefore cause for the wretchedness I exhibit ? ' ' Truly,' said one who was called Arrius, ' I wonder that you should weep at such an unusual instance of good fortune ! Give me, I pray you, two or three sprigs of that gentle tree, which I will divide with my neighbours, and thereby afford every man an opportunity of indulging the laudable wishes of his spouse.' Paletinus complied with his friend's request ; and ever after found this remarkable tree the most productive part of his estate." [1]

ELSBEER TREE

What is known in Germany as the Elsbeer tree is in some parts called the Dragon Tree. This appears to be a name for the Elder, or perhaps the Rowan, and it is said that branches of it were hung over houses and stables on Walpurgis Day in order to keep out the flying dragon.

CHRISTMAS TREE

The Christmas Tree, although known in Germany in the beginning of the nineteenth century, seems to have had its origin at a very remote period. December 24th has long been consecrated to Adam and Eve, and legend tells how Adam took with him from Paradise a cutting from the Tree of Knowledge, from which in due time was taken the wood to form the Cross. From this legend the Church appears to have laid claim to the Christmas Tree as an institution of its own. Another belief is that this tree owes its origin to the Scandinavian Ash Yggdrasil, and that the ornaments which are usually suspended from it are memorials of the stag, the eagle, and the squirrel, which had their abode on that cosmogonic Ash. A somewhat similar tree is found in Burmah called *Padaythabin*. It is formed from Bamboos, and, like its

[1] Dr. E. A. Baker, *History of the English Novel*, " The Age of Romance," etc., 1924.

European counterpart, is hung with presents, while at its base are piled blankets and other useful articles. According to Burmese mythology the original of this wonderful tree grew in the heaven of the Nats, and it bore on its branches whatever was wished for. The Christmas Tree and similar trees which bear gifts were thus known as Wishing Trees. In Burmah these trees were sometimes made of silver, and bore silver coins or silver jewellery on their branches, and they were frequently carried in Buddhist processions, being afterwards presented to the monasteries.

GENEALOGICAL TREE

The Genealogical Tree has been already mentioned (p. 157), and it, as well as De Candolle's idea of a tree as a republic, along with Homer's comparison of mankind to leaves on a tree, may all be referred to the primitive conception of man's origin from trees. That being so, it is not surprising to find trees figuring in the crests and armorial bearings of many families and countries, such as the now defunct Orange Free State in South Africa, which had a tree for its crest.

DEVIL TREES

In some parts of the world, notably in Africa and the Malay Archipelago, some trees bear the reputation of being trees specially dedicated to the Devil, and hence known as Devil Trees. These trees are looked upon as being peculiarly adapted for the reception of all manner of evils, and it has been suggested that the almost universal practice of hanging articles, touched or worn by a diseased person, on to trees, is in order to convey the disease to the tree. This practice is very common in Africa, the African Devil Trees being well known.

But many other trees apart from these Devil Trees have been employed as receptacles for diseases, as well as for ill-luck and for other troubles, and many methods of transference were adopted. Thus the Esthonians say that to pass bad luck on to a tree the person must embrace the tree, or walk three times round it at midnight biting a bit off the bark each time, and when the ill-luck has entered the tree, the tree withers.[1]

Among the Greeks and the Italians it was the custom to tie a thread round the neck or wrist of a sick person and hang the thread next morning on a tree, when the malady was believed to be shifted to the tree. Sometimes, as formerly among the French, the patient himself was bound to a tree, and the cords which bound him were left to rot on the tree, thus transferring the malady.[2]

Illnesses may also be transferred to a tree by tying a knot in its branches, or by boring a hole in the trunk and then knocking a peg in. Knocking nails into a tree was formerly a famous remedy for toothache, and many old trees may yet be seen studded with nails which had been driven in for this purpose.[3] Mr. W. Crooke tells that the Majhwars, one of the hill tribes of Mirzapur, believe all diseases to be due to ghosts, and when the plague is raging it is an evidence that the country is infested with these ghosts. They can, however, be shut up in a certain tree which grows on an island in the river, and this is done by a skilful wizard. He takes a piece of deer-horn which he has found in the jungle, and hammers it into the tree with a stone. The ghosts are then considered to be shut up, and Mr. Crooke says that this tree is covered with hundreds of these pieces of horn.[4]

GUARDIAN TREES

Trees were often believed to have a powerful influence on human life, and in the Middle Ages, when a person set out on a journey, he would frequently place his welfare in the keeping

[1] Dr. J. G. Frazer, The Golden Bough, Part iv, " The Scapegoat."
[2] Ibid.   [3] Ibid.
[4] The Tribes and Castes of the North-West Provinces and Oudh, Calcutta, 1896, vol. iii. p. 436.

of a tree, or rather in that of the spirit or genius of the tree. Thus, as long as the tree flourished he was well, but if the tree declined or withered, in like manner his health would decline or death overtake him. These trees were known as *Vård-träd*, or Guardian Trees. Mr. W. R. S. Ralston gives as an instance of these trees the sailors' quarters at Copenhagen, where, he says, each house has a protecting Elder tree. He mentions a Tyrolese legend which tells of a Guardian Tree which a peasant refused to sell, but one night a gale blew it down, and among its roots the peasant found a vast treasure.[1]

ABODE TREE

Another tree of a similar type, being one which grew more vigorously than the rest in the forest, was the Abode Tree, Habitation Tree, or *Bo-träd*. These trees were the home of Elves, and it was believed that in fine weather these Elves hung out their linen to dry on the branches, the cobwebs of different species of spider having no doubt given rise to this supposition. The Elf inhabiting the tree was called Rå or Rådande, and their generic name was Löfjerskor. They were invisible, but reposed in the shade of the tree, and showered benefits on those who were careful not to injure it. One tree, growing in Westmanland, was a Pine tree known as " Klinta tall," which stood for many years on a bare rock, at last falling from age. It was believed that a mermaid who lived in Lake Malar was the tree's Rå, and the country people had often seen snow-white cattle driven from the lake up to the meadows surrounding it.[2]

SPEAKING TREES

There was an old belief that trees could speak, and in Papua at the present day the natives believe that they do so. There has already been mentioned (pp. 152, 180) the belief

---

[1] *Forest and Field Myths.*   [2] Thorpe's *Northern Mythology.*

among the Bushmen of South Africa that a glance from a maiden's eye will change men into trees that talk, and several other instances of speaking trees will be found farther on. Professor Mannhardt says that, metaphorically, in the High Palatinate the trees speak in a whisper among themselves, sing loudly when the wind blows through their tops, and sigh sadly when cut down. He adds that this is why the woodcutter, before touching the trees destined to be felled—" before depriving them of life—prays them to please excuse him." [1]

LIFE TREE

An ancient and magnificent specimen of the *Arbor vitæ* for centuries flourished in the Imperial Garden in the midst of the Forbidden City at Pekin. It was the Life Tree of the Manchu Dynasty, the welfare of which was considered to be bound up in it. It has probably now fallen along with that dynasty. It may be noted here that a tree in Chinese characters is represented by 木, and two of these characters placed together, thus 木木, denote a forest.

BULL OAKS

What were known as Bull Oaks may yet be seen in many parts of England. These were very old and hollow trees, and it is said that they obtained their name from bulls taking shelter inside them. Loudon (*Trees and Shrubs of Britain*) mentions several of them. One, which gave the name of Oakley Farm to the farm on which it grew, was for long the favourite retreat of a bull ; and another, in Wedgenock Park, was probably the largest, and had long been substantially fenced round, with two of its projecting limbs supported by pieces of timber.

[1] *Der Baumkultus der Germanen.*

CHAPTER VII

TREES (*continued*)

Mythical Trees ; Sacred Trees ; Traditional Trees ; Famous Trees ; Curious Trees ; Marvellous Trees.

MYTHICAL TREES

IN the early strivings of the mind of primitive man to account for the scheme of creation, the tree took a foremost place, and the sky, with its clouds and luminaries, became likened to an enormous Cosmogonic Tree of which the fruits were the sun, moon, and stars. Many races of the earth evolved their own conception of a World Tree, vast as the world itself. They looked upon this tree as the cradle of their being, and it bore different names among different nations, and possessed different attributes.

Among the Scandinavian nations the World Tree was known as the Ash Yggdrasil. This tree, which typified existence, was believed to have sprung from the central primordial abyss, and to have had three roots—one for the past, one for the present, and one for the future. One root was situated in Niflheim, beside the well or fountain called Hvergelmir ; the second was placed near the well or fountain of Mimir in Jötunheim ; and the third grew beside the well or fountain of Vurdh or Urdar, which is in heaven, and was the spot where the gods were wont to hold their meetings. Three main branches sprang upwards, the centre one of which supported the earth, and, piercing it in the midst, issued from the mountain called Asgard, the home of the gods. The branches of this central stem overshadowed the entire universe. Their leaves were the clouds, and the flowers and fruits which they bore were the stars. A second branch sprang up by the fountain Urdar, and a third by the fountain Mimir. The fountain of Urdar, the water of which was supremely holy, was guarded by the three Norns or Fates, named respectively Vurdh, Verhandi, and Skuld, who represent the Past, the Present, and the Future. These daily water the roots of the tree with water drawn from the fountain in order to sustain and invigorate the tree. In this fountain swim two swans symbolising the sun and the moon. From the tree falls a clear honey-like dew called *hunângsfall*, which is the food of bees. The four winds are symbolised by four harts running to and fro among the branches, and they are for ever biting at the topmost shoots. An eagle sits in stately majesty on the topmost bough, with a keen-eyed hawk named Veðrfölnir perched on his head between his eyes and who gives him advice. The eagle symbolises the atmosphere, and the hawk symbolises the external ether. A monstrous serpent, or worm of the abyss, called Nidhöggr, lies coiled at the foot of the tree in the fountain of Hvergelmir, and it, along with other snakes, continually gnaws at the roots. These serpents represent the internal fires as ever anxious to overwhelm the earth. A squirrel named Ratatosk, symbolising rain and snow, constantly runs up and down the main stem, ever endeavouring to sow enmity between the eagle and Nidhöggr. A wise man, or giant, named Mimir, dwells in the fountain called by his name, and as the waters of that fountain, from which all streams had their source, are full of wisdom, he, from quaffing these, is the wisest of all. Here also, in Jötunheim, dwell the Frost-Giants, or Hrim-thyrs. Under the tree is hidden the horn called Giallr which is to be sounded by Heimdallr, the warder of the gods, in order to rouse gods and men for the last great conflict, known as the twilight, or doom, of the gods, in which time, life, and the world, are all to pass away. In the Edda known as the Wöluspa, or Lay of Wala the prophetess, we read :

" The sons of Mimir tremble, the tree in the middle takes fire
   At the startling sounds of the noisy horn ;
   Heimdal, horn in air, loudly sounds the alarm ;
   Odin consults the head of Mimir.

Then the Ash raised from Yggdrasil,
That old tree, shivers ; the Jotun breaks his chains :
The shades shudder upon the roads to the lower region,
Until the ardour of Surtur has consumed the tree." [1]

The poem, however, concludes by telling how the world
will be renewed, and how the tree will spring up again in all
its green beauty and grandeur, and how the gods will once
more congregate and deliberate on Idafield beneath its shade.
The earth will then be repeopled by a new race of men whose
parents had been carefully hidden in Hoddmimir's Grove,
that is, the World Ash itself, during the dread conflict. Their
names were Lif (Life) and Lifthrasir (Desire of Life), and they
were nourished on the morning dew.

The Volsunga Saga is an early Teutonic epic which relates
how on one occasion Odin, in the guise of a stranger,
thrust the great sword Gram into the trunk of the Oak
Branstock, saying " Whoso plucketh out this sword shall
have the same in gift from me, and will find that better
brand he never bare." There the sword remained until in
the world-war between light and darkness Sigmund succeeded
in drawing it out.[2]

The World Tree of the Germanic races bore the name of
Irminsul, and it, like Yggdrasil, reared its lofty head far into
the ether. The name Irminsul, however, would appear to
refer solely to the trunk of the tree, and to mean the columns
of the universe which support and uphold all. Three or four
great highways branched out from the foot of Irminsul towards
the four cardinal points, resembling the roots of Yggdrasil.
Professor de Gubernatis quotes the definition of it given by
Rodolphe du Fuld (*Pertz*, ii. 676) thus : " Truncium quoque
ligni non parvæ magnitudinis in altum erectum sub divo
colebant ; patria eum lingua Irminsul appellantes, quod latine
dicitur *universalis columna* quasi sustinens omnia." [3]

Later on, statues of the gods appear to have been erected

[1] *Asgard and the Gods*, ed. by W. S. W. Anson, 7th ed., 1891, pp. 314–15.
[2] Lewis Spence, *Dictionary of Mediæval Romance.*
[3] *Mythologie des Plantes*, vol. i. p. 180.

on wooden pillars, and these likewise bore the name of Irminsul. In support of this Grim [1] quotes from an ancient writer :

> " Upon an yrmensûl
> Stood an idol huge,
> Him they called their merchant."

And again :

> " On an yrmensûl he climbed,
> The land-folk to him all bowed."

meaning that the individual was worshipped as a god, and probably the Ancient Teutons worshipped a god bearing the name of Irmin, but who he was is unknown.

Grim suggests that probably Rodolphe du Fuld associated with his *truncus ligni* the thought of a choice and hallowed tree-stem rather than of a pillar hewn into shape by the hand of man, and says that as the image melts into the notion of tree, so does the tree pass into that of image.

A similar wooden pillar is found figuring in the mythology of Ancient Egypt. Each town or village of that land of mystery worshipped its own particular divinity, and these divinities manifested themselves in the form of some object in which they were supposed to dwell. One of these was the god of the town of Dedu, who was Osiris, and who manifested himself in the form of a wooden pillar, which thus became identified with him. Originally it was simply the trunk of a tree deprived of its leaves. Adolph Erman describes a festival, the representation of which he found in a Theban tomb. This was the feast of the " erection of the pillar Ded." [2] The Pharaoh began the festivities by offering a sacrifice to Osiris, the " lord of eternity," who was represented as a mummified figure wearing on his head the pillar Ded. A wooden pillar lying on the ground was then raised by the Pharaoh, assisted by his relatives and a priest, to an erect position, and this was symbolic of the moment when the dead

[1] *Teut. Myth.*, ed. Stallybrass, vol. i. p. 116.
[2] *Life in Ancient Egypt*, transl. Tirard, pp. 278-9.

Osiris came to life, and his backbone, in after ages represented by the Ded, again stood erect. Later on this pillar became symbolic of the four pillars supporting the heavens. In the royal tombs are often found objects resembling miniature pillars, or poles bearing four horizontal bars across the top, and coloured green, red, and blue. These little figures, known as the " ded " symbol, were hung round the neck of the deceased so as to ensure to the royal occupant a safe passage to the nether world, and also to endow him with life and strength. This sacred emblem of Osiris of Dedu was afterwards used in architecture, and charming effects were produced. Ded and Irminsul seem to have been of the same type as Asherah (q.v.).

The Omahas of North America had a " sacred pole " which seems to have typified the Cosmic Tree, and was known as the Mystery Tree. It was the centre of the four winds, and the home of the Thunder Bird.

Grim tells of a mythical tree known as a *Druden-baum*, or tree under which wizards were said to meet. He says : " A somewhat doubtful legend tells of a world-old *druden-baum* on the top of the Harberg near Plankstellen in Franconia, that its leaves from time to time shed golden drops, milk oozed out of its roots, and under it lay a treasure guarded by a dragon ; on the tree sat a great black bird, who clashed his wings together, and raised a storm when anyone tried to lift the treasure." [1]

The conception of the universe held by the Ancient Egyptians was that of an enormous box or chest, of which the lid formed the sky. As this lid required support they imagined it to be upheld at each of the four corners by a forked tree. Anticipating the danger that these trees would be blown over by some storm, the imagination of a later period replaced them by four lofty mountains, which were connected by a chain of lesser peaks.

The Cosmogonic or World Tree of Hindostan is the symbol

[1] *Teut. Myth.*, ed. Stallybrass, vol. iv. p. 1536.

of vegetation, of generation, and of universal life, and consequently of immortality. It bears various appellations, and is, in itself, considered to be actually the god Brahma, an elementary form of Brahma being known as the Tree of Skambha. All the other gods of the Hindu religious system were considered to be branches from this divine tree, which branches overshadowed the universe. In Hymn 81 of the Tenth Book of the Rigveda the question is asked : What was the Forest, what was the Tree from which the sky and the earth issued ?—the answer being that the Forest, the Cosmic Tree, was the god Brahma himself.

The sacred Vedas describe this Cosmogonic Tree under different names. As the *Açvattha* or *Pippala* it is said to be visited by two birds of heavenly beauty known as *Kapotâs*, and similar to doves. These come in turn, one merely hovering over the tree without eating and singing rapturously the while. This one symbolises Day, or the Sun. The other, symbolising Night, or the Moon, comes to feed on the fruit. When this tree is in danger all the universe is threatened with extinction. This appears to be the same tree which is described in the *Ornithologie* of Aldrovandi (xv) as follows : "There is a tree in India called *Peridexion*, whose fruit is sweet and useful, so that doves also delight to tarry in it ; and the serpent fears this tree, so that he avoids the shadow of it ; for, if the shadow of the tree go towards the east, the serpent flies towards the west ; and if the shadow of the tree reach towards the west, the serpent flies towards the east ; and the serpent cannot hurt the doves because of the virtue of the tree ; but if any of them straggle from the tree, the serpent, by its breath, attracts it and devours it. Yet, when they fly, or go together, neither the serpent nor the spar-hawk can or dares hurt them. Therefore the leaves or bark of the tree, suffumigated, avert all evil that is of venomous beasts." [1]

Under the name of *Kalpavriksha* this tree produced the fruit which nourished the first men ; but according to the *Agama*

[1] De Gubernatis, *Mythologie des Plantes*, vol. ii. p. 148.

Sûtra a tree named *Polo* was the first tree to be created after the sun and the moon, and it was intended to supply the want of nourishment on the earth as mankind had eaten all the savoury and sweet crust.

Bearing the name of *Parigâta* the Hindu World Tree was recognised as one of the five trees of the Hindu Paradise.

As *Ilpa* it grows in Brahma's own world, and is placed in the centre of Lake Ara, beyond the *vigarâ nadi*, that ever juvenescent river which produces the waters giving eternal youth. The tree likewise gives eternal youth, and to it Brahma gives his own perfume, and from it he took the vital sap. To the branches of this tree the dead cling, and by their aid only are they enabled to climb up to, and to enter into, the regions of immortality.

Under the name of *Kalpadruma* this tree fulfils all desires, gives knowledge, wisdom, and inconceivable bliss. It is a Cloud Tree, growing on a high mountain and surrounded by brilliant flowers and musical streams. It was on this mountain that, as the legend tells, Tathâgata, while doing penance, sacrificed himself by giving up his body to a starving tiger. Day and night were produced by the shadows of the tree before the sun and the moon were created. Among all the benefits which mankind was able to obtain from it that of knowledge was most sought after by Buddha and his followers.

Another name under which the tree is known is *Soma* or *Amrita*, and from its branches flows the life-giving ambrosia, the essence of immortality. It was believed to grow in the third heaven over which its mighty branches stretched, and under it the gods reclined, quaffing the immortalising juice. Two lovely birds, as in the case of the Pippala, sit on its topmost boughs, while other birds are occupied in pressing out the ambrosia. From this tree the gods made the heavens and the earth, and it bears all kinds of flowers and fruits now known on earth.

This great Cosmogonic Tree has also been known as the *Tree of Beautiful Leaves*, and under it the first father of men is said to have evoked the ancestors, i.e. the gods. The Vedas themselves are said to have been the leaves of this tree.

Several other mythical trees of the sky are described in the Hindu cosmogony. We find one called the *Kushtha*, which is mentioned in the Atharvaveda (v. V. 4, 3) thus : " Where the Açvattha stands, in the home of the gods, the third heaven from here, there the gods approach the Kushtha, revealer of the ambrosia." The legend relates how the gods set forth in a golden boat to recover the lost ambrosia, and how the boat was lit up by the tree Kushtha. From this it would appear that by the Kushtha is meant the moon, because it adds that the Kushtha grew the moment that the golden boat descended on the summit of the mountain Himavant.

Besides these above names the great Cosmogonic and Generator Tree has borne the appellations of the Tree of the Sky, the Solar Tree, the Lunar Tree, and the Tree of the Clouds. The milk, the water, the dew, and the rain which flowed from them was the ambrosia, that divine fluid or seed from which life was created.

Among the four principal great Cosmogonic Trees of India, the tree called *G'ambu* takes a prominent place. The other three were the *Ghanta*, the *Kadamba*, and the *Ambala*. These four colossal trees, along with four colossal elephants, represented the four cardinal points, and were believed to support and uphold the world. The G'ambu, it is stated, grew on the south side of Mount Méru, the summit of which mountain was thought to represent the zenith. In the cosmogonic forest of the Himalaya the enormous bulk of this tree towers to a stupendous height, and in itself represents the entire universe. Four great rivers, of which the waters are inexhaustible, take their rise at the foot of the tree and flow in different directions. The tree bears a golden and immortal fruit, as large as an elephant, and resembling in its proportions the vase called Mahâkala. The demons, under the form of wolves, continually long for the fruit, the Sanskrit name for the jackal being *gambuka*. The seeds of these fruits produce grains of gold which are carried down to the sea, and are sometimes found on the seashore. It is said that this gold is of incalculable value, there being none to equal it in the whole world. It is also said that the juice flowing from the fruit gives rise to one of the above-mentioned rivers called the Gambu, the waters of which, being gifted with salutary properties, are much sought after. The present representative on earth of this mythical tree is the *Eugenia jambolana*, of which the fruit is very large. The Septacataka of Hâla says that lovers often hide among the foliage of this tree, and tells how the young wife experienced the pangs of jealousy when she beheld her husband appear with his ears adorned with leaves of the G'ambu.

Another great Cosmogonic Tree of the Indian Paradise was the *Mandara*, while a tree called *Manorathadayaka* grew in the garden of the Vidyâdharas, which had the power of fulfilling all desires, and particularly the desire of obtaining children.

Very similar in its attributes was the World Tree of Buddha. It also was a Cloud Tree, the Tree of Ambrosia, the Tree of Wisdom, the Tree of the Wise, the Tree of Perfection and of Holiness. The Tree of Buddha was believed to have been a *Pippala* or *Açvattha*, though some consider it to have been a Palm, and many famous trees were conjectured to be either the identical tree, or a descendant or cutting from it. The mythological conception of this tree as a Cosmogonic Tree is a tree glowing and shining with divine jewel-like flowers, the whole tree being formed of gems of the rarest and richest description. The Buddhists relate that at the hour when Buddha was born a flash of light passed through all the world, and an enormous branch of the Açvattha grew up in the centre of the universe. The legend of Buddha is often found in the tales narrated by various Buddhist pilgrims of China. We are told that the only place indicated by the gods where one could acquire complete wisdom was under the tree *Peito*. This is the Chinese translation of the Hindu word for "leaf," and the Palm tree would

appear to be indicated as it is evergreen, but Mr. Beal remarks
that in all other respects it is said that the sacred tree in question
is the Pippala (*Ficus religiosa*). The same tale narrates that
the young prince Buddha went along the road during the night
surrounded by the Devâs, the Nâgâs, and other divine beings.
Under the tree Peito he walked from east to west, and for
seven days was adored by the gods. Then the gods built a
golden palace to the north-west of the tree, in which Buddha
slept for seven days. He then returned to the lake Mukhalinda,
where he sheltered in the shadow of the tree *Midella*. Thereafter the rain fell for seven hours, and the Nâgâ Mukhalinda
came from the lake and sheltered Buddha with his hood.
This tree was so identified with the existence of Buddha that
any injury done to it affected himself. The legend proceeds
to say that Buddha at the commencement of his conversion
habitually retired under the tree Peito to meditate and fast.
His queen was annoyed, and, in the hope of luring him back
to the house, gave orders to have the Peito cut down. At the
thought of this sacrilege Buddha's grief was so great that he
fell fainting to the ground. He was sprinkled with water, and
when, after much trouble, he was restored to consciousness,
he threw a hundred jugs of milk on the roots, and bending
his face towards the ground, pronounced this vow, " If the
tree does not revive, I shall never rise again." At that moment
the tree grew branches, and little by little extended upwards
until it attained the height of 120 feet.[1]

An amplification of the legend tells how Buddha sat for six
years in absolute solitude under the tree, in utter abandonment
to his sublime meditations. While there, the demoniacal hosts
assailed him, surrounding the tree, invoking hurricanes and
darkness, bringing deluges of rain, and hurling fiery darts at
him. Buddha triumphantly repelled their attacks, and in the
end the demons fled discomfited. Thus was Buddha enabled
to retain possession of the tree with all its knowledge and

[1] *Travels of Fahhian and Sung-yun—Buddhist Pilgrims from China to
India—400* A.D. *and 518* A.D., translated from the Chinese by S. Beal,
London, 1869.

wisdom and as the heart-shaped leaves of the Pippala are ever in motion, even during the profoundest calm, they are believed to be still trembling as if in recognition of the mysterious meditations of Buddha.

The Kadamba Tree (*Neuclea Kadamba*) has also been recognised as the Tree of Buddha. This tree bears orange-coloured flowers, and it is said to have an irresistible power to bring absent lovers back. The *Dîrghâyama Sûtra* (a Catena of Buddhist Scriptures from the Chinese) says that a great king of trees called Kadamba grows on Mount Sume. M. Senart (*Essai sur la légende du Buddha*) says that the Tree of Buddha sprang spontaneously from a nut from the Kadamba deposited on the ground. In a moment the earth cracked, a shoot appeared, and with inconceivable rapidity the colossal tree sprang up, its shadow covering a circumference of 300 cubits. Its fruit troubled the minds of the adversaries of Buddha, and the Devas let loose all the furies of the tempest against it, but in vain.

Another Cosmogonic Tree which grew in the Buddhist Paradise was the *Man'g'ushaka*, which of itself produced all the flowers of earth and water. It is sprinkled with the water of Anavatapta, and is covered with precious stones. The Pratyekabuddhas recline in meditation in the grateful shade cast by this tree.

In Cashmere a sacred mythical tree called Elâpatra is mentioned as having been killed by a Buddhist priest who became changed into a serpent in expiation of his sacrilege.

Among other mythic trees may be mentioned the Gaokerena, which is alluded to in the Zendavesta as having been created by Ahura Mazda, and it was the seat of immortality and ambrosia.

One of the mythic trees of torture, and growing in Hell, is the Salmali or Çalmalî (*Salmalia Malabarica*). It is a tree with very large and strong thorns, from which it has the Sanskrit name of *Hantakadruma* (the Tree of Thorns), and on this account seems to have been placed in the infernal regions under the name of the Tree of Hell, or the Tree of Yama, Yama being the Hindu god of death. Consequently his abode is believed to be situated near this tree. The Mahâbhârata (xiii. 5847) relates how Pitâmâha, the great father creator, after having created the world, rested under the tree, Çalmalî, the leaves of which no wind came to stir ; and in a Hindu poem the tree is reproached for showing its red flowers from afar, and offering nothing to the weary traveller who hastens to it in the hope of finding refreshing fruit.

Virgil, speaking of the vestibule of Hell, says : " In the midst a gloomy Elm displays its boughs and aged arms, which seat vain Dreams are commonly said to haunt, and under every leaf they dwell." From this the Elm has been called the Tree of Dreams, the Tree of Oneiros, or the Tree of Morpheus.

It is related that in the mythic Garden of Bakavali there grew trees of rubies with bunches of fruit so brilliant that they were equal to the clusters of stars which group themselves round the Tree of the Sun. Another mythic celestial garden is mentioned in the tale of the *Anvari Sohéili*, which has been translated by Garcin de Tassy : " A gardener, they say, possessed a garden more pleasant and voluptuous than the most celebrated gardens of the Orient. Its trees, of different species, were as beautiful as the variegated plumage of the peacock, and its flowers, of a thousand varieties, had the splendour of the crown of Kaous (King of Persia of the Second Dynasty). The surface of the soil was brilliant like the cheek of an elegantly clothed beauty, and the breezes of the atmosphere were perfumed like the store of an aromatic merchant. The branches, laden with fruit, were bowed down like an old man overwhelmed with years ; and the fruits, sweet and perfumed, were preserved without the heat of fire." [1]

Two fabulous trees which were said to grow on some part of the frontiers of India to the east of Persia, were called the Trees of the Sun and of the Moon. Sir John Maundevile

[1] De Gubernatis, *Mythologie des Plantes*, vol. i. p. 182.

says that in the deserts " weren the Trees of the Sonne, and
of the Mone, that spaken to Kyng Alisandre, and warned him
of his Dethe. And men seyn, that the folk that kepen the
Trees, and eten of the Frute and of the Bawme that growethe
there, lyven wel 400 Zeere or 500 Zeere, be vertue of the
Frut and of the Bawme. For men seyn, that Bawme growethe
there in gret plentee, and no where elles, saf only at Babylogne,
as I have told zou before." [1]

The Persian legend of these trees is to the effect that in his
progress towards India, Alexander came to a famous Plane
tree which grew near Damghan, standing alone and solitary
on a vast and arid tableland. This tree had a double trunk,
one trunk being male and the other female. The former
spoke during the day, and the latter during the night.
Alexander, taking counsel with these mystic Plane trees, was
warned in a boding voice that he would die while yet in his
prime, and that others would reap the fruits of his victories.

The legendary history of Alexander the Great describing
his campaigns for the conquest of the world refers to these
Trees of the Sun and of the Moon. In the French Prose
Romance of Alexander (A.D. 1180) it is related how Alexander
and his chief companions ascended a certain mountain by
2,500 steps, which were attached to a golden chain. At the
summit they found the golden temple of the Sun with an
old man sleeping therein. The Romance continues : " When
the old man saw them he asked them if they wished to see
the sacred trees of the Moon and Sun, which tell us of
future events. When Alexander heard this he was filled with
very great joy. They answered the old man, ' Yes, to be
sure, we wish to see them.' He said to Alexander, ' If you
are born of parents both royal, you may enter this place,' and
Alexander replied, ' We are born of parents both royal.' Then
the old man rose up from the bed whereon he was lying and
said to them, ' Take off your mantles and shoes.' And
Tholomeus and Antigonus, and Perdiacas followed him. Then

[1] *The Voiage and Travaile*, ed. by J. O. Halliwell, 1883, pp. 297–8.

they began to go through the forest which enshrouded many
marvels. There they found trees like unto Laurels and Olives.
And they were an hundred feet high, and there emanated from
them much incense called *ypobaume*.[1] Afterwards they
entered deeper into the forest, and found a very tall tree which
had neither leaf nor fruit. Perched on this tree was a large
bird, having on its head a crest like the peacock's, and the
feathers of its neck shining like pure gold. It was rose-
coloured. Then the old man said to him, ' This bird, which
astonishes you, is called Fenis. It has no peer in all the
world.[2] Then they passed on and went to the Trees of the
Sun and of the Moon. When they had reached them,
the old man said to them, ' Look up above, and think in your
hearts what you wish to ask, and do not speak it aloud.
Alexander asked him in what language the trees replied to
people. And he replied, ' The Tree of the Sun begins to
speak Indian.' Then Alexander kissed the trees, and began
to think in his heart whether he would conquer the whole
world, and return to Macedonia with all his army. Then the
Tree of the Sun replied, ' Alexander, you will be king of the
whole world, but Macedonia you will never see.' "[3] This
prediction was fulfilled as Alexander died at Babylon in
323 B.C.

These were interesting examples of Speaking Trees, and
Marco Polo has described the Tree of the Sun, or *Arbor Sol*,
but he appears to have confused it with another fabulous tree
called the Dry Tree or *Arbor Sec*. He says : " You arrive
at a province which is called *Tonocain*. . . . It also contains
an immense plain, on which is found the *Arbor Sol*, which
we Christians call the *Arbor Sec* ; and I will tell you what
it is like. It is a tall and thick tree, having the bark on one
side green and the other white ; and it produces a rough husk
like that of a chestnut, but without anything in it. The wood
is yellow like box, and very strong, and there are no other

[1] Opobalsamum.   [2] Probably the Phœnix.
[3] Probably these are the trees referred to as having spoken to Hea-bani,
v. p. 19.

trees near it nor within a hundred miles of it, except on one side, where you find trees within about ten miles distance. And there, the people of the country tell you, was fought the battle between Alexander and King Darius." [1]

Alexander, in his letters to Dindimus, relating his travels, gave an account of some wonderful trees which grew only in the daytime, when they were guarded by fierce birds that spat deadly fire and disappeared at night. [2]

The Dry Tree, Withered Tree, or *Arbor Sec*, has likewise been the subject of many fabulous legends which were much in vogue during the thirteenth century. It has been considered probable that the legend of the Dry Tree originated in the words of the Prophet Ezekiel (xvii. 24) : " And all the trees of the field shall know that I the Lord have brought down the high tree, have exalted the low tree, have dried up the green tree, and have made the dry tree to flourish : I the Lord have spoken and have done it."   Sir John Maundevile mentions the Dry Tree thus : " And a lytille fro Ebron [Hebron] is the Mount of Mambre [Mamre], of the which the valley taketh the name.   And there is a tree of Oke [oak], that the Sarazines clepen [call] Dirpe, that is of Abraham's tyme, the which men clepen the drye tree.   And thei seye, that it hathe ben there sithe the beginnynge of the world ; and was sumtyme grene, and bare leves, unto the tyme that oure Lord dyede on the cros ; and so dyden alle the trees that waren thanne in the worlde.   And some saye, be here prophecyes, that a Lord, a prince of the west syde of the world, shalle wyn the land of promyssyoun, that ys the Holy Land, with helpe of Cristene men ; and he schalle do synge a masse undir that drye tree, and then the tree schalle wexen grene, and bere bothe fruyt and leves.   And through that myracle manye Sarazines and Jewes schulle be turned to Cristene feythe.   And therfore thei don gret worschipe thereto, and kepen it fully besyly.   And alle be it so, that

[1] *Travels of Marco Polo*, ed. Colonel Yule, 1871, vol. i. p. 119.
[2] Lewis Spence, *Dictionary of Mediæval Romance*, p. 5

it be drye, natheles yet he berethe gret vertue : for certeynly he that hath a litille thereof upon him, it heleth him of the fallynge evylle ; and his hors schalle not be a foundred ; and manye othere vertues it hathe : wherefore men holden it full precyous." [1]

Jacob Grim gives several legends connected with a Withered Tree. He narrates how tradition says that the Emperor Frederick Barbarossa rests inside the mount of the Kifhaüser in Thuringia. He sits at a round table of stone, with his head resting on his hand, nodding, and blinking his eyes ; his beard has grown round the table twice, and when it has done so a third time he will awake. When he emerges from the mount he will hang his shield on a withered tree standing near by. The tree will then break into leaf, and a time of prosperity will dawn.[2] Grim also tells that in the Walserfeld is a withered tree which has been cut down three times, but has always sprung up again as luxuriant as ever. The next time it bursts into leaf the terrible fight will begin ; when it bears fruit Barbarossa will hang his shield on it ; all men shall rally round the shield, and the wicked shall be extirpated.[3] Another legend is quoted by Grim, who relates that in the manuscript called *Historia trium regum*, written by Joh. von Hildesheim in the fourteenth century, a temple of the Tartars is mentioned. Within this temple stands a withered tree closely guarded by men-at-arms. The legend says that whatever prince succeeds in hanging his shield on this tree will become lord of all the East. It is alleged that the Great Khan did succeed in doing so, and in consequence became irresistible.[4]

The World Tree of the Iranians or Persians was considered to have been the Haoma Tree, which bears the Homa, an immortalising and life-giving juice, similar to the Soma or Amrita of the Hindus. Windischmann, writing on the Zend-avesta, says : " Homa is the first of the trees planted by

---

[1] *The Voiage and Travaile*, ed. J. O. Halliwell, 1883, pp. 68–9.
[2] *Teut. Myth.*, ed. Stallybrass, vol. iii. p. 955.
[3] *Ibid.*, p. 956.   [4] *Ibid.*, p. 958.

Ahura-Mazda in the fountain of life. He who drinks of its juice never dies. According to the Bundehesh, the Gogard or Gaokerena Tree bears the Homa, which gives health and generative power, and imparts life at the resurrection. The Homa plant does not decay, bears no fruit, resembles the vine, is knotty, and has leaves like jessamin, yellow and white." In another part he says : "From this it appears that the White Homa or the tree Gokard is the Tree of Life which grew in Paradise." [1]

The Zend-avesta, however, speaks of two trees, the Haoma, and another one growing near it, which is called the "Impassive" or "Inviolable." The latter bears fruits containing the seeds of every kind of plant. The fountain of life, in which these trees grow, is called Vouru Kasha. A lizard, under the directions of Ahriman, the Persian Satan, is ever seeking an opportunity to destroy the sacred Homa, but is thwarted in its efforts by ten fish, who ceaselessly swim around the trees, protecting them from evil.

The Ancient Chaldeans and Assyrians likewise had their World Tree, coeval with Assur, the great First Source, which tree was located in the Forest of Eridhu. A fragment of a tablet containing a most ancient hymn, part of the Izdubar Epic, begins by saying that in Eridhu a stalk grew, its root of white crystal which stretched towards the deep. Its seat was the centre of the earth, while in its foliage was the home of Zikum, i.e. the heavens, the great primeval mother. One line on the fragment reads : "Into the heart of its holy house which spread its shade like a forest hath no man entered." This tree would appear to have been a Pine tree, or perhaps, more correctly, a Cedar tree, and Professor A. H. Sayce mentions that the "stalk" is indicated in the magical text to which the fragment about it has been appended. In this, he says, Ea describes to Merodach the means whereby he is to cure a man who is possessed of the seven evil spirits. He tells him first to go to "the Cedar-Tree, the tree that shatters

[1] *Zoroastrische Studien,* pp. 89, 167, 251.

the power of the incubus, upon whose core the name of Ea is recorded," and then, with the help of "a good masal," that is, a kind of phylactery which is placed on the sick man's head at night, to invoke the aid of the Fire-god to expel the demons. Professor Sayce adds that the mystic virtues of the Cedar were remembered long after the hymns of Eridhu were written, and mentions a tablet describing the initiation of an augur. Part of the initiation consisted in the novice being made to descend into an artificial imitation of the lower world, where he beheld "the altars amid the waters, the treasures of Anu, Bel, and Ea, the tablets of the gods, the delivering of the oracle of heaven and earth, and the Cedar-Tree, the beloved of the great gods, which their hand had caused to grow."[1]

This World Tree was looked upon as the personification of life and generation, and as such it was continually reproduced on the Assyrian sculptures and tablets. Several of these tablets appear to deal with the creation of man, and a very ancient one would seem to refer to the fall of man as recorded in the myth of creation in Genesis. In it a tree, similar to the Tree of Life which grew in the centre of the Garden of Eden, resembling a Pine, bears a fruit hanging down on either side. Seated on each side of the tree is a man and a woman who are stretching out their hands to pluck the fruit. To complete the resemblance to the Biblical account a serpent is reared erect behind the woman. Many other sculptures show animals, often bulls, kneeling in adoration in front of the Tree, or winged and eagle-headed cherubs in attendance upon it. It is curious to note the prevalence of the sacred number seven as the number of its branches, four being on one side of the stem and three on the other side.

The Tree Gokard has been mentioned above, and it, under the name Gharkad, is said to have been the tree of the Jews. A Mohammedan prophecy says that among the signs of the approach of the resurrection day will be war with the Jews,

[1] *Religion of the Ancient Babylonians.* The Hibbert Lectures for 1887.

of whom the Mohammedans are to make a great slaughter, the very trees and stones betraying those who hide themselves among them, except only the tree called Gharkad. This tree was an instance of a speaking tree, and it is said that in a dream Moslim b' Ocba heard its voice appointing him to command the army of Yazid against Medina.

The Koran mentions Mahomet's visit to Heaven, whither he was taken, he said, by the angel Gabriel, and where he saw " the Lote-tree beyond which there is no passing." This tree stands in the seventh heaven, on the right hand of the Throne of God, and is the utmost bounds beyond which the angels themselves may not pass.

A very thorny tree of Arabia is called the Zakkum tree, of which the fruit is extremely bitter, and these two evil qualities seem to have induced Mahomet to make it the principal tree in Hell, as the Koran says : " How different is the tree Al Zakkum from the abode of Eden ! We have planted it for the torment of the wicked." And again : " It is a tree which issueth from the bottom of Hell : the fruits thereof resembleth the heads of devils, and the damned shall eat of the same, and shall fill their bellies therewith. . . . Verily the fruit of the tree Al Zakkum shall be the food of the impious."

Plato describes a thorny shrub (*Calycotome villosa*) much resembling our Gorse, as one of the instruments of torture for tyrants in Hell or Tartarus.

In the Paradise of Mahomet, situated in the seventh heaven, the trunks of all the trees are of pure gold, and the branches are laden with gems and delicious fruits of a size and taste unknown on earth. The most remarkable of these trees is the tree called Tûba or Tooba, the Tree of Happiness, which stands in the palace of Mahomet.

It is of such a vast size that a person mounted on the swiftest horse would not be able to gallop from one side of its shadow to the other in a hundred years. A branch of it reaches to the house of every true believer, so that if a man desires to eat of any particular fruit it will be immediately presented to him by the boughs of the tree spontaneously bending down to his hand ; and not only so, but it will supply the blessed with silken garments, and animals ready saddled and bridled to ride upon, which will issue forth from the fruits. The rivers of Paradise all take their rise from the root of this tree, resembling the rivers issuing from Yggdrasil, and the Hindu World Tree G'ambu.

The Byzantine World Tree was composed of iron, which in the beginning spread throughout all space. The omnipotence of God formed its root, and on its summit were borne Heaven, Earth, and Hell.

Christianity itself is partly founded on a tree, the wood of which furnished the Cross. Many speculations have been put forth as to the identity of this tree, and several trees have been named. Thus it was said that the Cross was made from the Mistletoe, which at one time had been a fine forest tree, but has since then been degraded to the lowly position of a parasite. The Aspen has also been named, and tradition says that when it realised for what purpose it was being used, its leaves commenced quivering with horror, and continue doing so to this day. The Fig tree, the Oak, the Elder, and the Ash have also been credited with furnishing the wood.

The Book of Genesis tells us that God " planted a garden eastward in Eden," where He made " to grow every tree that is pleasant to the sight, and good for food ; the tree of life also in the midst of the garden, and the tree of knowledge of good and evil." Philon the Jew, in his book on the *Creation of the World*, wrote : " They say, it is written, that during the time when man was alone, and before woman was created, God planted a beautiful garden, not resembling ours in anything . . . ; but the trees which were planted in the terrestrial Paradise of God had a soul and were rational, bearing as fruit, virtues, immortal understanding, and vivacity of spirit, by which honesty and dishonesty, healthy life, immortality, and all similar things are distinguished and known."

It was by means of the fruit of the Tree of Knowledge

that the fall of man was brought about, and the Tree of Life
was to be the means of his redemption. This latter tree has
been also called the Tree of Adam or the Tree of the Cross.
As was natural to the mind of primitive man many legends
sprang up round these trees, all of which bore upon the
evolution of the Christian religion. What is more probable
than that early man in his strivings after a divinity should
imagine the erring pair, after having partaken of the forbidden
fruit from the Tree of Knowledge, to have taken shelter under
the colossal Tree of Life growing in the centre of the Garden ?
Here, granted the tree to have been a Fig tree or Banyan,
they would imagine themselves to be securely hidden among
the luxuriant foliage from the eye of their angry God, and,
conscious of their nakedness, would be constrained to make
themselves aprons of the large and broad leaves of the tree.

One of the legends referred to narrates that Eve, in absence
of mind, carried away with her from Eden a branch of the
Tree of Knowledge, which she planted ; while another tells
that the Archangel Michael handed to Eve a branch bearing
three leaves, detached from that tree, with instructions to
plant it on the grave of Adam. She did so, and it grew into
a tree, which was replanted as an ornamental tree by King
Solomon in the Temple, afterwards being plunged into the
pool of Bethesda, where it remained until it was drawn forth
to form the Cross.

Many variations of the legends surrounding the Tree of the
Cross or the Tree of Adam exist, and the Rabbinical tradition
of that tree was adopted by the Mohammedans, the account
in the Koran differing but little from the Bible story.

Among the tribes of Siberia the legend tells that at the
commencement of the world a tree was born without branches.
God caused nine branches to spring, at the feet of which were
born nine men, the predestined ancestors of the nine human
races. God permitted men and animals to nourish themselves
with the fruits of the five branches turned towards the east,
forbidding them to taste the fruit of the western branches,

and He appointed a dog and a serpent to guard these branches against men and against the seducing demon Erlik. While the serpent slept, Erlik climbed the tree and seduced Edji, the wife of Törongoi, who, having eaten of the protected fruit, gave part to her husband. The two were then instantly covered with hair, and becoming ashamed of their nakedness, hid themselves under the trees.

A tale of Little Russia gives some further particulars regarding the Tree of the Cross. It is said that the Virgin, when walking with Jesus one day, happened to stumble when passing near the tree, and sorrowfully remarked that on this thrice-blessed tree her son would be crucified. Jesus in reply said : " It is true, My Mother." The legend adds that the Jews tried to crucify Christ on certain other trees at first, but failed to do so, until at last they found the thrice-blessed tree.

In various countries of the world many other mythical trees were alleged to have grown, but these seem to have had their existence only in the excited imaginations of various early travellers, who were only too prone to put faith in all the marvellous tales they were told.

Certain mythical trees are mentioned in Russian Folklore, such as the vast Oak which grows on the island of Bujan, among the branches of which the sun disappears for repose every evening, to rise again therefrom refreshed in the morning. Another tale tells of an old man who once climbed an Oak of which the top reached the sky, and where a hind lived which could not be burned by fire nor drowned in water. Yet a third myth represents the thunder-cloud as a gigantic rainy and sonorous tree, which, while singing, that is, thundering, distils the water of life. The tales regarding this Singing Tree tell how the hero who wishes to reach it must whistle on a magic pipe, or flute, so as to imitate the sound of the tempest.[1]

Colonel Kenneth Mackay gives a charming conception of the belief in a future state held by the natives of Papua. He says that he was told that far up in the Astrolabe Range of

[1] De Gubernatis, *Mythologie des Plantes*, vol. i. p. 199.

mountains " there blooms, invisible to mortal eye, a great and
gracious tree, in and around which dwell for ever, free from
care and happy, all those who have lived good lives ere death
claimed them. There lovers and loved relations will be
reunited, while those already dwellers beneath its shade may
and do come back to watch over the living, so that each soul
yet on earth has an unseen but ever-present loving guide and
helper. The wicked have to pass through sickness, pain, and
trouble before they reach the tree, but eventually they, too,
are gathered beneath its branches. The natives of the
Astrolabe District say they know this sacred idyll is true
because those they loved and have lost have come back to
them and told them so." [1]

Among the Maoris of New Zealand the great father of
forests and of trees was known as Tane-Mahuta, and the
mythological conception of him was that of a colossal tree.
Originally, according to the Maori mythology, Heaven and
Earth were one, united in a close embrace, Heaven lying on
the top of Earth. As a consequence their children, the gods,
were forced to dwell in perpetual darkness, until they could
endure it no longer, and resolved to obtain freedom. One
of these gods was the Forest God, Tane-Mahuta, who remarked
to his brethren : " It is better to rend them apart, and to let
the heaven stand far above us, and the earth lie under our
feet. Let the sky become as a stranger to us, but the earth
remain close to us as our nursing mother." To him, accordingly, was deputed the task of separating heaven from earth.
He uprose in his might, planted his head in the earth, and
with his feet gradually forced the sky far upwards, where it
has remained ever since. This colossal tree may be imagined
as growing at a rapid rate, with its widespread branches
gradually pushing upward the atmosphere with its clouds in
the same manner as the rapid growth of broad-headed fungi
has been known to raise flagstones several inches. One of
Tane-Mahuta's brethren who had never consented to the

[1] *Across Papua*, 1909, pp. 25-6.

separation of his parents was Tawhiri-ma-tea, the father of winds and storms. He followed his father into the sky, and since then, in revenge, has never ceased to make war on the forest trees, the children of Tane-Mahuta. This New Zealand myth alludes to the Rainbow as a kind of monster, and tells that in the warfare between the forest and the storm the Rainbow arose, and placing his mouth close to Tane-Mahuta, the Father of Trees, blew so vigorously that the trunk was snapped in two, and the broken branches strewed the ground.

In the mythology of certain tribes of Mexico and Yucatan a great cosmogonic tree has a prominent place. It forms the centre of the Universe, its branches rising to the clouds, from which flows the fertilising rain, while it is rooted in the vase of the primeval waters, from which all things originated.

The Akawiros of Bolivia also have a mighty World Tree which bore not only all kinds of fruit, but also all organic beings.

The natives of Hawaii have mythical Kou trees, under the shade of which in the lower regions the dead recline and feed on lizards and butterflies.[1]

Among the natives of the islands of the South Pacific Ocean there is a belief in a certain point of departure for the Spirit World. The name of this Spirit World in different islands is Avaiki, Haw-aii, or Hawaiki, and on the island of Mangaia the point of departure is a cliff overhanging the sea. As soon as the departing soul reaches the edge of this cliff, a gigantic Bua tree (*Beslaria laurifolia*) springs up from Avaiki to receive the unhappy soul. The branches of this tree are covered with fragrant blossoms, and each tribe has a special branch reserved for it. The branch reserved for the soul's particular tribe is put forward nearest to him. By some miraculous force he is compelled to climb this branch, unless, as is sometimes the case, a mysterious voice calls him back to life and health. As soon as he is on the branch the Bua tree descends to the lower world bearing the soul with it. Beneath is a net spread

[1] Tylor, *Primitive Culture*, vol. ii. p. 283.

to catch the souls as they fall off the branches, which net is
held by the demon Akaanga and his assistants. After being
half-drowned in a great lake at the foot of the Bua tree, the
soul is taken into the presence of the hag Miru Kura, or " the
ruddy," so-called from her face reflecting the flames of her
hell-oven, in which she cooks the unhappy souls. In allusion
to this myth anyone who has recovered from a serious
illness is often wont to remark, " Yes, I have set foot
upon a branch of the Bua tree, and yet have been sent
back to life." [1]

The Samoans similarly believed that a Cocoanut tree grew
near the entrance to Pulotu, or the World of Spirits, and this
tree was called the Tree of Leosia or the Watcher. Should
a spirit strike against it, it had to go back to the body for
another term of earthly existence, and the relatives rejoiced
at this return from the gates of death, saying, " He has come
back from the Tree of the Watcher." [2]

In England at one time there was a belief in what was called
an Ymp tree, although it does not seem quite clear whether
this was a mythical tree, or an actual tree consecrated to the
imps or fiends, as Sir Walter Scott suggests. It appears,
however, to be generally accepted that an Ymp or Imp tree
is simply a grafted tree, and the fact or process of grafting
was considered to have imparted a peculiar character to
the tree. As such it figures in some of the early fairy
romances.

In the Isle of Man there was a mythical tree known as the
Blue Tree of Glen Aldyn. The legend relates how a Manx
fairy was once expelled from the Fairy Court because he had
been engaged in courting a pretty Manx maiden in a bower
under the Blue Tree of Glen Aldyn, and in consequence had
been absent from the Festival of the Harvest Moon, during
which period he had been dancing in the merry glen of
Rushen. His fate was to remain in a wild form covered with

---

[1] Rev. W. Wyatt Gill, B.A., *Myths and Songs from the South Pacific*,
1876, pp. 160–1.   [2] Turner, *Samoa*, p. 258.

hair, hence his name Phynnodderee, meaning the Hairy One, in the Isle of Man till Doomsday.[1]

A mystic Rowan tree was believed to grow in one of the Orkney Islands, with which their fate was bound up. It was said that should even a leaf of this tree be carried away from the island the whole group would pass under the dominion of a foreign lord.

SACRED TREES

As we have already seen, trees had formed the first and earliest temples for the gods, and as the centuries followed each other some individual trees came to be looked upon with greater reverence than others. Probably this arose from the great benefits which trees conferred upon mankind—from their fruit man obtained his first food ; from their bark his first clothing, if we except the skins of wild animals ; and by the aid of their leaves the couch of the cave-dweller was rendered soft and comfortable. A certain tree at length became closely identified with some particular divinity, and was often looked upon as the god himself, and was worshipped as such. In all countries of the world traces of this worship of particular trees are to be found, and even at the present day among uncivilised races trees are often worshipped as gods. Among the early Greeks this worship of trees was a widespread religious phenomenon, and Greek as well as Latin mythology teems with instances of a certain species of tree being sacred to a particular god or goddess. It is only necessary to mention the Oak, sacred to Zeus or Jupiter ; the Laurel, sacred to Apollo ; and the Olive, sacred to Athena. We have already spoken of the Nymphs or Dryads whose life was bound up with the life of the tree. The early worship of the Sacred Tree was conducted on the same principles which prevailed in the worship of the image of the deity in later ages. Thus,

[1] Keightley, *Fairy Mythology*, pp. 402–3.

the tree was crowned and decorated ; prayers were offered to it, and the people reverently kissed it ; religious processions were made to it, and sacrifices offered beneath it. No one dared to pass it, or even to enter its shadow, without the proper ceremonials, and when a sacred tree fell, it was considered to be the worst of omens. As the tree was believed to be the embodiment of the divinity, anyone injuring it was thought to have inflicted an injury on the god himself, which act merited the severest retribution.

Evelyn (" Sylva ") says that in Wales the Rowan tree was reputed so sacred that there was not a churchyard without one, and that on a certain day in the year everyone religiously wore a cross made from its wood. It used to be planted in these churchyards as a warning to Evil Spirits, and coffins on the way to the churchyard were frequently rested under one of the trees.

Scandinavian mythology relates that when Thor was crossing the River Vimur, which had been caused to overflow its banks by a sorcerer, on his way to the land of the Frost Giants, he was aided by a Rowan tree voluntarily bending to enable him to grasp it. Consequently that tree became known in Scandinavian countries as " Thor's Helper." The Norse ships used to have a piece of Rowan-tree wood inserted in them to protect them from the wrath of Ran, the wife of Ögir, the God of the Sea, who delighted in wrecking and drowning seamen.

A sacred Larch tree was said to have stood at Nauders, in Tyrol, down to the year 1859. Should it be cut it was thought to bleed, and the forester who cut it was believed to be wounded to the same depth. His wound would not heal until the scar in the tree filled up. So holy was the tree that no one would quarrel or swear near it, and quarrelsome ones were often rebuked by the injunction, " Don't, the Sacred tree is here ! " [1]

There was formerly an Oak tree at Kenmare dedicated to

[1] Dr. J. G. Frazer, *The Golden Bough*, " The Magic Art and the Evolution of Kings," 1911, vol. ii. p. 20.

St. Columba, which was blown down during a storm. The only person who would venture to touch the fallen tree was a tanner, who cured some skins with the bark, and made himself a pair of shoes. The first time, however, that he put them on he was struck with leprosy, and continued a leper for the remainder of his life.[1]

The Hawthorn tree was considered to be so holy that no evil spirit dare approach it.

At the present day certain Sacred Trees are worshipped by the Arabs. These trees are called *manāhil*, because it is believed that at the places where they grow the angels descend to dance and sing. It is very dangerous to pluck even a twig from one of these trees, but if a sick man sleeps in their shade he will, in a dream, receive instructions as to what measures to take for the restoration of his health.[2] Several of the Arabian tribes were said to have worshipped a particular specimen of the Acacia family. This tree was first consecrated by one Dhâlem, who built over it a chapel, which was so constructed that it gave forth a sound whenever anyone entered it. Tradition tells that in the eighth year of the Hejira, Mohammed sent an envoy to destroy the chapel. This was done, and the Sacred Tree was cut down and burned, while the priestess of the tree was slain. Mohammed himself was looked upon as such an intensely holy man, and endowed with such miraculous gifts, that when he went abroad the very trees went forth to meet and greet him.

In Yemen the sacred Date Palm of Negri, or Negra, was believed to be inhabited by a demon. This tree was adored at an annual feast, and decorated with fine garments and jewels ; while the demon had to be propitiated by prayer and sacrifice. A similar tree near Mecca was worshipped in like manner, being known as a *dhāt anwāt*, meaning " a tree to hang things on." Another tree, growing at Hodaibiya, was believed to impart a blessing to the pilgrims who came to it until it was

[1] O'Donnell, *Life of St. Columba*.
[2] Doughty, *Arabia Deserta*, i. pp. 448 *et seq*.

cut down by the Caliph Omar. The tribe of the Koreysh
revered a large tree which was called Zat Arowat.

In Palestine and Syria many particular trees were reverenced
as holy, and one of these seems to have been the famous Sacred
Tree near Shechem, which was called the Tree of Soothsayers,
or the Tree of the Revealer. Dr. W. Robertson Smith thinks
that this was probably the site of a Canaanite tree oracle, or
perhaps one tree in a sacred grove,[1] but there is no idea given
of how the soothsayers were guided to their predictions.

In Persia, certain large and venerable trees are held to be
sacred as it is considered they are inhabited by the souls of
the blest. These trees are known in Persian as *Pir*, which
means an old man, and in Arabic as *Iman*, meaning a sheik.[2]
There is a Persian story which tells of two vast Cypress trees
which were sacred among the Magians. These grew in
Khorasan, one at Kashmar near Turshiz, and the other at
Farmad near Tuz, and they were believed to have arisen from
shoots which Zoroaster had brought from Paradise. The
former of them was said to have been sacrilegiously cut down
by order of one of the caliphs in the ninth century. Probably
these trees had some connection with the trees of the Sun and
of the Moon mentioned previously.

The Persian geographer Hamdallah mentions a sacred tree
which distinguished the grave of a holy man named Abu
Abdallah at Bostam. This tree was fabled to have been at
one time the staff of Mohammed, which had been carefully
preserved through many generations until it was finally planted
on the holy man's grave, where it took root and produced
branches and leaves. It was said that he who injured this
tree in any way perished that same day.

It was one of the obligations of those who aspired to be
considered saints in Persia to plant useful trees, which appeared
to be afterwards considered sacred, and generally to work out
their salvation by engaging in all agricultural labour.

[1] *The Religion of the Semites.*
[2] " Pietro delle Valle's Travels in Persia," *Pinkerton's Voyages*, vol. ix.
p. 112.

In the great hall of the temple at Heliopolis in Egypt there once stood a very ancient Sycomore tree or Sycomore Fig (*Ficus Sycomorus*), of which it was said that Thoth and the goddess Sefchet, " the lady of writing, the ruler of books," wrote the name of the Pharaoh on its leaves, and that the god Atum, following her example, " wrote the name on the noble tree with the writing of his own fingers." [1] This Sycomore may have been identified with the mythical Sycomore which stood on the path to the other world, and from which the goddess who resided in it supplied the souls of the dead with food and drink while they were travelling thither. The Sycomore Fig along with the Date Palm, being the two great food producers of ancient times, were reckoned as the two most sacred trees of Egypt, and as such representations of them appear on many of the Ancient Egyptian sculptures. One of these shows several generations of a distinguished family receiving nourishment from the Tree of Life depicted as a Sycomore Fig. A goddess is shown issuing from the top of the tree, holding out a tray of figs with one hand and pouring out a stream of water from a vase held in the other. Another sculpture depicts a Date Palm, from the summit of which the two arms of the goddess Nepte issue. With one hand she presents a tray of dates to the soul of the deceased, which is standing in front, while with the other hand the water of life is presented.[2] Professor Maspero considers the tree at Matarîeh, known as the Tree of the Virgin, to have been the successor of the Sacred Tree of Heliopolis.[3] Various provinces or principalities of Ancient Egypt took their names from the trees which chiefly abounded there, and which were all considered to be sacred trees. Among these was the Principality of the Terebinth, the Principality of the Oleander, and the Land of the Sycomore. The most famous tree in the latter was the " Sycomore of the South," which was regarded as

[1] Adolf Erman, *Life in Ancient Egypt*, 1894, p. 348.
[2] R. J. King, *Sacred Trees and Flowers*. In *Quarterly Review*, July and October 1863.
[3] *The Dawn of Civilisation*, 1894, pp. 120 *et seq.*

the living body of the goddess Hathor, who was called the Lady of the Southern Sycomore.

India possesses many sacred trees, and in fact the fetish or local god of almost every village was usually a tree. The tree most widely worshipped in India is the *Ficus religiosa*, the Bo Tree or Tree of Buddha, also called the Peepul, Pipal or Pippala, or Açvattha. This tree personifies Buddha or universal wisdom, and it is also connected with his birth. It is said that when his mother Mâyâ felt her time was at hand she retired to the Lumbinî garden, and there, standing and holding on to the branch of a Pipal tree, or, as some say, of a Sal tree, she gave birth to the future prophet. The name Bo is that by which this tree is known in Ceylon, being a contraction of Bodhi, which means wisdom personified in the tree—the Tree of Knowledge.

The sacred Bo Tree of Ceylon stands in the sacred city of Anuradhapura, the fallen capital of the ancient Kings of Ceylon, and is believed to be one of the oldest trees in existence. M. Gerson da Cunha wrote in 1875 that this sacred tree was the most venerated object in all Ceylon. He says that it grew from a branch of the tree of Uruvela, which was considered to be the identical tree under which Buddha had meditated. This branch was sent to Ceylon by King Açoka to King Tissa 288 years before Christ. The latter planted it, and prophesied that it would flourish eternally and be for ever green. Kings had dedicated their dominions to this tree in testimony of their belief in its divine origin. It is so sacred that it is never touched by a knife, while the fallen leaves are eagerly collected by the Buddhist pilgrims as sacred treasures.

The Pippala was one of those trees sacred to Vishnu, who is often depicted as sitting on its heart-shaped leaves. He was born under one of these trees, and when Brahma appointed rulers over beasts, birds, and plants the holy Fig tree became the sovereign over all trees. A silk-worm, which feeds on its leaves, is called *dêva*, or divine, and shares in the sanctity of the tree.

In Tibet the Tree of Buddha received the name of *Tarayana*, meaning the " way of safety," because it grew beside the river separating earth from heaven, and by the aid of its overhanging branches mankind was enabled to pass from this world to the next.

The Banyan (*Ficus indica*) shares with the Pippala the distinction of being one of the most sacred trees of India. It is also known as the *Vaṭa*. One of these trees in particular, near the town of Surate, which is mentioned in the second book of the *Râmâyana*, as well as in others of the Indian sacred writings, had the utmost respect paid to it. There is a story of an elephant which one day ate a single leaf of it and perished in three days.

The Khonds of India believe that the Great Father or Pitabaldi dwells, in the likeness of a stone, beneath a very tall tree. This stone is daily smeared with saffron by the faithful as an oblation.[1] Their chief dwells in a cottage overshadowed by an enormous Cotton tree, in the centre of the village. This tree is planted by the priest, and is believed to be the abode or temple of the guardian divinity, and the welfare of the population of the village depends upon its growth and vigour,[2] it thus being an instance of a Life Tree.

In the town of Calicut, in Madras, there was a sacred grove of wild Fig trees, the scarlet berries of which were said to have been the cause of the fall of man. The largest of these trees was surrounded by a wall or terrace, on which the sacred serpents (*cobras*) sunned themselves, and they reared their young in the recesses of the stately sacred tree.

In some parts of China are to be found many sacred trees. Several of these bear inscriptions in large letters to the effect that " If you pray, you will certainly be heard."

The Japanese also possess their sacred trees, and Japanese women who have been betrayed by their lovers utilise these trees to bring about an enchantment on the faithless ones. To a sacred tree they nail a straw effigy of the lover, invoking

[1] Élie Reclus, *Primitive Folk*, p. 303.   [2] *Ibid.*, p. 268.

the gods to spare the tree, but to bring down retribution for the sacrilege on the traitor. There was formerly a Pine tree at a shrine at Kompira, which was covered with nails which had been driven in for this purpose.[1]

The Ainu of Japan look upon the Willow as a peculiarly sacred tree, and the Mistletoe which grows upon it is also held in special veneration.[2]

In the days of Ancient Rome the Emperor Claudius introduced the worship of the Sacred Tree into the established religion of Rome. This worship was conducted during the Festival of Cybele in the springtime.

The Prussian or Lithuanian Grove of Romowe (*vide* p. 79) contained a sacred evergreen Oak, under which a perpetual fire was kept burning, fed by Oak branches. This tree, standing in the centre of the grove, was decorated with drapery and images of the gods, the grove itself being so sacred that no twig might be broken nor beast slain within its precincts.

Africa, like India, possesses many sacred trees usually found in the vicinity of the native villages. The Hereros of Hereraland, in the neighbourhood of Lake Ngami, have a sacred tree, which they call Omumborombonga. It is a tall tree with a trunk of enormous thickness, and usually stands alone, although in some parts near Lake Ngami large forests composed of it are found. The Hereros look upon it as their ancestor, because they believe that from it they and all living creatures sprang.

Coomassee, the capital of the Ashantees, had a sacred or fetish tree growing in the centre of the town, which had its name from that tree. The tree had flourished for centuries, until one day it fell and was shattered to pieces. The people were so awed by this fearful portent that no one dared to pick up any of the pieces. The fall of this tree was truly an omen of evil for the nation, because early in February 1874 Coomassee was captured by the British, and the Ashantees came to an end as an independent nation.

[1] Dr. J. G. Frazer, *The Golden Bough*, " The Magic Art and the Evolution of Kings," vol. i. p. 60.
[2] M. Batchelor, *The Ainu and their Folklore*, p. 222.

In South America the most widely spread of the aboriginal races in Brazil, Bolivia, etc., is the Guaranis. These believe in a sacred tree to which the souls after death depart. The Great Spirit is called Tamoi, the grandfather and ancient of Heaven, who was their first ancestor, dwelling among them and teaching them how to till the soil. In the fullness of time he ascended into Heaven, after promising to aid them while they remained on earth, and when they died he would convey them from the Sacred Tree to a new life of everlasting happiness, and where they would all meet again, and enjoy perpetual hunting, which had been their favourite sport while on earth.[1]

An enormous Mimosa, known as the Zamang of Guaira, near Caracas, the capital of Venezuela, has from time immemorial been held in the utmost reverence.

TRADITIONAL TREES

Tradition has handed down to us accounts of many trees which, although some of them may be fabulous, would appear to have had an actual existence from the mere fact that the tradition must have had something to found upon. One of the most talked of trees in England at one time was the Glastonbury Thorn (*Cratægus oxyacantha præcox*). It is a variety of our common Hawthorn, and grows in Palestine and other Eastern lands, where it flowers towards the end of the year. The legend regarding it is that Joseph of Arimathea, in his journeyings to spread the Gospel, once visited England. He carried with him as a staff a branch of this thorn tree which he had obtained in Palestine. The story tells how he and his companions landed on the island of Avalon in Somersetshire, which is now far removed from the sea. When they arrived near the spot where the town of Glastonbury now stands, they proceeded to ascend a small eminence. Being weary and overcome with the heat of the day, they sat them-

[1] E. B. Tylor, *Primitive Culture*, 1871, vol ii. p. 283.

selves down to rest, and from this the eminence became
known as Weary-all Hill, now shortened into Worral Hill.
While resting, Joseph thrust his staff into the ground, where
it miraculously took root, grew, and flowered. Struck with
this circumstance, Joseph resolved to build a Christian church
on, or near, the spot. This was duly done, and from the
primitive edifice arose in time the Abbey of Glastonbury.
The tree grew and flourished amazingly, and the fact that it
flowered, as was said, only on Christmas Day, invested it with
a supernatural character, which gained ready credence in that
superstitious and credulous age. In after times the blossoms
produced by the tree were considered very valuable, and they
were exported to foreign Christian nations at a great price.
It was said that the tree at one time had a double stem, but
one of them was cut down by a religious zealot, whose sacrilege
was avenged by one of the thorns flying into and putting out
one of his eyes, or, as James Howell, who wrote *Dodona's
Grove* in 1644, puts it : " He was well serv'd for his *blind*
Zeale, who going to cut doune an ancient white *Hauthorne-
tree*, which, because she *budded* before others, might be an
occasion of *Superstition*, had some of the *prickles* flew into his
eye, and made him Monocular."

For many years the tree had been held in high repute, a
branch of it often being carried in various religious processions, while cuttings from it were planted in various parts
of the country, which still continue to flower about Christmas
time. The rest of the tree was said to have been cut down
during the Civil War in the reign of Charles I., but two thorn
trees, no doubt cuttings, still exist and flower at the Christmas
season among the ruins of Glastonbury Abbey. The stump
of the old tree, however, remained visible as late as the year
1750, and the spot where it grew was marked by a stone fixed
in the ground bearing the inscription " I.A.A.D. XXXI "
meaning Joseph of Arimathea, A.D. 31.

In A.D. 642 the battle of Maserfield was fought between
Oswald, the Christian King of Northumbria, and Penda

the pagan king of Mercia. Penda triumphed and slew Oswald. He suspended the dead body of his vanquished foe
from a tree, and this tree was said to have become famous in
after ages, and to have been known as Oswald's tree, while
a religious house was built in the vicinity. The town of
Oswestry in Shropshire gathered round this religious house,
the name meaning Oswald's tree. Another derivation is from
the Welsh *tre* or *tref*, meaning a home or town—thus Oswald's
town.

A tree is mentioned in the legend of Thomas the Rhymer,
which is known as the Eildon tree. The legend, as given in
the *Minstrelsy of the Scottish Border*, relates that

> "True Thomas lay on Huntly bank ;
> A ferlie (marvel) he spied wi' his ee ;
> And there he saw a ladie bright,
> Come riding down by the Eildon tree."

This was the Fairy Queen who carried him off to Fairyland,
where he lived for seven years, gaining all the knowledge
which he afterwards embodied in his prophecies. When seven
years had elapsed he was transported back to the Eildon tree,
but under an obligation to return to Fairyland when sum-
moned. The manner of his final departure as given in the
Minstrelsy was as follows : " While making merry with his
friends, in the tower of Ercildoune, a person came running
in, and told, with marks of fear and astonishment, that a hart
and hind had left the neighbourhood forest, and were com-
posedly and slowly parading the street of the village. The
prophet instantly arose, left his habitation, and followed the
wonderful animals to the forest, from whence he was never
seen to return."

A like tale is told of the wizard Merlin, who is said to rest
under an enchantment in an old tree in Cadzow Forest ; but
he has another resting-place in the Forest of Broceliande.

Mr. S. Baring-Gould gives a similar Norse legend relating
to one Helgi, who when exploring a forest came upon a party
of red-dressed women riding upon red horses. These ladies

were beautiful, but were Trolls. Helgi lived with them for
three days, and then went home. After a time he was again
fetched away one winter night, and for many years resided
with the Trolls in the mysterious abode of Gloesisvellir. By
aid of the prayers of King Olaf he was finally released, but
was blind.[1]

There was once a famous Fig tree in Rome which, so it
was said, had sheltered the infants Romulus and Remus while
they were being suckled by the wolf. The tree was thus
known as the Ruminalis, or the Ruminal Fig, and on one
occasion, so tradition avers, when it began to show signs of
decay, the utmost consternation prevailed in the City of Rome
at such an awful omen. Fortunately, however, for the tran-
quillity of the inhabitants, the tree eventually put forth new
shoots and regained its verdure.

Two Myrtle trees grew for a long time in front of the temple
of Quirinus in Rome. One of these was called the Patrician
Tree, and the other the Plebian Tree. For many years, so
long as the Senate retained its superiority, the former tree
throve exceedingly, while the latter was meagre and shrivelled.
When, however, the power of the Senate began to wane, the
Patrician Tree began to wane also, losing its vigour and
finally sinking into a state of decay. At the same time the
Plebian Tree increased in growth and vigour, eventually out-
growing the former.[2]

The Olive tree was much revered in Ancient Greece, and
it is said that Athena caused an Olive tree to spring from the
ground at the period of the foundation of the City of Athens,
and Pliny asserts that in his time that same Olive tree was
growing in the citadel of Athens.

One of the most famous of traditional trees was that one
known as the Oak of Mamre, or the Tree of Abraham. It
has never been really established what species of tree this was,
but it is generally accepted as having been a Terebinth

[1] *Curious Myths of the Middle Ages*, 1875, pp. 216–17.
[2] Pliny, *Nat. Hist.*, Bk. xv. c. 35.

(*Pistacia terebinthus*), also known as the Turpentine tree. It was averred that under this tree Abraham dwelt, and that in its shadow he entertained the angels, although another version of the legend states that the tree had sprung from the staff of one of Abraham's angelic visitors. Josephus says that this tree had flourished since the creation of the world, and that it still existed in his day. A very famous fair, known as the Fair of the Turpentine tree, was for long held under it.

This Oak of Mamre has also come into the category of a Dry tree (*vide* p. 205), and an old traveller named Montevilla wrote concerning it that "in the vale of Mambre, as one journeys from Ebron to Bethlehem, stands the woful withered tree that they call *Trip*, but we name it *Tree of Victory*; 'tis an *Oaktree*, and thought to have stood from the beginning of the world; and before Our Lord suffered, 'twas green and well-leaved, but when God died on the cross it withered it. . . . 'Tis found written in prophecies, Out of Netherland shall come a prince with many Christians, he shall win these lands, and let sing the mass under the *drytree*, then shall it gather green leaves again, and be fruitful, and Jew and Heathen all turn Christian. Therefore do they shew it great honour, and over it keep good ward."

Another of the traditional trees of Palestine is the tree on which Judas is said by St. Matthew to have hanged himself after the betrayal of Jesus, and several trees have been mentioned as having had that dubious privilege under the name of the Judas tree. According to a tradition found in Sicily the tree was a Tamarisk called *Vruca*. This is now a shrub, but formerly it was said to have been a large and beautiful tree. Since Judas hanged himself on it, it has become, by a divine malediction, a true shrub, unsightly, small, deformed, useless, and not even capable of kindling a small fire. They say that the ghost of Judas always flits around the Tamarisk, and he is tormented by seeing his body ever suspended from it.[1] Sir John Maundevile states that the tree was an Elder

[1] De Gubernatis, *Mythologie des Plantes*, vol. i. p. 194.

tree, and claims to have seen it during his travels. He says :
" And faste by, is zit the Tree of Eldre that Judas henge him
self upon, for despeyr that he hadde, whan he solde and
betrayed oure Lord." [1]

An enchanted tree at Gwalior in India grows over the tomb
of Fan-Sein, who was a musician of incomparable skill, and
who delighted the Court of the Emperor Akbar. It is said
that by chewing the leaves of this tree an extraordinary sweet-
ness will be imparted to the voice. The attendant ladies of
Lalla Rookh averred that the voice of the poet Feramorz, when
he spoke of love, was as sweet as if he had chewed the leaves
of that enchanted tree.

In parts of the American continent are likewise found some
trees which have their place in tradition. A venerable Cypress
tree is said to be still in existence on the road between Vera
Cruz and Mexico. Its trunk is 117 feet in circumference,
and beneath its mighty shade the whole army of Cortez,
comprising 600 men and 40 horses, was enabled to shelter.
De Candolle estimated the age of this tree to be six thousand
years.

FAMOUS TREES

Many individual trees have become famous in different
lands on account of their age, their size, or from some
traditionary or historical connection associated with them.
What may well be considered the oldest trees in the world
are some specimens of the species of Cypress known as *Sequoia*
or *Wellingtonia gigantea* of California, which are considered
as having probably been in existence during the Mesozoic
Epoch, and thus they will be the oldest living things on the
surface of the earth ; in fact the world as they knew it in their
youth has perished and they alone remain. It has been
computed that the largest of these trees, which is known
as the Big Tree of California, could not have attained

[1] *The Voiage and Travaile*, edit. J. O. Halliwell, 1883, p. 93.

to anything like its full maturity before 1,500 years had elapsed, and that it could not have been old before its four-thousandth year. During the centuries which these trees saw slip past before they were found by civilised man many curious things must have taken place under their shade. In the Mesozoic Epoch strange animals would have wandered past them, curious birds may have roosted among their branches, and other trees of long extinct types doubtless surrounded them. Could they but speak !

As compared with these giants of the vegetable world, the smallest tree known in the world is a Willow, the *Salix herbacea.* It is rarely higher than three inches, frequently not more than two, yet is in every respect a true tree, and is found growing on the highest mountains of Britain.

In addition to the famous and well-known Oak trees of England there are many other Oaks, as well as other trees, which have a certain fame, but which it is unnecessary to mention here. We must not, however, omit the famous Oak of Errol in Scotland, which has long since disappeared. It was alleged that the fate of the family of the Hays of Errol, in the Carse of Gowrie, was bound up in a Mistletoe plant which grew on this tree. One of the descendants of that family, writing in 1822, recorded the belief as follows : " Among the low county families the badges are now almost generally forgotten ; but it appears by an ancient MS., and the tradition of a few old people in Perthshire, that the badge of the Hays was the Mistletoe. There was formerly in the neighbourhood of Errol, and not far from the Falcon stone, a vast oak of an unknown age, and upon which grew a profusion of the plant : many charms and legends were considered to be connected with the tree, and the duration of the family of Hay was said to be united with its existence. It was believed that a sprig of the Mistletoe cut by a Hay on Allhallowmas eve, with a new dirk, and after surrounding the tree three times sunwise, and pronouncing a certain spell, was a sure charm against all glamour or witchery, and an infallible guard in the day of battle. A spray, gathered in the same manner, was placed in the cradle of infants, and thought to defend them from being changed for elf-bairns by the Fairies. Finally, it was affirmed that, when the root of the oak had perished, ' the grass should grow in the hearth of Errol, and a raven should sit in the falcon's nest.' The two most unlucky deeds which could be done by one of the name of Hay was, to kill a white falcon, and to cut down a limb from the Oak of Errol."

Thomas the Rhymer is credited with having uttered the above prophecy thus :

> " While the mistletoe bats on Errol's aik,
>   And that aik stands fast,
> The Hays shall flourish, and their good grey hawk
>   Shall nocht flinch before the blast.
>
> But when the root of the aik decays
>   And the mistletoe dwines on its withered breast,
> The grass shall grow on Errol's hearthstane,
>   And the corbie roup [croak] in the falcon's nest."

Another tree with a similar tradition grows at Howth Castle in Ireland. With its welfare is said to be bound up that of the St. Lawrences, Earls of Howth. It is believed that when the tree falls the direct line of the family will become extinct. To avert that catastrophe as long as possible, the branches of the tree are upheld by strong wooden supports.

The lower slopes of Mount Etna bear several ancient and colossal Chestnut trees. The largest and most celebrated of these is known as the *Castagno di Cento Cavalli*, or the Chestnut of a hundred horses. The trunk of this tree has a circumference near the ground of 190 feet. The inhabitants of the district tell that when Jeanne of Aragon was making a journey from Spain to Naples she stopped at Sicily in order to pay a visit to Mount Etna. She rode thither on horseback, as did all her suite. When on the way a heavy storm broke over them, forcing them all to take shelter under this tree. Its vast, spreading foliage was quite sufficient to shelter the whole company, horses included, from the rain, and from this circumstance the name originated. The enormous trunk is hollow, and inside it has been built a kind of house which shelters a shepherd and his flock.

After the battle of Morat, fought in 1476, which marked a brilliant crisis in the history of Switzerland, a Lime tree was planted at Fribourg to commemorate that victory. The tree, now over four hundred years of age, is encircled by a colonnade, and its venerable branches are upheld by a framework of wood.

Another famous Lime tree grew at Goldenkron in Bohemia. The *Botanische Zeitung* for September 1855 gave the following account of it : " In the court of the ancient abbey of the Cistercians at Goldenkron in Bohemia, there is a very aged tree, a venerable Lime. In spring, when the first impulse is given to vegetation and the earlier buds expand, the first leaf of each series is never perfectly unfolded, but always remains with its margins attached to each other, contiguous to the midrib and leaf-stalk.[1] The popular saying is that ' this tree bears *Capuzen* ' (monk's cowls or hoods), and the credulous believe that these hoods have grown on the tree since Ziska, at the destruction of the monastery in 1420, caused the monks to be hung thereon—to remind posterity of the atrocious act then committed."

The prodigious Lime tree at Neustadt, in the Duchy of Wurtemberg, gave a name to that town, which is known as *Neustadt an der grossen Linden* (Neustadt by the great Lime). On one occasion, during a siege, its wide-spreading branches were very much devastated, but they were afterwards propped up by columns and monuments of stone, which bore inscriptions, and the arms and devices of different princes and nobles.

An equally famous Lime tree was that which grew at Süderheistede in Ditmarschen, which was known as the " Wonderful Tree." There was an ancient prophecy that if

---

[1] This seems to be due to a leaf-rolling insect.

the freedom of the town was lost, the tree would wither, which was fulfilled. But the belief is still current that one day a magpie will build its nest on the branches, and that then the tree will revive and the town become free once more.

In former times there were several Plane trees growing in Greece and Asia Minor which were pointed out as having achieved immortal renown. The Plane tree is a native of Asia, where for ages it had been an object of religious veneration, particularly to the Iranians and the races of Asia Minor. As its wood was of no particular value it appears to have been introduced into Greece and Italy solely on account of the grateful shade which its luxuriant foliage afforded.

At Caphiæ, in Arcadia, grew a Plane tree of extraordinary beauty and size, which Pausanias, during his travels in Greece in the second century, mentions as having seen, and which at that period must have been about thirteen centuries old. This tree was called the Menelaid Plane, because, as the natives of the country said, it had been planted by Menelaus with his own hands when he came to Caphiæ to raise forces for the Trojan wars ; but Theophrastus was of opinion that it had been planted by Agamemnon.

A Plane tree in Lydia was, according to Herodotus, intimately associated with Xerxes. After Xerxes had declared war on the Greeks, while he was on his way to Sardis he saw a magnificent Plane tree, which so struck his fancy that he halted his whole army so that he might be able to admire it at his leisure. He called it his goddess, his mistress, his minion, and when finally he had to leave it, he encircled the stem with a golden collar, adorned its branches with golden bracelets and chains, and left one of the ten thousand to keep guard over it. In addition, he caused a medal to be struck, bearing a representation of it, which he continually wore. The traveller Hamilton, when in that region, found the half-decayed trunk of the most enormous Plane tree he had ever seen, and conjectured that it was the same which Xerxes had adored.

In Phrygia there used to be shown a large and ancient Plane

tree which was fabled to have been the identical tree from which Apollo had suspended his rival Marsyas.

Many conjectures have been put forward as to the identity of the Mustard tree mentioned in Scripture (St. Matthew xiii. 31, 32), and for long it was held that the *Salvadora Persica* had the best claim, as it was at one time thought to grow freely in Palestine from the writings of Messrs. Irby and Mangles, who travelled in that country and saw it growing near the Dead Sea. They said : " There was one curious tree which we observed in great plenty, and which bore fruit in bunches resembling in appearance the currant with the colour of the plum ; it has a pleasant, although strongly aromatic taste, exactly resembling mustard. The leaves have the same pungent flavour as the fruit, although not so strong. We think it probable that this is the tree our Saviour alluded to in the Parable of the Mustard-seed, and not the plant which we have in the north." Later on, however, Dr. Hooker pointed out that this plant grows only in the sub-tropical valley of Engedi, and during his sojourn in Syria he could hear of it in no other locality, and that no one had ever seen or heard of it elsewhere. It has now been considered that this Mustard tree was simply the common Mustard plant (*Sinapis nigra*) which in Palestine is very common and grows to a surpassing height. In fact Messrs. Irby and Mangles themselves said that it grew as high as their horses' heads, and Dr. Thomson said he had seen it as high as the horse and its rider. In Oriental hyperbole this would probably be called a tree, and it would be quite large and strong enough for small birds to rest upon, while there is no mention made of birds building nests in it.

One of the most famous trees in India is a Banyan, growing on the banks of the Nerbudda, and known to the Hindus as the Cubbeer-burr or Kabira-bâr. It is supposed to be the same as that described by Nearchus, the Admiral of Alexander the Great, as being able to shelter an army under its far-spreading shade.

In Africa, particularly in Senegal, and in some of the islands not far from the African coast, grows the Baobab (*Adansonia digitata*). Of all the trees in the world it is supposed to be the largest as regards the thickness of its whitish, conical trunk, which, however, rises only to a height of about fifteen feet before it branches, while its circumference is often more than one hundred feet. From the summit of this trunk numerous thick branches, from thirty to sixty feet long, branch off horizontally in all directions, and, as they gradually become shorter farther up the stem, the tree takes the appearance of a gigantic dome. The leaves resemble the fingers of the human hand, from which the naturalist Adanson gave it the specific name of *digitata*, its generic name being his own. The blossoms are of a proportionate size, are of a snowy white, and are regarded with a peculiar reverence the moment they burst into bloom. The fruit, large, oval, and resembling a cucumber, is a great favourite with monkeys, the tree being sometimes called Ape's-bread Tree, Monkey's Bread, and Ethiopian Sour Gourd. Adanson stated that these trees grow in plains of barren movable sand, and where the water of a river had washed this sand away, the roots were left exposed. These roots, he said, measured over 110 feet in length. The short thick trunk is necessary to support the overwhelming superincumbent mass of leaves, and seen from a distance the Baobab resembles a small forest rather than a single tree. Under the vast shadow, often 450 feet in circumference, cast by this tree, the negroes enjoy repose, and often find refuge from the storm. The negroes of Senegambia are said to worship these trees as divinities. When time, in the course of ages, has hollowed out the stem of one of these noble trees, it often becomes the abode of a negro family. Sometimes the hollow forms a place of amusement, sometimes a prison, and one tree is known in Senegambia which has been converted into a Council Hall, the entrance being covered with appropriate sculptures. Another use to which the negroes put these hollow trees is for the burial of their poets, buffoons, and

musicians in the cavity. They consider them to be inspired
by demons, so they will suffer the bodies neither to be buried
in the earth nor thrown into the sea, lest the fruit or the fish
should perish. Thus, to avert their doing harm to land or
sea, they are placed in these hollows, where they soon dry up.
As these trees commence to decay downwards at the point
where the branches spring forth, the hollow space thus formed
fills with water during the rainy season, and forms an excellent
cistern, the water being kept cool by the overhead foliage.
Those villages which are fortunate enough to possess such a
tree sell the water to travellers. Many of these trees in Senegal
are computed to be about five or six thousand years old. In
one of the Cape Verde Islands Adanson found a Baobab
bearing in its interior an inscription which had been traced
there by the English three hundred years previously. From
that, and by measuring the stems of many of the trees, he
calculated that the most vigorous specimens might be at least
five thousand years old.

Another very famous tree is the Dragon tree, or Dragon's
Blood tree (*Dracœna Dráco*) of the Canary Islands. Although
this tree is also found in Africa, China, and elsewhere, it is only
in the Canary Islands that it attains to such dimensions as
to render it famous. The trees are of such slow growth that
the enormous size to which some of them have attained gives
a certain proof of their vast antiquity. The most famous of
these trees was the Dragon tree at Orotava, in the island of
Teneriffe, which shared its fame with the Peak. The Canary
Islands were discovered by Bethencourt and his companions
in the fourteenth century. At that period this tree was carefully measured, and when Humboldt saw it in 1799 he found
that its size had in no way increased, it being then forty-five
feet in circumference and sixty-five feet high. At that time
it was considered to be the oldest and largest living tree, the
giant Sequoias of California being yet unknown. Humboldt
described it thus : " Its trunk is divided into a great number
of branches, which rise in the form of candelabra, and are

terminated by tufts of leaves like the Yucca : it still bears every year both leaves and fruit : its aspect feelingly recalls to mind that ' eternal youth of Nature,' which is an inexhaustible source of motion and of life." It was said that for many centuries this particular tree had been worshipped by the Guanches, who were the aboriginal inhabitants of the island, and during the fifteenth century Mass would appear to have been celebrated in the interior of its trunk as is attested by vestiges of a little altar found there. This tree no longer exists, having been utterly overwhelmed by a terrific storm in 1871. Gerarde,[1] in his description of the Dragon tree, and derivation of the name, says that in the fruit may be seen " the form of a dragon with a long neck and gaping mouth, the ridge or back armed with sharp prickles like the Porcupine, with a long taile and foure feet very easie to be discerned," and adds that if the bark is bruised or bored in the Dog Days it " yeelds forth drops of a thick red liquor, of the name of the tree called Dragons tears, or *Sanguis draconis*, Dragons bloud."

Charles Darwin has told how in South America, on the borders of Patagonia, he saw the famous Tree of Walleechu, which, he says, the Indians reverence as the altar of Walleechu, the inference being that Walleechu was a god. The tree was between the River Negro and the River Colorado. It was a somewhat low-growing tree, much branched and thorny, with a diameter of about three feet just above the root. It stood solitary, and was thus a landmark for a great distance round. As soon as a tribe of Indians come within sight of the tree they salute it with loud cries. When Darwin saw it, it had no leaves, being winter, but he mentions that votive offerings were suspended from it by numerous threads, while poor Indians who had nothing to offer simply tied on a thread. He adds that richer Indians " are accustomed to pour spirits and maté into a certain hole, and likewise to smoke upwards, thinking thus to afford all possible gratification to Walleechu."

[1] *Herbal*, ed, 1636, pp, 1523-4.

All around lay the bleached bones of horses which had been sacrificed to the sacred tree, the Indians believing that by this sacrifice they will insure prosperity for themselves, and that their horses will never become fatigued. This tree was a species of Acacia.[1]

CURIOUS TREES

In many parts of the globe there were at one time believed to exist certain trees which were considered to be very curious, perhaps on account of some natural phenomena connected with them, or from their associations or surroundings. One of these curious trees was known in Scotland as the Barnacle or Goose tree, it being believed to produce geese, or a fowl of some kind, as was solemnly averred by the older botanists. In fact the belief appears to have been prevalent prior to the thirteenth century, for we find Albertus Magnus expressing his disbelief in the tales of bird-bearing trees. In spite of that it continued for long to be the popular belief. Bishop Fleetwood mentions a tree of a similar nature growing at Guadeloupe, which he calls the Oyster tree.

Certain trees once grew in Scotland which were used by the Highland Chieftains to hang their refractory followers, and often their enemies, upon. These, many of which still exist, were known as Dool trees or Grief trees. They usually grew on a small hill known as the Gallows Hill, and the gallows itself in after times became known as the Gallows Tree, or simply the Tree.

Very often a young tree, frequently a Rowan tree, may be found growing in the fork of an old tree where the seed had been deposited by a bird. This, particularly in Norway and Sweden, was known as a *Flögrönn*, or Flying Rowan, and it possessed, in a superlative degree, all the magical virtues which were generally attributed to the Rowan. Dr. J. G.

[1] *Journal of a Voyage Round the World*, Minerva Library, 5th ed. pp. 49-50.

Frazer says that if anyone who is out in the dark chews a bit of a Flying Rowan, he is secure against witchcraft, and adds that in Sweden the Divining Rod was made from a tree of that kind. He also gives a Norwegian story which relates how some ploughmen were once so bewitched by a Troll that they were unable to drive straight furrows. Only one of them could do so, and that was because his plough was made from a Flying Rowan.[1]

In tropical countries the Mangrove (*Rhizophora mangle*) presents itself as one of the most curious of trees. Growing in the swampy lagoons, it is one of the great agents in the reclamation of land from the sea, and has been fancifully considered to be half-tree and half-fish. The tree grows about fifty feet in height, and from the circumstance that it spreads not only by its roots but also by its branches, which droop downwards, a single tree often covers the banks of the muddy rivers under the tropics in Asia, Africa, and America for over a mile. The seeds of the Mangrove germinate when still attached to the parent branch, forming young trees really, and drop a long slender rootlet into the water. These rootlets in time become a complicated series of arched or looped stems surrounding the parent stem, and as the process is continually repeated, interwoven groves are formed which, in the deltas formed at the mouths of the great rivers, serve to arrest the mould which is being constantly washed down from the higher land, and so muddy swamps are formed. As this goes on throughout the centuries the mud eventually dries somewhat, the Mangrove itself dies, and then Palm trees appear. Various creeping plants next come on the scene, which, as they wither and die, gradually add fresh mould, and finally a rich and fertile land is formed. In much the same manner the Landes of France were formed artificially. These Mangrove swamps were well known to the ancients, although they had an erroneous conception of their nature.

Parkinson describes a tree, under the name of the Sorrowful

---

[1] *The Golden Bough*, "Baldur the Beautiful," vol. ii. p. 281.

tree, which grows in Malabar. Its flowers, he says, never
open during the day, because when the sun shines the whole
plant becomes withered-looking and dead until evening, when
it revives. He says it is called Parizataco at Goa and elsewhere, from a nobleman of that name, whose daughter the sun
had loved and deserted. She, in despair, slew herself, and
from her ashes that tree arose, which ever since has been
ashamed to behold the face of the sun.[1]

In the island of Madagascar a curious Palm-like tree grows
which forms one of those wonderful sources of refreshment
which is provided by Nature for the thirsty wanderer through
the untrodden solitudes. It is known as the Traveller's tree
(*Ravenala Madagascariensis*). The trunk terminates in a
cluster of long leaves, among the largest in the world, the
stalks or petioles of which, often ten feet in length, embrace
the trunk with broad sheaths. In these sheaths the dew and
the rain trickling down the surface collect, and form a welcome
reservoir of pure and cool drinking-water.

As the cloudy sky has been mythologically compared to a
celestial tree, that metaphor has naturally given rise to the
popular belief in Rainy Trees. Many trees and other plants
have the power of absorbing a large quantity of water which
frequently distils in drops which fall off like rain. The best
known instance of a Rainy Tree, or, as it has been called,
Fountain Tree, is found in the Canary Islands, which were
first seen by European navigators in the fourteenth century.
Juan de Abreu Galindo, who in the seventeenth century wrote
a history of the conquest of these islands, says that there was
at Hierro (Ferro) a Laurel tree which furnished the natives
with drinking-water. This water distilled drop by drop from
the foliage, and was collected into cisterns. The historian
added that this marvellous vegetable fountain was, for a part
of the day, enveloped in a cloud, whence the water was drawn.
It is affirmed that the existence of this tree was first made
known to the Spaniards by a certain courtesan. When her

[1] *Theatrum Botanicum*, ed. 1640, pp. 1644-5.

treachery was discovered she was put to death by her own people. Parkinson mentions this tree and says : " In some parts of the world besides are found the like trees, the leaves whereof and branches doe perpetually droppe water (in the whole Island there being no other water to be had) a thicke mist as it were or cloud encompassing it continually, except when the Sunne shineth bright thereon ; which water being kept as it were in a fountain made for the purpose to retaine it, serveth the whole Island for their use." [1]

Certain curious trees are known as Bottle trees from the remarkable peculiarity they have of bulging out like a barrel in the centre of the stem. One, discovered by Mitchell in the tropical part of Australia, and known as the Delabecha, has wood of so loose a grain that when its shavings have boiling water poured over them a thick viscid mass results. Another, the *Pao Barrigudo* found in the Brazilian forests, draws the attention of every traveller. The centre of the trunk swells out, gradually tapering to the bottom and the top, while from the latter a few thin and scanty branches spring.

The Manchineel tree (*Hippomane Mancinella*) of the West Indies and Central America, where it grows to a vast size, has a very evil repute from the supposed poisonous emanations from it, and it has been called the Poison Tree. It was believed that certain death was the fate of those who slept under its branches, but this was found to be erroneous. The fruits, however, are highly poisonous, and the tree abounds with a white milky juice, which is very irritant, a single drop of it touching the skin causing a burning sensation and raising a blister.

MARVELLOUS TREES

Not so very long ago, and before travelling was rendered more rapid and easier by the advent of steamers, railway trains, and airships, any wild and improbable story which was

[1] *Theatram Botanicum*, ed; 1640, p. 1645.

brought home by those who had ventured into far countries was implicitly believed, and in most cases the travellers had themselves been duped, as invariably they had got their information second-hand. Tales of many marvellous and wonderful trees were told, among which the Upas tree of Java holds a foremost place. This tree (*Antiaris toxicaria*), which grows to the height of fully one hundred feet, belongs to the order *Urticaceæ* (the order containing the nettles), and its Javanese name is Antjar or Antsjar. It is one of the largest trees growing in the forests of Java, and bears no branches up to a height of from sixty to eighty feet, while the bark is white. When the bark is cut a yellowish sap oozes out which is of a very deadly character, and is used by the natives to poison the tips of small darts, which they discharge through blow-pipes.

For long this tree was looked upon as one of the horrors of creation. The one particular Upas tree of universal fame was said to grow in a sterile plain about twenty-seven leagues from Batavia. All around towered rocky mountains, and in the centre of the plain, known as the Valley of Death, the sinister tree stood alone. The king was said to have used the poisonous juice to poison the weapons used by his army, but as the emanations from the tree were so deadly, few could be found willing to go to gather the juice. The king, therefore, had recourse to criminals, on promise of pardon if they returned successful. Armed with long bamboo rods in which to collect the poison drops, many, it was stated, made the endeavour, but few returned. A Dutch physician named Foersche, who travelled in Java during the closing years of the eighteenth century, claimed to have seen this tree, and related how it grew in the midst of a frightful sandy solitude, and how the influence of its noxious exhalations extended for three or four leagues around. In that area nothing that breathes or vegetates could live. Only the skeletons of men and animals were to be seen, and birds which ventured to fly over it instantly fell to the ground. The Russian poet, Alexander

Pushkin, gives the following vivid impression of the horror
which this ghastly tree was said to inspire : " In an inhos-
pitable and sterile desert, on a soil burnt up by the sun,
the *Antchar*, like a threatening watch-tower, uplifts itself,
unique in creation. Nature, in these thirsty plains, planted
it in the day of her wrath, and supplied its roots and the pale
verdure of its branches with poison. The poison, melted by
the midday sun, percolates through the bark in drops, which
in the evening are congealed into a thick and transparent gum.
The birds avoid its very appearance, the tiger shuns it ; a
breath of wind rustles its foliage ; the passing wind is tainted.
A shower waters for a moment its sleeping leaves, and from
its branches a deadly rain falls on to the burning soil. But
an order is made and a man obeys ; he starts on an expedition
to the Antchar without hesitation, and next day brings back
from the branches and leaves the deadly gum, while from his
pallid brow the sweat pours in frozen streams. He, staggering,
brings it, falls on the mats of the tent, and expires at the feet
of his invincible prince. And the prince soaks his flexible
arrows in the poison. He wishes to carry destruction to his
neighbours on the frontier."

Dr. Darwin, in the *Loves of the Plants*, has also given a
forcible description of this Valley of Death with its sole and
menacing occupant. He wrote thus :

> " Where seas of glass with gay reflections smile
> Round the green coasts of Java's palmy isle,
> A spacious plain extends its upland scene,
> Rocks rise on rocks, and fountains gush between.
> Soft breathes the breeze ; eternal summers reign
> And showers prolific bless the soil—in vain !
> No spicy nutmeg scents the vernal gales :
> No towering plantain shades the midday vales ;
> No grassy mantle hides the sable hills ;
> No flowery chaplet crown the trickling rills ;
> No step, retreating, on the sand impressed,
> Invites the visit of a second guest.
> Fierce in dread silence, on the blasted heath
> Fell Upas sits."

Sir John Maundevile speaks of a marvellous tree which he says grew in the kingdom of Prester John, though he apparently does not claim to have actually seen it. In that kingdom, he says, there was a great gravelly plain, on which, every day at sunrise, small trees sprang up and grew till midday. They bore fruit, but no one could gather it as it was a thing of Fayrye. After midday these trees decreased gradually in size, and finally sank again into the earth.[1]

Sir John also mentions a tree of miraculous origin which he saw growing in the City of Tiberias. The tree originated from a burning dart which an angry citizen had thrown at Jesus. It stuck in the earth, became green, and grew to a great tree, of which the bark, Sir John said, was black, and like coal.[2]

When the traveller Odoricus du Frioul arrived at Malabar in the fourteenth century, he heard certain trees spoken of which, instead of fruit, produced men and women. These beings were scarcely a cubit in height, and their lower extremities were attached to the trunk of the tree. When the wind blew, their bodies were full of moisture, but they dried up wherever it lulled.

There is said to be a tree growing in a part of Central Australia to which the sun, taking the form of a woman, is fabled to have travelled from the east. If this tree should be destroyed, the natives believe that everyone will be burned up, and if anyone kills and eats an opossum which he finds on the tree, his whole inward parts will be burned, with death as a result.[3]

---

[1] *The Voiage and Travaile*, ed. J. O. Halliwell, 1883, p. 273.
[2] *Ibid.*, p. 117.
[3] Spencer and Gillen, *Northern Tribes of Central Australia*, p. 624.

CHAPTER VIII

FOLKLORE

Fossil or Petrified Forests and Trees ; Bark of Trees ; Leaves of Trees ;
Thorns, Spines, Prickles, etc. ; Origin of Fire ; Divination—Divining
Rod, Wands, etc. ; The Man in the Moon ; The Yule Log.

FOSSIL OR PETRIFIED FORESTS AND TREES

DURING the ages which have elapsed since vegetation first
appeared upon the face of the earth, the remains of many
trees and other plants have been found in a silicified state,
testifying to the fact of their former existence, and speaking
eloquently of the æons which have elapsed since they waved
green over the land. The vast vegetation of the Carboniferous
Epoch has already been mentioned, but many isolated instances
occur where the remains of forests of a later age are still
plainly visible.

Baldwin Mollhausen speaks of having seen a remarkable
formation of silicified stems of trees *in situ*, or partly prostrate.
At another spot the travellers saw what resembled masses of
wood which had been felled previous to the cultivation of the
land. Trees of all sizes appeared scattered around, some
more than sixty feet long, but a closer examination revealed
that these were fossilised trees which had been gradually
washed down by torrents. In long past ages these trees had
flourished on the high lands, had fallen, had been covered
over and silicified, and in after ages, possibly owing to con-
vulsions of Nature, had been raised once more as fossils which
torrents had swept downwards, breaking many in the process,
until they appeared as if sawn into logs two or more feet in
diameter. Many were hollow and of a dark hue, but the
rings, and even the bark, were quite discernible. A beautiful
blending of agate and jasper colouring appeared in some of

the blocks, while broken fragments presented truly lovely tints of various colours, but other pieces resembled simply rotten wood.[1]

In one of the expeditions to Bank's Land, in the Arctic regions, several hills were found which were formed of accumulations of wood, the remains of vast forests which had been flourishing there thousands of years previously. The records of the expedition tell that the ends of trunks and branches of trees were seen protruding through the rich, loamy soil in which they were embedded, while some of the hills were of a complete ligneous formation. They comprised the trunks and branches, some soft and dark, and in a state of semi-carbonisation, while others seemed to be fresh but hard, in which the structure of the wood was quite apparent. In other places the ligneous formation was hard and flattened, owing to the pressure which it had undergone for ages, and in this case traces of coal were observed. The trunk of one tree was twenty-six inches in diameter, and that of another was three feet in circumference. Both appeared to have belonged to the *Coniferæ*.

Charles Darwin says that in the Uspallata range of the Andes he noticed some snow-white, projecting columns on a bare slope, and closer observation revealed that they were petrified trees. Eleven of them were silicified, and from thirty to forty were converted into a coarsely crystallised white calcareous spar. These trees were of the Fir tribe, with affinities to both the Araucaria and the Yew.[2]

Professor Agassiz, when travelling in Brazil, found on the seashore the remains of forests now covered with sand. One of these submerged forests was at the mouth of the Igarapé Grand, where evidently it had grown in one of those marshy lands constantly inundated, and in it the stumps of the trees, still standing erect in the peat, had been laid bare on both sides of the river by the encroachments of the ocean. At

---

[1] *Diary of a Journey from the Mississippi to the Coasts of the Pacific.*
[2] *Journal of a Voyage round the World in H.M.S. " Beagle."*

Vigia, just where the Pará River meets the sea, there was another submerged forest with the stumps of innumerable trees standing in it, and encroached upon in the same way by tidal sand. No doubt, Agassiz remarked, these forests were once all continuous, and stretched across the whole basin of what is now called the Pará River.[1]

During Dr. Livingstone's first expedition to Africa, in 1840–56, he mentions that after leaving Chipong he skirted a range of hills, at the base of which he observed a forest of large petrified trees of the Araucarian type. He also observes that numerous fossil trees abound in the district of Chicova, many lying prostrate, and others standing upright, while others were shattered into fragments. The explorer gives other instances of having observed petrified forests and trees.

At low tide submerged forests may be seen at various places round the coasts of the British Islands, the stumps and roots becoming visible. They may be seen in Mounts Bay, Cornwall, the Bristol Channel, at the mouth of the Humber, in the Firth of Forth, and as far north as the Orkney Islands. The most of these appear to be remains of ancient forests of *Sigillarias*. The forests of which all these are the vestiges seem to have flourished during interglacial periods, and to have perished when the ice-cap again covered the land. Man appears to have wandered in their shade, as weapons of stone and of bronze have been found in them, along with bones of the Elk, the Beaver, and other animals not now known in these islands.

BARK OF TREES

The bark of various trees has been widely taken advantage of for many purposes—for clothing, food, writing, etc., and has even been used in lieu of coin. In very ancient times, in the northern parts of Europe, mankind had apparently no other garments than the bark of trees, and it was not until

[1] *A Journey in Brazil*, by Professor and Mrs. Louis Agassiz in 1865, pub. 1868, pp. 434–5.

later on that he began to clothe himself in the skins of animals. Even yet in many parts of the world, notably in the islands of the South Seas and in the Malay Archipelago, the bark of trees is formed into a kind of cloth. The process of manufacture is very much the same everywhere. Large cylinders of bark are cut from the tree and beaten with mallets till it separates from the wood. It is then repeatedly soaked and beaten till it becomes extremely thin and very tough. Sometimes the sap from the bark of a certain tree is used to stain this cloth, and it also renders it waterproof. This cloth was known as *ahu* in Tahiti, and in the Tonga Islands it was called *gnatoo*.

In India, anchorites, as a penance, sometimes covered themselves with the bark of trees when they returned from their ablutions, in order to keep the moisture in their bodies.

A remnant of the aborigines of Ceylon still inhabit the forests of that island. These are the Veddas, or " hunters." They live in caves, or in huts made from bark, and formerly their clothing consisted of bark. Ages ago they seem to have inhabited hollow trees, as in Singhalese the word for a hollow tree is *rukula*, and the same word now means a house.

Bark has even been used as food in emergencies. Thus we are told that during the retreat of Xerxes, his army being in sore straits for provisions, they stripped off the bark of trees and ate it along with the leaves. A pestilence, however, followed this strange diet, and destroyed large numbers of them.[1]

Boats were frequently made of bark. Among the Tinneh tribes of North America the canoes were formed from strips of bark sewn together with fibre, and the seams were filled with pitch made from Fir trees. In Russia, boats are still made from the bark of the Birch. The aborigines of Australia, according to Captain Cook, used sheets of bark crimped up at the ends as canoes.

In very early times the inner bark of trees was used for writing upon. This is the layer called in Latin *liber* ; hence a book, consisting as it did of leaves made from that inner

[1] *Herodotus*, Cary's transl., Bk. viii. 115.

bark, was termed *liber*, from which the word " library " is derived. Dictys Cretensis was an author supposed to be contemporary with the siege of Troy, of which he wrote an account in Punic letters on linden-bark paper. This manuscript was said to have been found in a tin case by some shepherds in Dictys's tomb at Gnossos, and was afterwards translated into Greek, but the story seems to be somewhat apocryphal.

Some nations, such as the Chinese, still in many instances use this inner bark of trees for pencraft. Sir Thomas Holdich, speaking of Captain H. Bower's journey across Tibet in 1893, says : " It was Bower who first astonished the world of Oriental scholars with the birch-bark manuscript dug out of the Turkestan desert near Kashgar, which proved to be one of the most ancient manuscripts in the world, and has set scientists exploring and working in the same direction ever since." [1]

The bark of the Birch tree is the most durable of all, and was largely used by the ancients for writing purposes before the invention of paper. A striking instance of the durability of this thin pellicle was found in the mines of Dworetzkoi, in Siberia, where a piece of Birch wood was disinterred completely fossilised. The thin outer skin of the bark was exactly in its natural state, and had a white satiny shimmer, precisely as may be seen on Birch trees growing at the present day.

As bark was used for writing upon in ancient times, so in more modern times bark was the means of the discovery of printing. We are told that Gutenberg one day amused himself by carving out letters from the bark of a Beech tree. Wrapping them up when still damp in paper, he was astonished to find the impression of them on the paper when he reached home. This gave him the idea. Carving out others, he was delighted to find that they gave clear impressions, and so the art of printing was evolved.

The bark of several trees abounds in medicinal properties. Such, for instance, is the Cinchona or Peruvian Bark, known

[1] *Tibet the Mysterious.*

as quinine, from the Peruvian name for the bark, *quina-quina*, meaning bark of barks. Another equally efficacious remedy for fevers is obtained from the bark of Willow trees, which is known as salicine. As the Willow abounds in marshy and wet districts where fever and ague are very prevalent, it would appear that Nature had provided the remedy in close proximity to the disease, and it has been found that an infusion of Willow bark has almost the same curative effect as the salicine of the druggist.

Marco Polo tells how the great Kublai Khan caused the bark of trees to be made into something like paper, and to be used as money all over his dominions. The bark used was that of the Mulberry tree, and was the layer next the wood.[1]

The smooth shining bark of some trees offers an irresistible invitation to carve letters and figures on it, which for long has been a sentimental pastime of lovers, who usually carve their own and their sweethearts' names or initials, along with the date, so that in after years they may be reminded of a long and joyous summer day spent in the woodlands in loving company. The bark of the Beech tree is the favourite, and in Shakespeare's day, and probably long before, the practice was as prevalent as it is now. In *As You Like It* (Act iii, Scene 2) Orlando enters the Forest of Arden, and exclaims :

> " O Rosalind ! these trees shall be my books,
>   And in their barks my thoughts I'll character ;
> That every eye, which in this forest looks,
>   Shall see thy virtue witness'd every where.
> Run, run, Orlando ; carve on every tree,
> The fair, the chaste, and unexpressive she."

Evelyn [2] quotes several poetic effusions on the same subject thus :

> " My name on bark engraven by your fair hand,
> Oenone, there, cut by your knife does stand ;
> And with the stock my name alike does grow,
> Be't so, and my advancing honour show."

[1] *Travels of Marco Polo*, ed. Colonel Yule, 1871, vol. i. pp. 378–9.
[2] *Sylva*, vol. ii. p. 233.

"There on the tender bark to carve my love ;
And as they grow, so may my hopes improve."

"Repeat, thy words on cherry-bark I'll take,
And that red skin my table-book will make."

LEAVES OF TREES

Homer compares the race of mankind to leaves upon a
tree thus :

"Like leaves on trees the race of man is found,
Now green in youth, now withering on the ground ;
Another race the following spring supplies ;
They fall successive and successive rise :
So generations in their course decay ;
So flourish these, when those are past away." [1]

The leaves of trees were, and are, often utilised in various
ways for many different purposes. The most ancient method
of writing was upon leaves of which the papyrus rolls of
Ancient Egypt are outstanding examples. The disciples of
Mahomet recorded his sayings on Palm leaves, and on the
shoulder bones of sheep. These were all placed in a chest
and left in charge of one of his wives. Five years after his
death they were arranged and published.[2]

In ancient times there were supposed to live certain women,
ten in number, in different parts of the world, who were
believed to be inspired and to utter prophecies. These women
were known as Sibyls, and the most celebrated of them was the
Sibyl of Cumæ, in Italy, who inscribed her warnings on
leaves. Virgil speaks of her thus : " When, wafted thither,
you reach the city Cumæ, the hallowed lakes, and Avernus re-
sounding through the woods, you will see the raving prophetess,
who, beneath a deep rock, reveals the fates and commits
to the leaves of trees her characters and words. Whatever
verses the virgin has inscribed on the leaves, she ranges in

[1] *Iliad*, Bk. vi. 181-6 ; Pope's translation.
[2] Gibbon, *The Decline and Fall of the Roman Empire*, ed. 1847, vol. iii.
p. 411.

harmonious order, and leaves in the cave enclosed by themselves : uncovered they remain in their position, nor recede
from their order. But when, upon turning the hinge, a small
breath of wind has blown upon them, and the door [by opening]
has discomposed the tender leaves, she never afterwards
cares to catch the verses as they are fluttering in the hollow
cave, nor to recover their situation, or join them together.
Men depart without a response, and detest the Sibyl's
grot." [1]

It was said that a stream of prophecy flowed from the
Castalian fountain of Daphne, and it is recorded that the
Emperor Hadrian read the history of his future greatness on
a leaf dipped in the Castalian stream.

Fruits as well as leaves are connected with inscriptions.
Thus in one of the rooms of the Memnonium a painting
shows the Pharaoh Rameses II. seated under a Persea
tree, on the fruits of which the goddess of wisdom, Ra-tum,
and the sacred scribe, Thoth, are writing his name. Another
painting at Medinet Habou shows Thothmes III. being led by
Hathor and Thoth before the Tree of Life, and on its fruits
the god Amen-Ra is inscribing a sacred formula.[2]

Leaves of trees were believed to know all secrets and
to give them up to those who knew how to consult them,
and hence the ancient magicians used to encircle their heads
with leaves so as to obtain wisdom. Leaves speak and
sing—the harmony of the spheres is the singing of the
leaves of the Celestial Tree. A Swedish ballad tells how,
when a young nymph played, the leaves of the trees accompanied her harmoniously. An ancient writer says that
Japhet invented the first musical instrument after hearing
the rustling of leaves in the wind.

Leaves have been thought to possess souls, or to be inhabited by some kind of beings, and certain sects of the
Guzerate stretched the Pythagorean doubt so far that they

---

[1] *Æneid*, Bk. iii, Davidson's translation.
[2] Professor Rendel Harris, *The Ascent of Olympos*, p. 41.

would not eat green leaves lest they should swallow some of the living beings inhabiting them.

Thales the Greek imagined the earth to be a cup floating on a leaf of the Plane tree.

The Scandinavian legend of Brandan relates how he met a tiny man floating on a leaf on the sea. In one hand he held a little bowl, and in the other held a pointer. Dipping the pointer into the sea he then let the water drip off it into the bowl, and so on until the bowl was full. He then emptied out the bowl and began filling it again, and so on continually, as he was doomed to measure the sea until the Judgment Day.[1]

A female saint, called St. Noyala, accompanied by her nurse, is alleged to have crossed the sea to Brittany on the leaf of a tree.[2]

In India there are several legends of a similar kind, one representing Brahma seated on a Lotus floating on the sea in deep contemplation, and another showing Vishnu as an infant floating on the sea of milk on a Pippala leaf, and sucking his toe.

One of the trees of India is called the Arka tree, which means " having a thunderbolt for leaf," on account of the cuneiform shape of the leaves. The word *arka* is also a name for the sun, and during the Vedic period the leaf of this tree was used in sacrifices to that luminary. There is an Indian tradition that those who approach this tree will become blind, which probably had its origin in the name, as lightning and the sun both dazzle the eye.[3]

Some of the ancient writers tell of wonderful trees whose leaves produced animals and even serpents, and in one case the leaves as they fell off became changed into butterflies. The Italian traveller Pigafetta, during his voyage round the world with the Squadron of Magellan in the beginning of the sixteenth century, was the first to find the famous animated leaf in the forests of Borneo, and his account of it was such

[1] Grim, *Teut. Myth.*, ed. Stallybrass, vol. ii. p. 451.
[2] Lewis Spence, *Legends and Romances of Brittany*, p. 360.
[3] De Gubernatis, *Mythologie des Plantes*, vol. ii. p. 15.

that his narrative was looked upon as fabulous, though afterwards proved to be true. He said : " What to me seemed most extraordinary was to see trees, the leaves of which as they fell became animated. These leaves resemble those of the Mulberry tree, except in not being so long. Their stalk is short and pointed ; and near the stalk, on one side and the other, they have two feet. Upon being touched they make away ; but when crushed they yield no blood. I kept one in a box for nine days ; on opening the box at the end of this time, the leaf was alive and walking round it. I am of opinion they live on air." These leaf insects, which have also been called Walking Leaves, belong to the order *Orthoptera*, and all the members of the family *Phasmidæ* bear a resemblance to natural objects. The genus *Phyllium* bears the strongest likeness to a leaf, but it is only the female which does so. The wings, in their shape, colour, and venation, strongly resemble the leaves among which it lives and on which it feeds, and, as if to increase that resemblance, the leaves have leaf-like expansions.

In the Malay Peninsula leaves are used as a charm when hunting the Gaur or Indian Bison. To prevent the animal when pursued from turning to charge its pursuers, the hunter takes a couple of leaves from the nearest tree, folds each in two, and then slips one inside the other so that the upper half of the one encloses the lower half of the other. He then pegs down these leaves into a footprint of the animal, uttering a charm over them, which is believed to prevent the animal from turning. The idea is that, as an insect which had crawled along the folded leaf from its stem to its tip would find itself no farther advanced on its journey than at the beginning, so the pursued animal would be unable to proceed farther, but would be forced to return in its tracks, and the charm would prevent it from charging its pursuers.[1]

In the Nicobar Islands a man believed to be possessed by devils is released from their presence by being first smeared

[1] George Maxwell, *In Malay Forests*, 1911, pp. 104–5.

over with pigs' blood, and then beaten with leaves. The devils are understood to go into the leaves, which must be at once thrown into the sea before the dawn appears.

When the natives of the Island of Timor are making long journeys, and are heated and fatigued, they use leafy branches to fan themselves with, and when they are finished with them they throw them down on some particular spot. All generations of travellers have done the same, and thrown the branches on the same spot, with the result that numerous heaps of withered branches are seen all over the island. The idea at the bottom of this process is that the fatigue which is felt is supposed to pass into the leaves and to be left behind.

The Fijians had a custom of throwing a leaf on the spot where a man had been clubbed to death, as a sign of respect for him, and also to avoid a like fate.

William Mariner says that in the Tonga Islands green leaves were worn by the priests round the neck, as marks of submission and humility as well as of fear, not towards the enemy, but towards the gods.[1]

At a certain ford on the Calabar River in West Africa much frequented by crocodiles, there is a large oval stone which is said to be an altar of a goddess named Nimm. She is very powerful, and often takes the shape of a crocodile or of a snake. When a native wishes to assure himself of a safe passage through the river he plucks a leaf, rubs his forehead with it and says : " May I be free from danger ! May I go through the water to the other side ! May I see no evil ! " He then throws down the leaf on a heap of similar leaves in front of the oval stone, and says : " I am coming across the river, may the crocodile lay down his head." Being thus satisfied that the goddess will appreciate this offering, and allow him to cross unmolested, he plunges boldly into the river. The natives of this same district treat the dead body of a chameleon with the utmost respect. If a native kills one he leaves it by the wayside, and every passer-by plucks a few leaves

[1] *The Tonga Islands*, Constable's Miscellany, 3rd ed. 1827, vol. i. p. 194

and drops them on the body saying : " Look ! here is your mat." Mr. Talbot says that this observance is intended to pacify the shade of the chameleon, which would otherwise go to the Earth-god Obassi Nsi and clamour for vengeance on his slayers.[1]

In other parts of Africa, as well as in many other parts of the world, similar practices are prevalent, and travellers in remote regions often come across heaps of leaves or branches which have accumulated by every passing native adding his quota.

THORNS, SPINES, PRICKLES, ETC.

Thorns, spines, prickles, *et hoc genus omne* are the natural defences of plants—against mankind, who wishes to pluck their flowers or fruit, or against animals which desire to browse on their foliage. An interesting example of protective measures against browsing animals is afforded by the Holly. When this tree is young the leaves are well protected by spines, but as it increases in height and the leaves are at last beyond the reach of animals, they lose their spines, and their edges are smooth all round. The poet Southey refers to this peculiarity in his poem called " The Holly Tree." He writes :

> " Below a curling fence its leaves are seen
>   Wrinkled and keen ;
> No grazing cattle through their prickly round
>   Can reach to wound.
> But as they grow where nothing is to fear,
> Smooth and unarmed the pointless leaves appear."

Thorns, etc., are credited with having a certain magic power owing to their capacity to lay hold of a thing. On Walpurgis Night, that night on which all the witches met to hold their unholy revels, it was customary in Bohemia to place branches of Hawthorn, Gooseberry, Wild Rose, and other

[1] P. Amaury Talbot, *In the Shadow of the Bush*, London, 1912, p. 242.

prickly plants on the thresholds of the cow-houses, in order to catch the witches and prevent them from entering.

The Persian Epic tells that, although Isfendiyar cannot be wounded by any weapon, yet he is at last slain by a thorn thrown by Rustam, which penetrated his eye.

Many have been the conjectures as to which plant furnished the Crown of Thorns. Thus the Hawthorn, the Holly, the Barberry, and the Libyan Thorn, among others, have been named as being probably the plant. Sir John Maundevile says that it was formed of " Jonkes of the See, that is to say, Rushes of the See that prykken as scharpely as Thornes." But he further tells how Jesus was led into a garden where the Jews " maden him a Crowne of the Braunches of Albespyne, that is White Thorn [Hawthorn], that grew in that same Gardyn, and setten it on his Heved, so faste and so sore, that the Blood ran down be many places of his Visage, and of his Necke, and of his Schuldres. And therfore hathe White Thorn many Vertues : For he that berethe a Braunche on him thereoffe no Thondre ne no maner of Tempest may dere him ; ne in the Hows that it is inne may no evylle Gost entre ne come unto the place that it is inne." Maundevile says that the Crown was afterwards divided into two, one part being kept in Paris and the other in Constantinople, and he adds : " And I have one of the precyouse Thornes, that semethe licke a White Thorn ; and that was zoven to me for gret Specyaltee." [1] The whole crown had been originally preserved in Constantinople, but it is said that Louis IX. of France, having aided Baldwin II., the last Frankish Emperor of Rumania, he received from him part of it, which he bore triumphantly to Paris.

In Normandy the peasants wear a sprig of the Hawthorn in their caps, for the reason that the Saviour's crown was formed from it ; and in Brittany there is a legend to the effect that when Christ was bearing His Cross a small bird endeavoured to relieve His sufferings by plucking one of the thorns

[1] *The Voiage and Travaile*, edit. J. O. Halliwell, 1883, pp. 10-13.

from His brow. The bird's breast became stained with blood, and it became known ever afterwards as Robin Redbreast.

In the West Indies the legend is that the Crown was made from the Cashew tree, and that one of its yellow petals became black in consequence of the blood staining it.

A French legend tells that Jesus being once pursued by the Jews, rested in a wood, when the magpies mischievously covered Him with thorns, but the swallows came and removed them.

ORIGIN OF FIRE

There was an ancient tradition that fire first appeared on the tops of trees, which may have been an allusion to St. Elmo's Fire. The Ancient Persians saw the fire-generator in the Cypress or Konar Tree, because its needles point to the sky, and from it flashed the first spark. They say it was the first tree planted in their Paradise, whence it was brought to earth by Zarathustra, who saw in it the image of Ahuramazda himself. On account of this it was planted before all the fire temples and elsewhere, in an endeavour to recall, however feebly, the memory of the lost Paradise.[1]

Ancient myths tell that the Hawthorn originated from lightning, and Jacob Grim says that the Ancient Germans made their funeral pyres from its wood. Dr. Grill, referring to this, remarks : " It is thought that by virtue of the sacred fire which flows from the thorns the souls of the dead are received into the sky, and it is clear that this sacred fire is the image of the celestial fire, and the burning of the corpse a symbol of the storm, since the funeral pyre and the hammer were both consecrated to the god Thor." [2]

In various countries the usual way of producing fire is by rubbing two pieces of wood together, which is in many cases successful, even if the wood be green. It has been conjectured that many forest fires, apparently causeless, have had their

[1] De Gubernatis, *Mythologie des Plantes*, vol. ii. p. 117.
[2] *Die Erzväter der Menscheit*, i. 182.

origin by the branches of trees rubbing together, and probably primitive men, being forest-dwellers, obtained their first ideas of fire from that phenomenon. It may be that a divinity was believed to reside within the branches. Sir John Lubbock mentions that in De Brosse's *Cult des Dieux fétiches* reference is made to a passage in *Sanchoniatha* quoted by Eusebius, in which the first thirteen generations of men are described. The third generation had the names of Phos, Pur, and Phlox, meaning Light, Fire, and Flame, and these discovered how to generate fire by the rubbing of two sticks of wood against each other, and they taught men the use thereof.[1]

Evelyn, speaking of the probable origin of sociability among mankind, tells how Vitruvius described the process (Vitruv. 1, 2. c. 1) when he says that the violent impact of one tree against another, owing to a furious wind, setting them into flames, these flames did not so much surprise the savages as the heat which was produced. Finding this warmth so comfortable, they would be induced to approach nearer, and as the fire waned they would encourage one another, by signs and barbarous tones, to heap on fresh combustibles, and these tones would in time be formed into words. Thus, from this accident, the savages would find the benefits of society, and would mutually agree to live in company with each other, instead of in solitude as before.[2]

When it is recognised, as said on page 161, that the Ivy, personifying Dionysos, is a subordinate thunder-god containing the sacred fire, it can be easily understood how Ivy wood was one of the earliest woods used as a fire-stick. Oak wood was also used by primitive man, probably in conjunction with Ivy, one piece, the borer, being male, and the other female ; but primitive man would not trouble about sexuality ; he wanted fire, and probably experimented until he found woods suitable for his purpose. Dr. Frazer points out [3] that among the northern nations " perpetual fires, kindled with the wood

[1] *The Origin of Civilisation*, 5th ed., 1889, pp. 210-11.
[2] *Sylva*, Reprint of 4th ed., vol. ii. pp. 205 *et seq.*
[3] *The Magic Art*, etc., vol. ii. p. 366.

of certain oak-trees, were kept up in honour of Perkunas : if such a fire went out it was lighted again by friction of the sacred wood."

The Beltane Fire of olden times, which marked the commencement of summer, was kindled by this method, and the fire produced was known as " Need Fire."

Should the sacred fire in the Forum of Ancient Rome be allowed to expire through the negligence of the Vestal Virgins, it could only be re-ignited by the Pontifex Maximus rubbing two pieces of wood together.

In Arabia and other Eastern countries the trees furnishing the wood for fire production are known as Markh and Afâr, and a passage in the Koran referring to this practice reads : " For He is skilled in every kind of creation : who giveth you fire out of the green tree, and behold ye kindle your fuel from thence." [1]

In Hindu Mythology, Agni is the God of Fire, and in some of the old Vedic hymns he is mentioned as dwelling in two pieces of wood, which, when rubbed together, produce fire. Dr. J. Muir, in a poem, refers to the birth of Agni thus :

> " Sprung from the mystic pair, by priestly hands
> In wedlock joined, forth flashes Agni bright ;
> But, oh ! ye heavens and earth, I tell you right,
> The unnatural child devours the parent brands."

The Mahābhārata speaks of Agni as desirous of recruiting his vigour by consuming the whole Khandava Forest, but being prevented from doing so by Indra. In the end, however, with the aid of Krishna and Arjuna, he accomplished his object. [2]

Dr. Muir, in the above-mentioned poem, speaks of the destruction of forests by fire, and, addressing Agni, says :

> " Thou levellest all thou touchest ; forests vast
> Thou shear'st, like beards which barber's razor shaves ;
> Thy wind-driven flames roar loud as ocean's waves,
> And all thy track is black when thou hast past."

[1] *The Koran*, transl. by George Sale, 1825, vol. ii. chap. xxxvi. p. 308.
[2] Dowson, *Dictionary of Hindu Mythology.*

In his *Original Sanskrit Texts* Dr. Muir has collected numerous expressions and sentences alluding to the ancient fire-worship, or worship of Agni in Aryan India. One of these says : " Fed by wood, with blazing tawny mane, he sends up his smoke like a pillar to the sky, or like a wavering banner." Another most expressive sentence, descriptive of a forest fire, reads : " When he has yoked his wind-driven coursers to his car, the beautiful, fleet, ruddy steeds that can assume all shapes, he bellows like a bull and invades the forests ; the birds are terrified at the noise when his grass-devouring sparks fly round, and his wheels mark his path with blackness."

Among the Hindus the kindling of the sacred fire on the altar was a most holy ceremony, two peculiarly shaped pieces of wood being used. One of these was from the *Ficus religiosa*, itself a sacred tree, and the other was of some softer wood, usually the Sami (*Acacia suma*), with a hollow in it. The process consisted in rapidly twirling the former in the hollow of the latter, symbolising generation, when by the friction a spark appeared, and thus Agni was born.

An ancient Chinese philosopher was once credited with having invented the fire-drill by seeing a bird peck at the branches of a tree until sparks came.

In the Caroline Islands there is a legend that Olofaet, the god of fire, instructed the bird Mwi to carry fire in his bill down to earth. The bird did so, storing fire in each tree, so that, when required, it could be brought forth by friction.[1]

The Hervey Islanders have a legend telling how Māui obtained the secret of making fire from Mauiki the Fire-god. Māui went to the underworld and picked a quarrel with Mauiki, whom he worsted, but promised to spare him on condition that he imparted to him the secret of fire—where it was hidden and how it was produced. Mauiki accordingly did so by the aid of his fire-sticks, but Māui, having now obtained the grand secret, in revenge for the trouble he had had, set fire to Mauiki's

[1] Dr. J. G. Frazer, *The Golden Bough*, " Balder the Beautiful," vol. ii. pp. 295–6.

abode. The legend tells how the rocks split and cracked with the heat, and how the flames burst through the earth at Teaoa, and were with difficulty extinguished. This spot for long was waste ground, and was held sacred until, after the advent of Christianity, it was cultivated. Māui, now owning the secret, kept it to himself for a long time, but in the end he compassionately let the inhabitants of the world share it with him.[1]

In the Island of Peru, one of the Gilbert Group, the natives say that an old lady obtained fire from heaven and put it in a tree, and then told them they could bring it out by friction.[2]

DIVINATION—DIVINING ROD, WANDS, ETC.

The foretelling of future events, or discovery of something concealed, by means of a rod or wand, or sometimes from the fruit of a tree, has been for long practised among many races, and even yet, experts in this art claim to be able to discover the whereabouts of water or the presence of precious metals by means of the Divining Rod. In all mythologies wands or rods had obviously a magic power, and were used to drive away the powers of darkness, serpents, and other evils, as well as to discover hidden treasures. In fairy tales we find the wand mentioned, and the Fairy Queen is invariably shown bearing her wand and with it performing her marvels.

The Divining Rod proper was used to discover the whereabouts of treasures or the presence of water. In olden times it was essential that these rods should be handled by sorcerers, or by persons with a knowledge of the magic formulæ. Different trees have been called upon to furnish this rod. One of these was the Willow, it being believed to be full of magical properties. In Sicily branches of the Pomegranate tree were considered the best, while in Sweden the Mistletoe was sometimes used. The most efficacious of all these wands, however,

---

[1] Rev. W. Wyatt Gill, *Myths and Songs from the South Pacific*, 1876, pp. 56–8.　　　　　　[2] Turner, *Samoa*, 1884, p. 297.

was that supplied by the Hazel, and it was also called the
Wishing Rod. M. Chéruel describes the method of using the
Divining Rod thus : " Since the eleventh century we find
mentioned the use of the divine wand for discovering springs
and treasures. It is a forked branch of Hazel, Alder, Beech, or
Apple. This is how it should be held. One of the forks of
the branch is held, not too firmly, with the palm of the hand
turned up. By holding the other fork of the branch in the
other hand, the main stem will be parallel to the horizon. The
holder advances gently towards the place where water is
suspected to be. When he arrives there, if water is below, the
rod turns in the hand and bends towards the earth like a needle
which has been magnetised. Such is the account of those
who believe in the virtue of the Divining Rod. They add,
that it has also the property of discovering mines, hidden
treasures, thieves, and fugitive murderers." [1]

The Divining Rod seems to have had some connection with
the Elves or Pixies, who have all the treasures of the earth in
their keeping. In Cornwall it is said that the Pixies guide
the rod to the mine, and that a rich lode has often been
discovered by hearing the singing of the Elves on the moors
at night.

In very ancient times, when the races of the earth were
pastoral peoples or shepherds, the patriarch bore his shepherd's
crook, and in time, as he assumed greater authority over his
tribe, this crook or wand developed into the insignia of royalty
known as the sceptre. The chiefs of many savage races still
bear a wand as a symbol of their rank. The rod was also the
emblem of discipline, and many ancient sculptures, particularly
in Egypt and Assyria, show the ruler wielding the rod over his
subjects and his captives. In some parts of the East Indies
it is said that a single branch of a tree placed over the door of a
house by the police prevents anyone from leaving the house
until the branch is removed, and a single branch placed in the
middle of a public march is sufficient for all those who find

[1] *Dictionnaire historique des institutions, mœurs, et coutumes de la France.*

themselves within the march to consider themselves as prisoners of the king.[1]

The rods of Moses and of Aaron were considered to have been the origin of the Crosier or Pastoral Staff of bishops. Adam is said to have once cut a staff from a tree which grew in the Garden of Eden, and this staff descended to Noah. It became in turn the property of Abraham, Isaac, and Jacob. The latter, when in Egypt, gave it to Joseph, and in due time Moses obtained possession of it. According to the Book of Numbers (xvii. 8) the rod of Aaron appeared to have been made from the Almond tree. There, we are told that Moses put twelve rods, representing the twelve tribes of Israel, into the Tabernacle, to choose from among them which tribe was to furnish the high priest. Next day the rod representing the tribe of Levi was found to be covered with leaves and blossoms, and accordingly that tribe was set apart for the priesthood. This rod was from the Almond tree.

The above is one of the many instances of which we read respecting wands and staffs which have miraculously borne leaves and flowers. Mr. S. Baring-Gould, relating the legend of Tannhäuser, says that after Tannhäuser had escaped from the Venusberg he confessed his guilt to Pope Urban IV., desiring absolution. The Pope, horrified at the enormity of the sin, spurned the penitent, saying : " Guilt such as thine can never, never be remitted. Sooner shall this staff in my hand grow green and blossom than that God should pardon thee ! " On hearing this fiat Tannhäuser sadly retraced his steps to the Venusberg, as the only refuge open to him. He had been gone for three days when Urban suddenly discovered his staff to have budded and flowered. Messengers were at once sent after Tannhäuser, but they could only ascertain that a weary and haggard man had been seen to enter the Hörselloch, and since then Tannhäuser has been heard of no more.[2]

A somewhat similar tale is told in Sweden of a water-spirit

---

[1] De Gubernatis, *Mythologie des Plantes*, vol. i. pp. 56–7.
[2] *Curious Myths of the Middle Ages*, 1875, pp. 213–14

known as the Neck, who appeared either as a young or an old man. A Swedish tradition tells that a priest once saw the Neck as a young man playing on the harp. He said to him : " Why dost thou so joyously strike thy harp ? Sooner shall this dried cane that I hold in my hand grow green and flower than that thou shalt obtain salvation." The young man was very sorrowful and wept bitterly. The priest continued on his journey, but had not ridden far when his staff began to put forth leaves and lovely flowers. Hastily returning to the Neck he showed him the flowering staff, and said : " Behold ! now my old staff is grown green and flowery like a young branch in a rose garden ; so likewise may hope bloom in the hearts of all created beings ; for their Redeemer liveth ! " The Neck was thus comforted, and gaily resumed his harping.[1]

Classical Mythology tells how Prometheus brought fire down from heaven enclosed in a hollow wand.

Dionysos or Bacchus, the God of Wine, is always represented as bearing a particular wand known as a *thrysus* or *caduceus*. Mercury is also represented as carrying one, and in the Homeric hymn it appears as having three leaves, hence its appellation of *Tripethlou*. This *caduceus* had two snakes twining round it, but originally these were Olive boughs. With this wand the god touched the dwellers on the earth, teaching them how to speak, and endowing them with all good qualities.

St. Patrick drove out the serpents from Ireland by means of his sacred rod ; and in Sicily a branch from the Elder tree is considered to be far superior to any other rod for killing serpents and driving away thieves.

In Scandinavia the belief was held that no child could be born in safety, and no soul could depart in peace, if a Willow wand was suspended anywhere near by. The Sallow (*Salix caprea*) was the Willow in question, and it seems to have been very full of magical properties. In these countries also the wand, or rod, of Woden, " Wuotan's Wand," was used for measuring land, and in some other countries a rod was used

[1] Thorpe's *Northern Mythology*.

to give sasine of properties. In addition to a sod of " earth and stone," a branch of a tree was thrust into the sod, and the whole was presented to the new proprietor.

There is a very ancient tradition which tells that after Adam had been banished from Paradise, God gave him the power to create any animal he desired by striking the sea with a Hazel rod. The first animal he produced was a sheep, and Eve, jealous of his power, thought to go one better. Her stroke unfortunately produced a wolf, which at once devoured the sheep. Adam, to redress matters, then created the dog, which instantly attacked and overcame the wolf.

Long ago in Europe omens were taken from the manner in which rods, when thrown up, fell—backwards or forwards, to the right or to the left.[1]

The Hazel nut, like the tree itself, was formerly believed to possess divining powers, and even still the magic power of the nut is held to be all potent on All-Hallows Eve or Halloween, also, in England, called " Nutcrack Night." This was the night on which the fate of lovers was determined by the behaviour of Hazel nuts when placed on the fire. The poet Gray wrote :

> " Two hazel nuts I threw into the flame,
> And to each nut I gave a sweetheart's name.
> This, with the loudest bounce me sore amazed,
> That, with a flame of brightest colour blazed.
> As blazed the nut, so may thy passion grow,
> For 'twas thy nut that did so brightly glow."

Burns likewise celebrated the rites of Halloween in Scotland :

> " Some merry, friendly, countra folks
> Together did convene,
> To burn their nits, an' pu their stocks,
> An' haud their Halloween
> Fu' blithe that night."

Sometimes each unmarried person had a nut named after them, and the manner in which it burned was believed to

---

[1] Brand, *Popular Antiquities*, vol. iii. p. 332.

prognosticate certain events in the after-life of the person whose name it bore.

In the South Sea Islands generally, and particularly in Polynesia, the Cocoanut was much used for divining purposes. Probably the reason lay in its alleged origin, it being said to have originated from the head of a man, the marks on it giving it a remote resemblance to a human face.

The Man in the Moon

From the earliest ages the markings or spots observed on the surface of the moon had been a subject of much speculation until the telescope revealed their true nature. When the moon is full a resemblance is alleged to be traceable to the features of the human face, or to the figure of a man bending, bearing a burden on his back. From this various legends arose making the moon the habitation of a man, almost all of which account for his appearance there as being a penance imposed on him for certain crimes committed while he was on earth. Different countries have their own characteristic legends. In Central Europe the legend ascribes the banishment to different crimes ; in Westphalia it takes different forms. Some affirm that Cain was taken to the moon while carrying a bunch of briars which he intended offering to the Lord, that being the cheapest produce of his fields ; or that the man represents Isaac bearing the wood for his own sacrifice. Another tells that a man who was working in his fields on Good Friday had just lifted a bunch of thorns on his fork when he was suddenly transported to the moon, where he still remains in company with a woman, who was also banished there for churning butter on a Sunday. Yet another legend says that the man was banished to the moon for decorating the church with thorns on a Sunday.

The Swabian legend tells how a man, accused of pruning his vines on a Sunday, exclaimed : " If I am guilty, may I be exiled to the moon ! Having, in fact, committed the crime, he was duly transported thither, carrying his bundle of prunings.

The Black Forest tale runs that a man stole a bundle of wood from the forest on a Sunday, knowing that all the foresters would be absent on that day. Soon after he had left the forest he was accosted by God Himself, Who reproved him for his sacrilege and gave him his choice to be banished either to the sun or to the moon. Objecting to being burned in the sun he said he would rather freeze in the moon, and there he remains, still bearing his stolen bundle in his hand and his axe over his shoulder.

An Ancient Chinese tradition says that a man who had committed various sins when he was an anchoret was banished to the moon, and condemned to eternally drive his axe into a Cassia tree, known as the giant tree Kuei, but that the gashes he makes always close up directly.[1] The Cassia is thus known in China as the Moon tree.

When Captain Ross first visited the Esquimaux of Baffin's Bay, they imagined him and his crew to be phantoms come from the sky. They believed, as they were told by their wizards, that the dead inhabited the moon, where wood was very abundant, and when they saw the vessel with its boats, masts, oars, etc., they were filled with amazement, and whispered with mystery to each other : " How much wood there is in the moon, how very much ! "[2]

The Yule Log

In ancient times a huge log of wood used to be laid across the fire, with many ceremonies, on Christmas Eve. This appears to have been a survival of the still more ancient custom of lighting fires at the Winter Solstice to celebrate the commencement of the return journey of the sun. Brand, in his *Popular Antiquities* (vol. i, pp. 467 *et seq*.) gives a great deal of information regarding this Yule Log, or Yule Clog, as he calls it. M. Fertiault, in his *Coup d'œil sur les Noëls en*

[1] Grim, *Teut. Myth.*, ed. Stallybrass, 1882, vol. iv. p. 1505.
[2] Elie Reclus, *Primitive Folk*, pp. 2–3.

Bourgogne," describing Christmas in Burgundy, speaks of the Yule Log, which is there called *suche*, thus : " This is a huge log which is placed on the fire on Christmas eve, and which is called in Burgundy on this account *lai Suche de Noei.* Then the father of the family, particularly among the middle classes, sings solemnly Christmas carols with his wife and children, the smallest of whom he sends into the corner to pray that the yule-log may bear him some sugar-plums. Meanwhile, little parcels of them are placed under each end of the log, and the children come and pick them up, believing, in good faith, that the great log has borne them."

CHAPTER IX

LEGENDARY

Forest and Tree Legends

THE forest is full of romance, mysterious voices echo in the shadowy glades, filmy forms glide along them, and consequently forests throughout the world have become the theatre of superstition and of miraculous events ; while round many of the trees of the forest legend has spread its imaginary lore. A legend connected with the Forest of Dooros in Sligo tells how the Rowan tree was believed to grow in Fairyland or the Land of Promise. This land was one of the chief dwelling-places of the Dedannans or Fairy Host. These had brought some of the scarlet Rowan berries from Fairyland, and in passing through the Wood of Dooros one of them fell to the ground unnoticed or unheeded by the Fairy Host. From this berry a great tree sprang up which had all the virtues of those Rowan or Quicken trees which grow in Fairyland. Its berries tasted of honey, and those who ate them became very cheerful as if they had partaken of wine, and even a centenarian, if he ate three of them, returned to the age of thirty. This tree was guarded by a giant called Sharvan, and no one ventured to approach the wood, so greatly was he dreaded. Consequently for many miles around the tree the country was practically a wilderness.[1]

In the reign of King Richard II. one of the keepers of Windsor Forest was known as Herne. He owned two black hounds of the St. Hubert breed, and on account of his great knowledge of woodcraft and skill in hunting King Richard held him in particular esteem. His fellow hunters consequently hated

---

[1] *Old Celtic Romances*, transl. from the Gaelic by P. W. Joyce, LL.D., 1879.

him and plotted his destruction. One day the king, when hunting, was almost slain by an infuriated stag, but was saved by Herne interposing his person and receiving the blow instead. Herne, to all appearance, was dead, when suddenly a tall dark man appeared, giving the name of Philip Urswick, who, for a reward offered by the king, declared he would effect a cure. He first cut the stag's head off, and bound it upon the head of Herne, who was then conveyed to Urswick's hut on Bagshot Heath. The king announced his intention of making Herne his chief keeper if he recovered, and Urswick promised faithfully to look after him. The other keepers regretted that he had not died, and Urswick offered them revenge if they would grant the first request he made. They agreed, and Urswick told them that, though Herne would recover, he would lost all his skill. Herne duly recovered and was appointed chief keeper, but found his former skill gone from him. King Richard, annoyed at this, revoked the appointment, whereupon Herne, in despair, hanged himself upon an Oak tree, from which his body mysteriously disappeared. The two immediate successors as chief hunter also lost their skill, and appealed to Urswick to remove the spell. He informed them that the curse of Herne's blood was upon them, and told them to repair to the Oak, where they would learn what to do. When they reached the tree the spirit of Herne appeared to them, and told them to bring horses and hounds for the chase the next night. This they did, and Herne, leaping on a horse, ordered them to follow. He led them to a Beech tree where he invoked Urswick, who burst forth in flames from the tree. In fulfilment of their promise he ordered them to form a band for Herne the Hunter, and made them take a fearful oath to serve him as their leader. Afterwards, night after night, this band ravaged the forest and thinned the deer. King Richard heard of these doings and repaired to the Oak where Herne appeared to him desiring vengeance on his enemies, which, if done, he would trouble the forest no more in his reign. They were accordingly hanged, and

Herne vanished. After King Richard's death Herne and his band reappeared, and during the following eight reigns ravaged the Forest of Windsor.

Another version of the legend is that Herne had committed some heinous crime and in remorse hanged himself; while a third says that it is a forest demon in the shape of Herne, with stag's horns on its head, which haunts the forest and endeavours to persuade the keepers to sell their souls to him.

The Oak itself fell from natural decay on the night of August 31, 1863, and on the spot where it had stood Queen Victoria planted a young Oak.

Many weird tales were told of Herne the Hunter, and Shakespeare, in *The Merry Wives of Windsor*, alludes to the legend thus :

> " There is an old tale goes, that Herne the hunter,
> Sometime a keeper here in Windsor forest,
> Doth all the winter time at still midnight,
> Walk round about an oak, with great ragg'd horns ;
> And there he blasts the tree, and takes the cattle ;
> And makes milch-kine yield blood, and shakes a chain
> In a most hideous and dreadful manner."

And again :

> " Why, yet there want not many, that do fear
> In deep of night to walk by this Herne's oak."

The Faröe Islanders have a tradition that the lack of trees on the islands is due to St. Olaf. On one occasion he inquired of the islanders if they had any woods at home, but they, suspecting he had the design to tax them, replied that they had none. " So be it," said the saint, and at that moment the Faröe woods vanished into the ground.[1]

A legend is current in Little Russia that once, on the Eve of St. John, a peasant lost his cattle. In looking for them he passed through a forest near to a fern at the moment of its

[1] Thorpe's *Northern Mythology*.

flowering, and the flower fell into his shoe. Immediately he saw where the cattle were hidden. The fern-flower being in his shoe he could see certain places where treasure was concealed, and on his return he declared to his wife that he would go to look for it. " Change your stockings," his wife said, observing that they were wet. It was the advice of the devil. He listened to her ; took off his shoes ; the fern-flower fell on the soil, and at the same instant he forgot everything.[1]

Buddha was one of the god Vishnu's incarnations, and it is told that in his youth he was never so happy as when sitting alone in the depths of the forests lost in meditation, and it was in the midst of a beautiful forest that he was shown the four great truths.

The natives of Guiana and some of the Central American countries have tales of a wonderful flower which grows in the forests. This flower is called Hata, and is large and white. The legend is that there is only one Hata flower in the world, and that it is found in one place only during the duration of a moon. Then, when the moon disappears, it disappears also, to be seen again in some other part of the forest, or, it may be, in some distant forest. Whoever discovers this flower in the forest will obtain all his desires, will be enabled to overcome all his enemies, and will live for many years.

Numerous legends have gathered around trees, but only a few can be narrated here. The majority of these tree legends have a family likeness in which mythology and superstition are inextricably intertwined with one another.

In the *Life of St. Brandan*, edited by Thomas Wright, it is narrated how St. Brandan made a journey to Paradise, and the legend continues : " But soone after, as God wold, they sawe a fayre ylonde, full of floures, herbes, and trees, whereof they thanked God of his good grace, and anone they went on londe. And whan they had gone longe in this, they founde a full fayre well, and thereby stode a fayre tree, full of bowes, and on every bough sate a fayre byrde, and they sate

---

[1] De Gubernatis, *Mythologie des Plantes*, vol. i. p. 189.

so thycke on the tree that unneth ony lefe of the tree myght be seen, the nombre of them was so grete, and they songe so meryly that it was an hevenly noyse to here." There are narratives of other journeys made to Paradise, in all of which the beauty of the trees and birds of that celestial land has been eloquently described.

St. Genevieve was born in A.D. 422, at a place about four miles distant from Paris, and she became highly renowned for saintliness. She resolved to build a church and dedicate it to St. Denis, but when she asked the priests to supply her with building materials they were unable to do so, saying they could get neither chalk nor lime. She told them to go to the bridge of Paris, where they would find what was necessary. They accordingly went to the bridge, when, two swineherds happening to pass, one said to the other that he had found a bed of lime, whereupon the other remarked that he had found one also under the root of a tree which the wind had blown down. The priests, having ascertained where these discoveries were, informed St. Genevieve, and the building was proceeded with.

Another legend relates that when this saint was on a voyage to Spain she arrived at a port where ships were always wrecked. This was due to a tree which grew in the water, so Genevieve commanded it to be cut down, and commenced praying, when, as the old Chronicler says, just as it commenced to sway, "two wild heads, grey and horrible, issued thereout, which stank so sore that the people that were there were envenomed by the space of two hours, and never after perished ship there ; thanks be to God and this holy saint." [1]

A French legend tells how St. Lucy of Scotland fled from her father's court to Lorraine, where she lived in solitude and piety. She became a shepherdess to a rich farmer, who left her all his wealth, and this she devoted to building a church on the hill on which for so long she had watched her master's flocks. When she died she was canonised and became the

[1] Hone's *Every-Day Book*, 1838, vol. i. p. 26.

guardian saint of the country-side. On one occasion she had planted her distaff in the ground while she was kneeling to pray, and when her prayer was over she found her distaff had been converted into a living tree, which still stands upon the hill. Several other legends of Lorraine are connected with her.

A Russian fairy tale narrates how the Tsar had promised his daughter in marriage to whoever would construct a flying-ship. The " Fool of the Family " thought he might have a chance to win the princess, and set out to seek his fortune. He showed hospitality to an old man whom he met, and to whom he confided his desires. In gratitude the old man said to him : " Go into the wood, right up to the first tree, cross yourself thrice, and strike the tree with your axe, then fall with your face to the ground and wait till you are aroused. Then you will see before you a ship quite ready ; sit in it and fly wherever you like, and gather up everything you meet on the road. So it befel, and among others whom he picked up was a man carrying a bundle of wood. This man, on being questioned, said that the wood he bore was not common wood, but of such a sort that if you scatter it a whole army will spring up." Accordingly, with the aid of his ship and his army, the youth overcame all difficulties and gained his bride.[1]

The Finns have a legend regarding a certain box or casket called Sampo which had been made by the god Ilmarinen in Pohjola, which land, owing to its presence, was abundantly fertile. But the jealous gods were desirous of possessing the box, and Wäinämöinen and Ilmarinen himself succeeded in stealing it. Louhi, the princess of Pohjola, taking the shape of an eagle, pursued and overtook them on the sea. In the struggle which ensued Sampo fell into the sea and broke, the lid only remaining in Louhi's hand, and she returned with it to Pohjola. In the meantime Wäinämöinen found fragments

---

[1] R. Nisbet Bain, *Russian Fairy Tales*, from the Skazki of Polevoi, 2nd ed., 1893, pp. 14, 16, 21.

of the casket on the shore. These he placed in the ground, and they grew up into lofty trees—one of them, which became an oak, growing so tall that it darkened the sun.[1]

In Tyrol, the Alder tree was a favourite with sorcerers, and a Tyrolean legend tells that a boy once climbed a tree and saw a number of sorcerers at the foot who cut up a woman's corpse, and threw the pieces into the air. The boy caught one, and when the sorcerers counted the bits and found one missing, they replaced it by a piece of Alder wood, whereupon the dead came back to life.[2]

The Greek word κερκίς, meaning a shuttle, was given to the Aspen tree on account of its vibrating leaves. Several legends sprang up round the tree to account for the continual quivering of the foliage. The most popular one is that which says that the Aspen was one of the trees chosen to furnish the wood for the Cross, and that its leaves have trembled with horror ever since. A German legend relates how the Holy Family once walked through a forest, all the trees of which bowed in reverence except the Aspen. Then the Holy Child cursed it, when its leaves began to quiver, and have continued to do so ever since. The legend has been poetically rendered thus :

> " Once as our Saviour walked with men below,
>   His path of mercy through a forest lay ;
> And mark how all the drooping branches show
>   What homage best a silent tree may pay !
> Only the Aspen stands erect and free,
>   Scorning to join the voiceless worship pure ;
> But see ! He casts one look upon the tree,
>   Struck to the heart, she trembles evermore ! " [3]

Another legend says that at the hour of the Passion all the trees bowed down in sympathy except the Aspen, which was immediately seized with a trembling which everlastingly con-

---

[1] Grim, *Teut. Myth.*, ed. Stallybrass, 1882, vol. ii. p. 873.
[2] De Gubernatis, *Mythologie des Plantes*, vol. ii. p. 30.
[3] Henderson, *Folklore of the Northern Counties.*

tinues. The tremulousness of the Aspen is referred to in a Russian proverb, which says : " There is an accursed tree which trembles without even a breath of wind."

Sir Walter Scott wrote :

> " O woman ! in our hours of ease
> Uncertain, coy, and hard to please,
> And variable as the shade
> By the light quivering Aspen made."

Gerarde, however, ungallantly compares the leaves of the Aspen to women's tongues, as they " seldome cease wagging " ; in fact, he says the report goes that women's tongues were made from these leaves.

Jacob Grim mentions a Low Saxon legend of an Ash tree which, it is believed, will one day grow in the churchyard of Nortorf in Holstein. It has never been seen yet, but every year a small shoot comes up, and every New Year's Night a white horseman on a white horse cuts it down. A black horseman on a black horse tries to prevent him, but is put to flight. One day, however, the black horseman will prevail, and the shoot will grow up into a tree. When it is tall enough for a horse to be tied under it, the king with a mighty army will come, and a terrible battle will be fought. The king's horse will be standing under the tree during that battle, after which the king will be more powerful than ever.[1]

The Norwegian love-story of Axel Thordsen and the Fair Valdborg relates how they never were united in life, but that on each of their graves, not far removed from each other, an Ash tree was planted. These trees grew to an equal height, in time inclining towards each other, until at last they entwined their boughs together.[2]

A Scandinavian legend tells how some people once got an Ash tree from a giant, who told them to set it on the altar of a church which he wished to destroy. Instead of doing this

---

[1] *Teut. Myth.*, ed. Stallybrass, vol. iii. p. 960.
[2] Thorpe's *Northern Mythology*.

they placed it on a mound over a grave, which instantly burst into flames.[1]

The French romance called *Lay le Fraine*—the Adventure of the Ash or the Lay of the Ash Tree—deals with twins, one of which was deserted by its mother and placed under an Ash tree at the door of an abbey. When discovered the abbess called the child Le Fraine, as being found under the Ash.[2]

According to a tradition of the Pyrenees a man, while one day beating hot iron on his anvil, raised such sparks that they reached the eye of God Himself, Who cursed him and condemned him to become a bear. He was allowed to climb all trees except the Beech, whereupon he at once endeavoured to uproot that tree.[3]

Classical legend tells how Athena and Apollo, taking the shape of vultures, sat on a Beech tree, and watched the conflict between the Greeks and the Trojans.

There is the Russian tale of a Birch tree which once showed its gratitude to a young maiden for tieing a red thread round it, by saving her from the tyranny of her witch-stepmother; and another mentions a Birch tree which grew in the island of Buian, on the top of which the Mother of God was thought to be seen seated. Yet another tale speaks of a young shepherdess who spun in a Birch wood. To her came a wild woman, who made her dance during three whole days till sunset. At the end of the dance the wool was all spun, and the shepherdess was rewarded with a pocket full of Birch leaves, which changed into gold coins.

Among the Esthonians the Birch tree is the living personification of their country. It is said that a peasant who once saw a stranger sleeping under a tree at the moment when a storm was about to burst awakened him. The stranger, in gratitude, said to him: "When, far from thy country and experiencing homesickness, thou shalt see a crooked Birch, strike it and ask: 'Is the crooked one at home?'" Long

[1] Grim, *Teut. Myth.*
[2] Lewis Spence, *Dictionary of Mediæval Romance*, p. 115.
[3] De Gubernatis, *Mythologie des Plantes*, vol. ii. p. 171.

afterwards, when the peasant, who was now a soldier in Finland, felt very melancholy, he suddenly saw a crooked Birch and was reminded of his former experiences. He struck the tree, and asked : " Is the crooked one at home ? " The stranger instantly appeared, called one of his familar spirits, and ordered him to transport the soldier to his own home, with his knapsack full of silver.[1]

In a folk-tale of Brittany the life of a giant was bound up in an ancient Box tree which grew in the garden surrounding his castle. Anyone who wished to kill him had to sever the tap root with one stroke of an axe, but had to be careful not to injure any other root. This task the hero of the tale successfully accomplished, and no sooner was the root severed than the giant dropped down dead.

Mr. Richard Folkard, in narrating the legend of the building of the monastery of St. Christine in the Pyrenees, says that the builders had great difficulty in finding a suitable foundation, until one day they saw a white pigeon flying, carrying a cross in its beak. They pursued it until it alighted on a Box tree. When they approached, it flew away, but left the cross among the branches. This being considered a good omen, they laid the foundations on the spot where the tree had stood, and so the building was completed.[2]

Scandinavian folklore tells of an Elder tree which once grew in a farmyard and had the unpleasant habit of taking a walk in the twilight and peeping in through the window at the children when they were alone.

Two Scottish youths were one day ploughing in a field, in the centre of which stood an ancient Hawthorn tree reputed to be a trysting-place for the Fairies. One of the youths drew a circle round the tree, within which the plough was not to go. As soon as it was drawn, a green table laden with bread, cheese, and wine miraculously appeared within it. The youth who had drawn the circle sat down to the table and

---

[1] De Gubernatis, *Mythologie des Plantes*, vol. ii. pp. 45–6.
[2] *Plant Lore, Legends, and Lyrics*; 2nd ed., p. 257.

partook heartily, saying " Fair fa' the hands whilk gie," but the other scorned the Fairy-food and continued at his work. The former, however, it was said, " thrave like a breckan," and became renowned for wisdom ever after.[1]

There is a popular tale of the Middle Ages called the Romance of *Maugis d'Aygremont et de Vivian son Frère*. Tapinel and a female slave stole the two children of Duke Bevis of Aygremont. Tapinel sold the one he had taken, while the slave wandered off with the other. She lay down to rest under a Whitethorn or Hawthorn tree, when she was surprised and devoured by a lion and a leopard. These two animals then fought for the infant and killed each other. The Romance continues : " And the babe lay under the thorn, and cried loudly, during which it came to pass that Oriande la Fée, who abode at Rosefleur with four other fays, came straight to this thorn ; for every time she passed by there she used to repose under that White-thorn. She got down, and hearing the child cry, she came that way and looked at him and said : ' By the god in whom we believe, this child here is lying badly [*mal gist*], and this shall be his name ' ; and from that time he was always called Maugis." The Fairy took him to Rosefleur, where she brought him up, and after he came to man's estate he had many adventures, one of them being the gaining of the enchanted horse Bayard.[2]

A legend of the Roman Catholic Church tells that when Charlemagne knelt in reverence before the Crown of Thorns it suddenly burst forth into bloom, and the scent of Hawthorn filled the air.

Mr. W. R. Ralston, in *Forest and Field Myths*, mentions the following folk-tale of Modern Greece : " There was once a childless wife, who used to lament, saying : ' If only I had a child, were it but a Laurel berry ! ' And heaven sent her a golden Laurel berry, but its value was not recognised, and it was thrown away. From it sprang a Laurel tree which gleamed with golden twigs. At it, a prince, while following

[1] Keightley's *Fairy Mythology*, pp. 352–3.　　[2] *Ibid.*, pp. 32–3.

the chase, wondered greatly. And determining to return to it, he ordered his cook to prepare a dinner for him beneath its shade. He was obeyed. But during the temporary absence of the cook, the tree opened, and forth came a fair maiden, who strewed a handful of salt over the viands and then returned into the tree, which immediately closed upon her. The prince returned and scolded the cook for over-salting the dinner. The cook declared his innocence, but in vain. The next day just the same occurred. So on the third day the prince kept watch. The tree opened and the maiden came forth. But before she could return into the tree the prince caught hold of her and carried her off. After a time she escaped from him, ran back to the tree, and called upon it to open. But it remained shut. So she had to return to the prince. And after a while he deserted her. It was not till after long wandering that she found him again and became his royal consort." [1]

The Lime tree, or Linden, was, in Scandinavia, one of the favourite haunts of Elves, Fairies, and such-like beings, and it was considered unsafe to be near one of these trees after sunset. Some verses of the Swedish ballad of Sir Thynnè run :

" And it was the knight Sir Thynnè
Went the hart and the hind to shoot,
So he saw Ulva, the little Dwarf's daughter,
At the green Linden's foot.

" And it was the knight Sir Thynnè,
From his horse he springs hastily,
So goeth he to Ulva, the little Dwarf's daughter,
All under the green Linden tree.

" And it was Thora, the little Dwarf's wife,
She at the hill-door looked out,
And there she saw how the knight Sir Thynnè,
Lay at the green Linden's foot." [2]

[1] *The Contemporary Review*, vol. xxxi., February 1878.
[2] Keightley's *Fairy Mythology*, p. 97.

A German legendary hero is named Horny Siegfred or Sigurd, so named because, after he had slain the dragon Fafnir and bathed himself in its blood, he became horny and invulnerable all over except one spot between his shoulders, on which a Linden leaf had stuck.[1] Ancient Scandinavian lore says that the mythical dragon Fafnir lives ninety years in the ground, ninety in the Lime tree, and ninety more in the desert.[2]

Elberich was a very famous dwarf in legendary lore, and assisted the Emperor Otnit of Lombardy to win the Soldan of Syria's daughter for his bride. The Emperor had heard of her, but the queen, his mother, tried to prevent him from seeking her. Her efforts were in vain, so she gave him a ring, and told him to ride towards Rome till he came to a spot where a Linden tree stood in front of a hill from which a brook flowed. The ballad then tells how he set off on his journey :

" Till he found the fountain, and the green Linden-tree,
  And saw the heath wide spreading, and the Linden branching high.

" And when the Lombarder had looked on the Linden,
  He began to laugh loud ; now list what he said then :
  ' There never yet from tree came so sweet breathing a wind,'
  Then saw he how an infant was laid beneath the Lind.

" Who had himself full firmly rolled in the grass ;
  Then little the Lombarder knew who he was :
  He bore upon his body so rich and noble a dress,
  No king's child upon earth e'er did the like possess.

" His dress was rich adorned with gold and precious stones ;
  When he beneath the Linden the child found all alone :
  ' Where now is thy mother ? ' King Otnit he cries ;
  ' Thy body unprotected beneath this tree here lies.' "

This child was Elberich himself, who revealed to the Emperor that he was his father, and aided him to win the hand of the Princess, which he did after many adventures.[3]

---

[1] Keightley's *Fairy Mythology*, pp. 207–8.
[2] Grim, *Teut. Myth.*, ed. Stallybrass, vol. iv. p. 1493.
[3] Keightley's *Fairy Mythology*, pp. 208–13.

A story is told in Switzerland of a number of dwarfs who were in the habit of coming to look on at the haymaking. They used to sit on a long thick branch of a Maple tree among the foliage. One evening some evil-disposed people came and sawed the branch half through. Next morning the dwarfs, fearing no evil, came and sat down as usual, when the branch broke in two, and they were thrown to the ground. On the people laughing at them they became very angry, and exclaimed :

> " O how is heaven so high
> And perfidy so great !
> Here to-day and never more ! "

After that they were never seen again.

An Alsatian fable tells that once upon a time the bat was credited with the power to render the eggs of the stork abortive. In order to avert this calamity the stork placed some branches of the Maple in its nest, and these by their power prevented the bat from entering the nest. It was once believed that if a Maple branch was placed under the entrance to a house, the bat could not enter.[1]

Several classical legends account for the origin of the Myrtle tree. One relates how the nymph Myrsine or Myréne beat the goddess Pallas or Athena in a race. The goddess, being angry, slew her, and from her body the Myrtle grew. Pallas ever afterwards loved the tree, probably through remorse. Another legend tells that a priestess of Venus named Myréne was changed into a Myrtle tree because she wished to marry a youth whom she loved. Yet a third legend is to the effect that Myréne, having offended Venus, the latter changed her into a Myrtle tree, but, to show that her affection was un-diminished, ordained that it should remain evergreen and odoriferous. There is still a fourth legend, which narrates that when Venus in the Island of Cytheræa was ashamed of

[1] De Gubernatis, *Mythologie des Plantes*, vol. ii. p. 129.

her nakedness, she concealed herself behind a Myrtle tree, and in gratitude to it adopted it as her best-loved tree. The Myrtle was thus sacred to Venus, the Goddess of Love, because it was thought to possess the virtue, not only of inspiring love, but also of retaining it. When Venus first sprang from the sea she wore a wreath of Myrtle on her head, and her temples were always surrounded by Myrtle groves. In Greece she was adored as Myrtilla.

From time immemorial the Oak tree has been enveloped in a cloud of romance and mystery, and innumerable legends connected with it carry one back to the remotest antiquity. A Greek festival called the Daedala was instituted to commemorate a quarrel between Zeus and Hera, whom Zeus had deceived by giving out that he was to marry another. He had caused a wooden image of a bride to be made, which was called Daedala. Hera came down from Olympos in a fury, and, tearing off the bridal clothes, discovered the deception. She was then reconciled to Zeus. Pausanias tells us that there was a certain wood in Bœotia where the finest Oaks grew, and when the time for making the image for use in the festival drew nigh some cooked meat was placed in front of the wood, and the ravens were watched to see which one took it, and on which tree it perched. That tree was then cut down and the image made from its wood.

Mr. R. Folkard mentions a Greek legend connected with the Ilex or Evergreen Oak. He says : " When it was decided at Jerusalem to crucify Christ all the trees held a council and unanimously agreed not to allow their wood to be defiled by becoming the instrument of punishment. But there was a second Judas among the trees. When the Jews arrived with axes to procure wood for the cross destined for Jesus, every trunk and branch split itself into a thousand fragments, so it was impossible to use it for the Cross. The Ilex alone remained whole, and gave up its trunk for the purpose of being fashioned into the instrument of the Passion. So to this day the Grecian woodcutters have such a horror of the tree. that they fear to sully their axe or their hearthstones by bringing them into contact with the accursed wood." [1]

Dean Stanley speaks of a Jewish legend connected with a row of seven Oaks in Palestine. It tells how, after Cain had murdered Abel, he was compelled to carry the dead body about with him for seven hundred years, and then to bury it at that spot. After burying it he stuck his staff in the ground to mark the place, and from it sprang up the seven Oak trees.

According to tradition King Harold survived the Battle of Hastings, and took an oath extorted from him by William under an Oak tree at Rouen. He broke his oath, and at that moment the Oak tree shed its leaves. [2]

There was formerly the remains of an Oak wood at Store Heddinge, in Zealand, the trees of which were said to be the Elle-King's (Fairy King) soldiers. By day they were trees, but at night they became warriors.

A Russian legend given by Afanassieff (*Narodniya Russkiya Shaszki*, i. 13) and mentioned by Professor de Gubernatis, tells the tale of Basile Bestchastnoï. It relates that the wicked stepfather sent Basile to the Kingdom of Serpents (meaning the night time), in the belief that there he would perish. Basile found an Oak tree three hundred years old in that kingdom which told him to ask the serpent how many years it would still stand. The serpent replied that the Oak would fall when one came from the East and kicked it. Then it would be uprooted and the treasure would be found under its roots. This myth, says de Gubernatis, possibly means that the tree represents the darkness, or night, of heathen superstition which is uprooted by Christianity coming from the East, and exposing beneath it the treasures of true religion. [3] Professor de Gubernatis gives several other legends or fables connected with the Oak. Thus, about two centuries ago a shepherdess named Jeanne, who was caught one day in a storm, called all the shepherds and their flocks to gather round her. She then

[1] *Plant Lore, Legends and Lyrics*, 2nd ed., 1892, p. 385.
[2] Lewis Spence, *Dictionary of Mediæval Romance*, p. 223.
[3] *Mythologie des Plantes*, vol. ii. p 66.

stuck her shepherd's crook in the earth, whereupon an Oak tree at once sprang up which was so umbrageous that the whole company remained in dry security underneath. In after years a little chapel to the Virgin was erected near this Oak. The tree still stands, and those who are rash enough to climb it in order to cut branches are miraculously thrown off, but it seems to be permissible to cut little twigs as talismans. These guard from all storms, provided that, standing in front of the twig, the owner invokes the names of Jesus and Mary thus :

> " Col nome di Gesù e di Maria,
> Questa tempesta la vada via."

A Scandinavian legend narrates how the giant Skrŷmir went to sleep under an Oak. Thor came and with his hammer struck him on the head, whereupon he awoke and asked if a leaf had fallen on him. He then lay down under another Oak, where he snored till all the forest reverberated. Thor struck him a harder blow, on which he asked if an acorn had fallen on him. For a third time he lay down and slept, when Thor struck him still harder, but he merely stroked his cheek and said : " There must be birds roosting on these boughs, I fancied when I woke they dropped something on my head." [1]

Grim mentions a mediæval tradition of Herodias, alleging that she sits on Oak and Hazel trees from midnight till cock-crow, and floats in the air the rest of the time. She had been hopelessly in love with John the Baptist, and when his head was on the charger she would fain have covered it with kisses, but it drew back and blew hard at her. She was then whirled into empty space, where she hangs for ever, except when resting on the above trees.[2]

A story regarding Destiny is given by Grim [3] thus : " A poor knight sits in the forest consuming a scanty meal ; he looks up and spies in the tree overhead a monstrous being, who cries

[1] Grim, *Teut. Myth.*, ed. Stallybrass, vol. ii. pp. 541–2.
[2] *Ibid.*, vol. i. pp. 284–5.   [3] *Ibid.*, vol. ii. p. 878.

to him, ' I am thy *ungelücke*.' He invites ' his ill-luck ' to share
his meal, but no sooner is it down than he seizes it firmly and
shuts it up in an *eicher* (hollow oak). From that moment
all goes well with him, and he makes no secret of what has
happened. One who envies him, wishing to plunge him into
misery again, goes to the wood and releases *ill-luck* ; but
instead of burdening the knight any longer, it jumps on the
traitor's back, just as a kobold would. This fable was known
to H. Sachs, iii. 2, 72[c.] ; *Misfortune* shall be made fast with
chains and ropes to an oaken stake, so it may visit no house
more unless some man be so fond to let it loose again."

Grim also tells how Misfortune, like a demon, sat on a tree,
and that it was said of a hollow tree

> " There are saints in there,
>   That hear all people's prayer."

Old Bohemian songs speak of an Oak tree that springs
from a murdered man's grave, on which holy sparrow-hawks
perch and publish the foul deed.[1]

The Olive tree, one of the most valuable trees of Greece
and Italy, was fabled to have been created by the goddess
Athena, Pallas-Athene, or, as she was known to the Romans,
Minerva. The legend of the foundation of the city of Athens
relates that when the gods began to choose cities for themselves, both Athena and Poseidon (Neptune) chose Athens.
The former created and planted an Olive tree, and the latter
created the horse, as symbols of possession. Twelve of the
gods decided the matter and awarded the city to Athena, as
her gift was the more useful one, and she then named the city
after herself, handing the tree over to the care of the serpent
god Erechthonios. The Olive to which Athena had thus
given origin became her favourite tree, and the identical tree
was said to have grown in Athens. This tree was much
venerated and cherished by the Athenians, severe penalties
being imposed on anyone who injured it, and Pliny avers that

[1] Grim, *Teut. Myth.*, ed. Stallybrass, vol. ii. p. 675.

it was still alive in his time. After the burning of the city by
the Persians under Xerxes, the people were reassured by seeing
this Olive tree put forth a new shoot. Horace, speaking of
Athens, says : " There are some whose sole employment is to
chant in endless verse the city of the spotless virgin goddess
Pallas, and to prefer the Olive to every other leaf that is gathered." [1] The Olive tree to which Argus fastened Io after
she had been transformed into a cow was said by Pliny to have
been then still in existence, as was the Wild Olive from which
Hercules was fabled to have obtained his first wreath.

In the Forum at Megara an Olive tree once grew on which
distinguished warriors were wont to suspend their arms.
In the course of time the bark grew to such an extent as to
cover up these weapons, and at last their existence was forgotten. An oracle, however, had announced that when a
tree should produce arms the fall of the city was impending.
It was so. When the tree was cut down the weapons were
found within it, and the enemy conquered the city.[2]

The Mount of Olives, or Olivet, near Jerusalem, from which
it is separated by the narrow vale of Jehoshaphat, has an
inexpressible charm about it when one recollects that it was a
favourite resort of the Saviour. The most interesting of the
Olive trees which clothed the slopes of Olivet were those
which grew in the Garden of Gethsemane. The Christians
of Jerusalem believe that the trees now growing there have
sprung from the roots of those under the shade of which the
Saviour often wandered. An Olive tree which once grew
in the Valley of Jehoshaphat was said to have been the tree
on which Judas hanged himself.

Professor de Gubernatis gives an Andalusian legend regarding the Orange tree. When the Virgin was travelling with
the infant Jesus and Joseph, she came to an Orange tree which
was guarded by an eagle. She begged the tree to give her
one of its fruits, whereupon the eagle miraculously fell asleep.
She then plucked three oranges, giving one to Jesus, one to

---

[1] *Odes*, Bk. i. 7.   [2] Pliny, *Nat. Hist.*, Bk. xvi. c. 76.

Joseph, and keeping the third for herself.[1] The golden apples of the Hesperides were in all probability oranges.

In a Scandinavian legend a female spirit dwelt under a Pine tree. To this tree one might see snow-white cattle being driven up from the lake across the meadows, and no one dared to touch its boughs.[2]

A fairy tale relates how a giant ordered a young prince to ascent to the top of a Fir tree to look for magpies' eggs. His sweetheart marked the steps of a ladder on the stem of the tree with her fingers, and so he was enabled to obtain the eggs, and at the same time found his sweetheart, whom he recognised by the absence of one of her fingers.

Nork [3] mentions that once at Ahorn, near Coburg, a wizard sent a terrible wind which bent the steeple of the church. Everyone laughed at its appearance, until a shepherd fastened it by a rope to a Pine tree, and by using magic invocations and imprecations, succeeded in straightening it. Nork also tells that in the year 1300 an image of the Virgin, which had been hidden in a Pine tree, made itself audible to a priest, and thereafter a church dedicated to the Virgin was erected in the vicinity.

At one time it was believed to be very injurious to sleep beneath a Walnut tree, probably on account of its connection in some cases with witches. For long a Walnut tree at Benevento was held in the utmost horror, being regarded as frequented by the devil and the witches, who were believed to hold an annual dance under it which was called the Beneventine wedding. The citizens were in the habit of performing many heathenish rites under it, until, according to the mediæval legend, when Christianity was introduced, St. Barbatus had the tree cut down. When this was done the devil was seen creeping away in the form of a serpent from among the roots. But, despite that, it was said that Satan, whenever a witches' dance was to be held, caused an exactly

---

[1] *Mythologie des Plantes*, vol. ii. p. 267.
[2] Grim, *Teut. Myth.*, ed. Stallybrass, vol. ii. p. 652.
[3] *Mythologie der Volkssagen und Volkmärchen.*

similar tree to appear on the same spot, and the unholy revels continued.

In Classical Legend the Greek goddess Hera was born under a Willow tree in the island of Samos. This tree was for long preserved within the precincts of her temple there. This temple contained a wooden image of the goddess which disappeared every year, and, being diligently sought for, was found on the seashore bound to a Willow, the branches of which concealed it. The priestess then unbound it, washed it, and conveyed it back to the temple. Another legend says that some Tyrrhenian pirates stole the image, but as soon as they took it on board, their ship refused to move. In terror they took it back and left it on the shore, where the people finding it thought it had run away of its own accord, and tied it to a Willow to prevent a similar escapade in future. The priestess then found it and restored it to the temple. From this the annual ceremony of disappearance and restoration was supposed to have arisen.[1]

The Arabs give the following legend to account for the Weeping Willow : " They say that, after David had married Bathsheba, he was one day playing on his harp in his private chamber, when he found two strangers opposite to him, though he had given strict orders that no one should intrude upon his privacy. These strangers were Angels, who made him convict himself of his crime, nearly in the same manner as is related in Holy Writ. David then recognised in the strangers the Angels of the Lord, and was sensible of the heinousness of his offence. Forthwith he threw himself upon the floor and shed tears of bitter repentance. There he lay for forty days and forty nights upon his face, weeping and trembling before the judgment of the Lord. As many tears of repentance as the whole human race have shed and will shed on account of their sins, from the time of David till the judgment day, so many did David weep in these forty days, all the while moaning forth psalms of penitence. The tears

[1] Keightley's *Classical Mythology*, 4th ed., 1890, pp. 88–9.

from his eyes formed two streams which ran from the closet into the anteroom and thence into the garden. Where they sank into the ground there sprang up two trees, the Weeping Willow and the Frankincense tree ; the first weeps and mourns and the second is incessantly shedding big tears in memory of the sincere repentance of David." [1]

What is known in pottery as the Willow Pattern had its origin in a Chinese legend of two lovers.

Early Irish romance has a tale similar to the Greek legend of King Midas. The hero of this romance was King Maon, also known as Labra the Mariner, and he, like his Greek prototype, had the ears of a horse. On the occasions when he had to have his hair cut, the man who performed that office was at once put to death lest the secret should leak out. On one occasion a poor widow's son was chosen, and he, through his mother's entreaties, and on the strength of his own oath to keep the secret, was spared by the king. Finding the weight of the secret very burdensome, he acted on the advice of a Druid, and whispered it to the first Willow tree he came to, returning home much relieved. Not long afterwards a harper named Craftiny required wood to construct a new harp and cut down this tree. When the harp was finished he performed upon it before the king, when, to the latter's amazement, the harp sang out, " Labra the Mariner hath two horse's ears." The king, perforce, had to bow to circumstances, and no one was again put to death when tonsorial operations had been performed.[2]

One of the many Hindu legends of the god Vishnu, under his name of Krishna, during his boyhood, tells how he and his companion and brother Balarāma, an incarnation of the serpent Shesha, were very fond of playing with the young cowkeepers and tormenting the calves belonging to his mother Yasodā. She, becoming angry, tied Krishna to a heavy wooden mortar and continued at her work. In Krishna's efforts to

[1] Loudon, *Trees*, vol. iii. p. 1463.
[2] Lewis Spence, *Dictionary of Mediæval Romance*, pp. 73, 217–18.

free himself he managed to wedge the mortar between two Arjuna trees, and by a final effort these trees were uprooted. The inhabitants of the place, seeing the trees fall although no storm was blowing, deemed the place unlucky and removed to Vrindāvana. According to the *Bhāgavata* these trees were two sons of Kuwera, the God of Riches, who had been cursed by the sage Nārada and transformed into trees. It was said that Krishna had purposely put himself into the position he was for the purpose of liberating the brothers from the spell.[1]

In the Hindu Paradise, the heavenly garden of Indra, the principal tree is said to be the Pârijâta tree, which was produced at the churning of the ocean. The reason for this churning was that Indra's power began to wane on one occasion, being threatened by the rising power of the *asuras*, or demons. The gods became alarmed, and were advised by Vishnu to collect all plants and throw them into the sea of milk. They were then to take the mountain Mandara for a churning-stick and with it to churn the sea. This churning would produce the divine ambrosia, which the demons were forbidden to partake of. The churning was then proceeded with, Vishnu himself, in the form of a tortoise, acting as a pivot for the churning-stick, and after a little while

> " from the whirlpool sprang
> Fair Pârijâta, tree of Paradise, delight
> Of heavenly maidens, with its fragrant blossoms
> Perfuming the whole world."

Then at last

> " Came forth Dhanvantari, the gods' physician,
> High in his hand he bore the cup of nectar—
> Life-giving draught—longed for by gods and demons."

After drinking this divine ambrosia the gods were reinvigorated and routed their enemies.[2]

The *Vishnu Purāna* gives the legend of a great conflict

---

[1] W. J. Wilkins, *Hindu Mythology*, 1882, pp. 171–2.
[2] *Ibid.*, pp. 109–10.

between Indra and Krishna (Vishnu). The latter once
visited Indra, and, incited by his wife, coveted the Pârijâta tree,
which then grew in Indra's garden. Krishna overcame Indra
and took possession of the tree. Despite all the efforts of the
gods he succeeded in bearing it away, and planted it in his
own garden.

Another legend in which the Pârijâta tree, under the name
of Pârigâtaka figures, is given by the Portuguese physician
Garcia da Horto as follows : " A ruler called Parizatacos
[Pârigâtakas] had a very beautiful daughter with whom the
Sun fell in love. But, soon after, he became enamoured of
another, and the poor abandoned one conceived such despair
that she killed herself. From her the tree Parizatacos grew,
the flowers of which hold the sun in horror, as is shown by
the way in which they always turn away from him.[1]

Balarāma, before mentioned, the brother of Krishna, having
been sent by Krishna to pay a visit to his old playmates, the
cowkeepers, Varuna told his wife Varuni to go and help him
in his enjoyments. Varuni accordingly proceeded to the
forest of Vrindāvana, and there took up her abode in a Kadamba
tree. Balarāma, when strolling in the forest, happened to
smell the fine fragrance of the liquid produced by that tree,
and this aroused in him his former passion for strong drink.
While under its influence he demanded that the River Yamuna
should come to him, and on her refusal he seized her and
dragged her about after him until his passion abated.[2]

A legend of Cambodia relates how Prince Phra Thong was
banished from his country, and after a long sea voyage landed
on an island on which a wonderful Talok tree (*Grewia in-
æqualis*) grew. He ascended the tree in order to view his
surroundings, but the farther up he got the more the tree grew
in height, until he began to fear he would never see the earth
again. Accordingly he ventured no farther, but began to
descend. On his way down he discovered a wonderful grotto

---

[1] De Gubernatis, *Mythologie des Plantes*, vol. ii. p. 254.
[2] W. J. Wilkins, *Hindu Mythology*, pp. 186–7.

in the hollow trunk of the tree, and in that grotto he met the Dragon King's daughter and married her. Another version of the legend says that it was the king, Pathumma Surivong, who, while reposing under that wonderful tree, saw the maiden bathing in a neighbouring lake, and, promptly falling in love with her, wedded her.[1]

The Hindu legend of the origin of the Mango tree is as follows : On one occasion the daughter of the Sun, to escape the persecutions of an enchantress, threw herself into a pool, and at once became changed into a yellow Lotus. The king, seeing the lovely flower, desired to possess it, but the enchantress burned it. From its ashes arose the Mango tree, and the king, enamoured of the flower and the fruit, desired the latter to be kept for his own use. When the fruit was ripe it fell, and from it came the daughter of the Sun, whom the king recognised as having been his former wife.[2]

The fruit of the Mulberry was once white, and took its present colour from the blood of Pyramis and Thisbe. Ovid tells how these two were prohibited from marrying, but agreed to meet under a white Mulberry tree. Thisbe arrived first, and on a lioness appearing, took refuge in a cave. She dropped a veil, which the lioness covered with blood. When Pyramis came and saw the blood-stained veil, he believed Thisbe had been killed, and stabbed himself. Thisbe returning, and seeing him dying, threw herself on the dagger, praying that their ashes might be mingled together, and that the fruit of the Mulberry should ever after take on the colour of their blood, as a witness to their constancy. Rapin (*De Hortorum Cultura*, Gardiner's transl., 1665) wrote regarding this tragedy as follows :

> " Hence Pyramis and Thisbe's mingled blood
> On Mulberries their purple dye bestowed.
> In Babylon the tale was told to prove
> The fatal error of forbidden love."

[1] James Fergusson, D.C.L., *Tree and Serpent Worship*, 2nd ed. 1873, pp. 53-4.
[2] R. Folkard, *Plant Lore, Legends and Lyrics*, 2nd ed., p. 428.

In tropical and semi-tropical regions of the earth the various species of Palm trees constitute the universal provider—in fact

> " The Indian nut alone
> Is clothing, meat and trencher, drink and pan,
> Boat, cable, sail, and needle—all in one ; "

while a Persian hymn sings of the three hundred and sixty blessings of the Palm tree, so the tree in consequence became surrounded with many legends and much lore. Classical Mythology said that the Palm was the offspring of Terra and Phœbus (Earth and Sun) ; and Linnæus asserted that the region of Palms was the first country inhabited by the human race, and that mankind is essentially *Palmivorous*.

Arabia is one of the principal habitats of the Palm, and the Arabs say that Mohammed on one occasion affirmed Adam to have been as tall as a high Palm tree. The Koran relates that previous to the birth of Christ the Virgin retired to a distant place, and the pangs of childbirth came upon her when she was near a Palm tree. This was a withered tree, and it was the winter season. She leaned on it during her travail, whereupon it miraculously revived, shot forth green leaves along with a head laden with ripe fruits which supplied her with nourishment and refreshment. Mohammed was also said to have leaned against the trunk of a Palm tree when he prayed and delivered his weekly exhortations.

The City of Palmyra was built by King Solomon, who named it Tadmor, meaning the City of Palm Trees, owing to the numerous Palms surrounding it. The name Tadmor was translated Palmyra by the Greeks.

An Eastern legend says that Cain, after killing Abel, had to bear about the body for many days, not knowing how to dispose of it. At last he found out how to bury it by seeing a raven scrape a hole and inter another raven which it had killed. Cain, following this example, buried Abel at the foot of a Palm tree, of which the branches, then erect, drooped sadly ever afterwards. The raven had watched this proceeding, and flew off to Adam, whom he told of the murder of his younger son. Consequently the raven from that time became a bird of evil omen.

We read (Judges iv. 5) that the prophetess Deborah uttered her oracles under a Palm tree near Bethel. This same tree was said by tradition to mark the grave of the nurse of Rebecca.

In Ancient Chaldea the Date Palm was tended with a loving care. It was believed that the gods themselves had taught to men the artifice of shaking the flowers of the male Palm over those of the female one in order to facilitate reproduction, and in the ancient sculptures these gods were frequently represented with a bunch of flowers in their right hand in the attitude assumed by a peasant in fertilising a Palm tree.[1] Burckhardt mentions that in Persia Date trees were sold by the single tree, and that the price paid to a girl's father on her marriage often consisted of such trees. In some parts of Persia when dates are shaken from the trees by the wind they are not gathered, but are left lying for those who possess no Date trees, or for wayfarers. Moore refers to this pleasing custom in *Lalla Rookh* (*The Fire-Worshippers*) thus :

> " 'Twas stillness all—the winds that late
> Had rush'd through Kerman's almond groves,
> And shaken from her bowers of date
> That cooling feast the traveller loves."

The Date Palm, known as the Tree of the Virgin (*vide* p. 220), which bent down for the Virgin to pluck the fruit, was rewarded by the Divine Infant saying to it, " Lift thee up, O Palm, and be thou companion of the trees which are in the Paradise of my Father."

In the legend of St. Christopher the Date Palm has a prominent place. After carrying the Holy Child across the river aided by his Palm staff, he asked the Child who he was, adding, " Had I carried the whole world on my shoulders,

---

[1] Maspero, *The Dawn of Civilisation*, p. 555.

the burden had not been heavier." Then the Child replied,
Wonder not, Christopher, for thou hast not only borne the
world, but him who made the world, upon thy shoulders. Me
wouldst thou serve in this thy work of charity ; and behold,
I have accepted thy service ; and in testimony that I have
accepted thy service and thee, plant thy staff in the ground, and
it shall put forth leaves and fruit." Christopher did so, and
his staff immediately flourished as a Palm tree, bearing clusters
of dates, while the Child vanished from his sight. He then fell
on his knees and confessed and worshipped Christ.[1]

Another legend tells how just before the death of the
Virgin Mary an angel brought to her a Palm branch from
Paradise, the leaves of which sparkled like the stars of the
morning.

The *Indian Antiquary* for the year 1872 mentions a legend
regarding the Palm tree of the Lake of Taroba in Central
India. It was said that this tree was visible only during the
day, and in the evening it went underground. One morning
an imprudent pilgrim climbed up to the top of the Palm, which
thereupon grew so high that the rays of the sun burned up
the adventurous one while the tree itself vanished into dust.
On the spot where it once grew now stands the idol of the
guardian of the lake, also called Taroba.

The Chinese name for the Cocoanut is *Ye-tsu*, and also
Yüe-wang-t'ou, meaning, the head of the Prince of Yüe. This
has been explained by Dr. Bretschneider in the *Chinese
Recorder* for 1871 as follows : " According to the *Nan-frang-
t'sao* a tradition exists that Prince Lin-yi was at strife with the
Prince of Yüe. The former sent to kill his enemy, and while
the latter was intoxicated his head was cut off. The head was
hung on a tree, and was changed into a cocoanut with two
eyes in its shell. This is why the fruit is called *Yüe-wang-
t'ou*." [2]

There is a Mongolian legend of a tree called *Asambu-*

[1] Mrs. Jameson, *Sacred and Legendary Art*, ed. 1891, vol. ii. pp. 439–42.
[2] De Gubernatis, *Mythologie des Plantes*, vol. ii. p. 104.

bararkha, the fruit of which, when it drops into the water, utters the word *sambu*.[1]

Professor de Gubernatis mentions two folk-tales regarding the Bilva or Vilva tree (*Aegle marmelos*). The first is of a Bilva or Bel tree, on which two flowers grew and then two fruits. In these latter were concealed two children who had been killed by sorcerers. These children were, as may be, Prince and Princess, husband and wife, brother and sister, and so on. The other tale, called *The Beautiful Princess*, relates how the Prince, when looking for the Princess, encountered a fakir. The latter told him that the Princess would be found in a garden situated in a great plain. In the centre of the garden grew a Bilva tree bearing one solitary fruit, in which was hidden the Princess. He was told to pluck the fruit, not to let it fall, and not to look back. Unfortunately, when leaving, after being successful, he did look back, the sorcerers overtook him, changed him and his horse into stone, and replaced the fruit on the tree.[2]

An Indian legend says that the Akaulea tree died by order of the Creator in order to furnish the boat for the dead to cross the River of Death.[3]

According to a Persian legend the first Pomegranate tree sprang from the haft of the axe with which the unhappy Ferhád, the lover of the fair Sheereen, slew himself.[4]

In Classical Mythology the Pomegranate was sacred to Hera or Juno. Zeus permitted Pluto to carry off Persephone to Hades to be his queen, but on the representations of her mother, Demeter, relented, and endeavoured to persuade Pluto to allow Persephone to return to earth. Pluto agreed, but gave her a Pomegranate seed, which she heedlessly swallowed. After meeting her mother the latter anxiously asked if she had tasted anything when in Hades, and Persephone confessed to having swallowed one seed. This entailed her

---

[1] Grim, *Teut. Myth.*, ed. Stallybrass, 1882, vol. ii. p. 873.
[2] *Mythologie des Plantes*, vol. ii. p. 42.
[3] *Ibid.*
[4] Malcolm, *Sketches of Persia*, ii. 98.

having to spend one-third of the year with Pluto, but the rest of it she could spend with her mother among the gods. Another version of the myth says that she had plucked a pomegranate in the garden of Hades, and put seven of the seeds in her mouth.

The fruit of the Pomegranate was embroidered on the hem of Aaron's robe, as well as on the robes of the ancient kings of Persia, and the capitals of the pillars of the Temple at Jerusalem had pomegranates carved on them.

A Japanese goddess called Kishi Bojin was credited with a propensity to eat young children until Buddha cured her by giving her the fruit of the Pomegranate to eat. She is thus represented in Japanese Art as carrying a child along with a pomegranate.

According to the Brahmins, Brahma created Adam and Eve, and placed them in the island of Ceylon. They were forbidden to leave that island; but one day in the course of their wanderings they arrived at the extremity of the island, where a narrow and rocky pathway connected it with the mainland. On the other side they saw, as they thought, beautiful and stately trees with birds of a thousand brilliant colours flitting about among the foliage. This was a device of the Spirit of Evil to tempt them to disobedience. Thinking that that land looked lovelier than their own, they succumbed to the temptation, and Adam carried Eve across. No sooner, however, had he set foot on the land than a terrific clamour arose, and trees and everything vanished from their sight, while the rocks on which they had crossed sank beneath the sea. They could no more return to their Paradise, but were at last forgiven for each each other's sake, and it was promised that Vishnu would come in the future with the hope of a reward in a future life.[1]

In Egypt the legend of Osiris tells how he was slain by his brother Set, who placed his body in a coffer and threw it into the Nile. The coffer, after being carried down to the sea,

[1] Max Müller, *Chips from a German Workshop*, ed. 1895, vol. iv.

floated for a long time until it was washed up on the coast of Syria at Byblus. Here an Erica tree grew up round it, completely enclosing it. This tree was cut down some time afterwards and made into a pillar. Isis eventually got that pillar and cut out the coffer. She then gave the trunk of the tree to the King and Queen, who placed it in a temple of Isis, where it was worshipped by the people of Byblus.

A shrine of Osiris was situated at Busiris, where his sign was a hieroglyph originally thought to represent a leafless tree, but in later ages interpreted as meaning the god's back-bone.

A legend, or rather popular tale, in which a Cedar tree takes a prominent part, entitled the *Tale of the Two Brothers*, was no doubt often recounted in the homes of Ancient Egypt. The tale is written on a papyrus now in the British Museum, and the papyrus was at one time the property of the Pharaoh Seti II., of the Nineteenth Dynasty. The author was the scribe Anna or Enna, who seems to have been a prolific writer of his day. The story goes much on the same lines as that of Joseph and Potiphar's wife, but is too long to be narrated here.[1]

The Zulus have a legend of a girl who was stolen by cannibals, and shut up in the great rock called Itshelikantunjambili, which opens or closes at the word of those who know its secret. The girl succeeded in finding out the secret and was enabled to escape. The cannibals, however, pursued her, but she threw on the ground a calabash full of sesame, which they stopped to eat. Being at last tired of running, the girl climbed a tree, where she found her brother, who, warned in a dream, had come to look for her. The two then went higher up the tree till they came to a beautiful country full of fat oxen. They killed one, and while it was roasting they occupied themselves in making a stout thong from its hide. Meanwhile one of the cannibals, allured by the savoury smell of the roasting meat, came to the foot of the tree and

[1] *Records of the Past*, pub. 1875, vol. ii. "Egyptian Texts," pp. 138–51.

saw the boy and girl. They invited him up to share their feast, and let down the thong to aid his ascent. When he was half-way up they let go, and down he fell with a terrible crash.[1]

During Stanley's second expedition into Africa he heard an interesting legend of Uganda connected with the Banana. It is called the *Legend of the Blameless Priest*, and tells that one Kintu came forth from the north and became the founder of the Kingdom of Uganda. At that time the land was sterile and uninhabited, but Kintu had brought with him one Banana root. He planted it, and the legend narrates that it " sprang up almost instantly into a stalk of vast girth, from the top of which hung pendent such a cluster of fruit as is not seen in Uganda nowadays, and the root spread itself over a large area, from which hundreds of bananas shot upward with great stalks, and all the leafy luxuriance of a large plantation." [2]

All Bananas and Plantains bear the fruit hanging downwards with the exception of the Mountain Plantain, which shoots its bunch of fruit erect to the heavens. The Samoan legend says the reason for this is that of old all the Bananas held their heads erect. They, however, quarrelled with the Plantain, fought, and were beaten. Ever since, in token of defeat, they hang their heads, while the Plantain still continues erect as a symbol of its victory.[3]

In Polynesia there are different legends told to account for the origin of the Breadfruit tree. One of them relates that at the time when the people ate red earth, a husband and wife had an only son, whom they dearly loved, but who was very weak and delicate. One day the husband said to his wife, " I compassionate our son, he is unable to eat the red earth; I will die and become food for our son." His wife asked, " How will you become food ? " and her husband replied, " I will pray to my god ; he has power, he will enable me to do it." Accordingly he petitioned his god and got a

[1] Callaway, *Zulu Nursery Tales.*
[2] *Through the Darkest Continent*, 7th ed. 1889, p. 219.
[3] Dr. George Turner, *Samoa*, 1884, pp. 216–17.

favourable answer. He then said to his wife, " I am about to die ; when I am dead take my body, separate it, plant my head in one place, my heart and stomach in another, etc., and then go into the house and wait. When you shall hear first a sound like that of a leaf, then of a flower, afterwards of an unripe fruit, and subsequently of a ripe round fruit falling on the ground, know that it is I, who am become food for our son." He died shortly afterwards, and his wife did as she had been instructed. She heard the various sounds, and as it was now daylight she awoke her son, and they went into the garden. There they beheld a large and handsome tree, with broad shining leaves, and profusely laden with breadfruits. She told her son to gather some, offer the first to the family god, and roast and eat the rest. This he did, and was healthy ever after.[1]

A legend of the Tonga Islands says that long ago a canoe returning from Fiji was blown out of its course and stranded on the shores of the Island of Bolotu, the home of the gods and of the dead. The crew landed, and, being hungry, endeavoured to pluck the breadfruits from the trees which abounded there. These trees, however, proved to be but shadows which they could pass through, and they were counselled to return home. They did so, but the deadly air of Bolotu had so affected them that they all soon died.

William Ellis, speaking of the Aoa tree, which somewhat resembles the Banyan, says that the Polynesian account of its origin is one of the most fabulous of the native legends. According to the legend the moon is like our earth, diversified with hill and valley, and adorned with trees. The Aoa is one of these trees, and it is its shadow which forms the dark spots on the surface. In very ancient times a bird flew to the moon and picked some of the berries of the Aoa. Then returning, and when flying over the islands, it dropped some of the seeds, which, germinating in the soil, produced the Aoa tree.[2]

---

[1] William Ellis, *Polynesian Researches*, 2nd ed. 1832, vol. i. pp. 68–9.
[2] *Ibid.*, pp. 34–6.

The Hurons of North America believe that the founder of their race was a woman named Ataentsic, who had been banished from the sky for having committed some fault. In the Huron heaven there are woods and plains as on earth, and one of the various crimes alleged as the cause of her banishment was that she had cut down a Heaven tree and fell along with it. She chanced to fall on the back of a turtle in the middle of the sea, who consulted the other animals as to what was to be done with her. One of them fished up some soil, and from it made the earth on which Ataentsic lived, and gave birth to twins who were the ancestors of the human race.[1]

On one occasion a Dog-Rib Indian chased a squirrel up a tree until he reached the sky, where he set a snare for the squirrel and descended. Next day, instead of the squirrel, the sun was caught, and darkness at once ensued—in other words, the sun was eclipsed. " Something wrong up there," thought the Indian, " I must have caught the sun," so he sent up a number of animals to try to release it, but they were all burned to ashes. Finally a mole, burrowing through the ground of the sky, succeeded in gnawing the cords asunder, but just as it put its head through the ground, a flash of light put its eyes out, and it has been blind ever since. The sun, however, after this experience, travels more carefully.[2]

A Mexican legend tells that during the great deluge, Coxcox, or Teocipactli, the Fish-god, rescued himself by means of a Cypress trunk, and afterwards repeopled the world.

The principal god of several Brazilian tribes was called Jurupari, and one of the Uapes legends regarding him is that on one occasion he devoured the children of the tribe because they had eaten the fruit of the Uacu tree, which was sacred to him. The enraged parents threw him into a fire, from the ashes of which sprang up the Paxiuba tree. This tree is the bones of Jurupari. The god has an intense dislike to women,

---

[1] A. Lang, *Myth*, etc., vol. i. pp. 176-7.
[2] Tylor, *Early History of Mankind.*

and the sacred musical instruments made from that tree must never be seen by them. Should a woman accidentally happen to see them she is at once poisoned, and whenever the women happen to hear the " Jurupari music " during festivals they at once conceal themselves until the danger is past.[1]

Professor Agassiz, during his journey in Brazil in 1865, heard the legend of the origin of mankind with which a Cotton tree was intimately associated. It was said that the first man, who was named Caro Sacaribu, was also divine. He had a son, an inferior being, named Rairu, who was also his prime minister, but to whom he was inimical. He tried to get rid of him in various ways, and among other stratagems he made a figure resembling a tatu or armadillo, which he buried in the ground, leaving only the tail exposed, which he covered with a kind of oil. This oil when touched adheres to the skin. He then ordered Rairu to pull the tatu out of the hole and bring it to him. Rairu accordingly seized the tail, but his hand stuck to it, and the tatu, being suddenly endowed with life by the Supreme Being, plunged into the earth and dragged Rairu with it. Rairu in time succeeded in reaching the surface again, and told Caro Sacaribu that in the earth there were great numbers of men and women, and that it would be an excellent thing to get them out to till the soil and make themselves generally useful. Caro Sacaribu was pleased with this idea, and planted a seed in the ground, from which sprang a Cotton tree, and from the cotton it bore he formed a long thread. Rairu, then, holding one end of the thread, descended once more into the earth through the same hole that he had been dragged previously. He collected all the people together, and they were drawn up through the hole by means of the thread. The first lot were small and ugly, but they gradually improved in appearance, until finally the men were handsome and the women beautiful. Unfortunately the thread by now had

[1] Marian Edwardes and Lewis Spence, *A Dictionary of Non-Classical Mythology.*

become worn and weak, and broke, so that the great majority of the last lot fell back into the hole and were lost, and this, say the Mundurucus, is the reason why beauty is such a rare gift in the world. Caro Sacaribu then arranged the population he had drawn from the earth into different tribes, and marked or tatooed them with different colours and patterns. After this was done, a residue of the smallest and ugliest specimens of the human race were left, and, drawing a red line over their noses, he said to them, " You are not worthy to be men and women—go and be animals." Accordingly they were changed into the birds called Mutums, and these, with their red beaks and melancholy voices, still wander through the forests.

INDEX

INDEX